THE ROAD

or, Under the

by S. J.

SIMON AND

NEW

TO MILTOWN

Spreading Atrophy

PERELMAN

(

SCHUSTER · 1957

YORK

All of the stories in this book appeared originally in *The New Yorker*, except "The Swirling Cape and the Low Bow," "I'll Always Call You Schnorrer, My African Explorer," and "Who Stole My Golden Metaphor?"

"The Swirling Cape and the Low Bow" and "I'll Always Call You Schnorrer, My African Explorer" appeared originally in *Holiday*.

LIBRARY OF CONGRESS CATALOG CARD NUMBER: 57-5681
MANUFACTURED IN THE UNITED STATES OF AMERICA

TO *E. McKnight Kauffer*

Contents

⊂⋸

And Thou Beside Me, Yacketing in the Wilderness   1

Short Easterly Squall, with Low Visibility and Rising Gorge   10

CLOUDLAND REVISITED: When to the Sessions of Sweet Silent Films . . .   17

No Starch in the Dhoti, *S'il Vous Plaît*   27

De Gustibus Ain't What Dey Used to Be   37

I Am Not Now, Nor Have I Ever Been, a Matrix of Lean Meat   44

CLOUDLAND REVISITED: Roll On, Thou Deep and Dark Scenario, Roll   51

The Saucier's Apprentice   59

Whereas, the Former Premises Being Kaput—   66

vii

Contents

My Heart's in the Highlands, and My Neckband,
Too 74

CLOUDLAND REVISITED: Vintage Swine 82

Long Time No Sheepskin 89

The Swirling Cape and the Low Bow 96

Genuflection in the Sun 107

CLOUDLAND REVISITED: The Wickedest Woman
in Larchmont 116

Swindle Sheet with Blueblood Engrailed, Arrant
Fibs Rampant 124

Come On In, the Liability's Fine 131

This Little Piggy Went to Market 138

CLOUDLAND REVISITED: I'm Sorry I Made Me Cry 146

Danger—Molting Plumage 154

Sorry, No Phone or Mail Orders 162

Don't Tell Me, Pretty Gypsy 169

CLOUDLAND REVISITED: By the Waters of Razz-
Ma-Tazz 177

Next Week at the Prado: Frankie Goya Plus Monster Cast 184

I'll Always Call You Schnorrer, My African Explorer 191

One Comely Babe, Piping Hot 202

CLOUDLAND REVISITED: "M" Is for the Migraine
That She Gave Me 210

You're My Everything, Plus City Sales Tax 218

Contents

Is There a Doctor in the Cast?   226

CLOUDLAND REVISITED: Hungarian Goulash, with
    Battered Noodles   236

Who Stole My Golden Metaphor?   244

CLOUDLAND REVISITED: It Takes Two to Tango,
    But Only One to Squirm   251

Calling All Addlepates   259

CLOUDLAND REVISITED: Shades of Young Girls
    among the Flummery   266

And Thou Beside Me, Yacketing in the Wilderness

IF I EVER sit down like a retired Scotland Yard inspector to write my memoirs, which I have provisionally entitled "Forty Years a Boob," one of the episodes I plan to gloze over is the night of pub-crawling I spent in Hollywood last summer with a beautiful, Amazonian extra player named, for purposes of this indiscretion, Audrey Merridew. For nine tumultuous hours, her destiny and mine were interwoven. (No more than our destinies, I hasten to add; we never even progressed to the point of lacing fingers.) The encounter was so brief, our lack of rapport so conclusive, that when I received a postcard from her recently—an aerial view of San Bernardino, with a tiny shrunken lemon wired to it—I could not recall the creature for a few seconds. Then the whole gruesome affair came back, and I realized with an uprush of pique that the card had an ulterior significance. So I was a wizened little fruit long past its prime, was I? That was feminine gratitude for you; you danced attendance on them, flattered their vanity, listened to their preposterous confidences, subordinated everything to their whims, and in return they made you a laughing stock across the country. Standing at my rural-delivery box in the Pennsylvania bush, I could hear the personnel of the entire postal system, from coast to coast, guffawing at the gibe. Well, I thought as I flung the postcard into the weeds, it's damn lucky a continent lies between us, or I'd hang a shiner on Audrey's eye, for all the eight inches she towers over me. When my dander's up, I lash out irrespective of size or sex.

I got embroiled in the thing through Norman Spindrift, a budding producer at Metro who entered show business by the back door as a dice hustler at Las Vegas. He had taken me to lunch at his commissary and devoted most of it to soliciting my opinion of Frank Harris's *My Life and Loves* as a potential movie. "How can it miss?" he kept demanding. "It's got girls, situation, jeopardy—everything."

"That it has," I conceded. "But why not try something more current in the same vein—the new Kinsey, for instance? You could get boffs out of those statistics if you animated them."

Norman contemplated the tip of a Larrañaga he had exhumed from its cedarwood coffin. "Not a bad idea," he said thoughtfully. "Assuming it could be cleared legalwise, would you be interested in an assignment like that?"

"Hell, I'm just opening a can of kumquats," I said. "I believe in giving a man the handle bars and letting him ride the bicycle."

"Well, it's worth a fast mull," he said, his eyes narrowed. "Look, walk me back to my office and let's see if we can't synthetize our thinking."

We had traversed an expanse of burning concrete fully the length of an airstrip when Norman abruptly broke off his speculations and propelled me toward the door of a sound stage.

"Mind if I check on this unit a second?" he asked. "I got a company here doing a ballroom sequence." Molelike in the pitch dark, I followed him through a labyrinth of cables and props to the set, a dazzling affair of chromium staircases and tufted leather that exactly simulated, said my companion, the lounge of the Reform Club in London. A sizable crowd of dress extras in the last stages of tedium loitered about waiting for the technical crew to complete a setup, and while Norman engaged in a colloquy with the director, I picked up a script and updated my glossary of Hollywood subjunctives. A minute or two later, he returned, looking, I thought, unbearably arch.

"Listen," he said, in a guarded tone. "Is the little woman in town with you?" I explained that the two of us had been unable to fit into a roomette on the Chief but that I wrote her daily copious letters that would give anyone the illusion of being in the movie capital. "Yes, yes," he said impatiently. "Well, I know how lonely a man can get in this burg, so I got you a date for tonight. Now, don't start giving me that Nujol," he said, hushing my objections. "She's a hep dame, a million laughs, good-looking, just your type. And, what's more, not a gold digger. Take her out, buy her the blue plate, a couple of drinks—you can *talk* to Audrey. She isn't one of these china dolls." Since the man had obviously gone to considerable trouble in my behalf, I yielded, and accompanied him around the rear of the set to meet the lady. She was undeniably striking—a bold, wide-eyed brunette, with dimples and a smoldering quality, who reminded me somehow of one of my early screen deities, Priscilla Dean. Her white evening gown, accented at the bodice with pompons, appeared at first glance to have been improvised from a candlewick bedspread, though it admittedly complemented her olive skin and pneumatic *balcon*. She did not rise from the camp chair she was seated in but extended her hand in a fashion, at once comradely and languorous, that won me.

3

"Why hasn't Norman brought you around before?" she asked reproachfully. A long-time partisan of contraltos, I recognized at once that hers was instinct with moonlight and camellias. "I love people from the East," she went on. "There's so much more *to* them." Uncertain whether I was supposed to hail from Jubbulpore or Newark, I decided to play it safe and adopted an inscrutable global expression. Audrey—our match-maker had instantly put us on a first-name basis—jotted down her home address, where I was sweetly enjoined to call for her no later than seven, and stood up in response to the assistant's whistle. My inscrutability curled around the edges when I saw she was a good head and a half taller than me.

"Pretty slick, eh?" Norman commented as she waved adieu. "You're in solid, man. I can tell."

I seemed to have a frog in my throat temporarily. "Tall girl, isn't she?" I wheezed. "I mean sitting down she gives the impression—"

"I told you she wasn't any china doll, for Crisake," he snapped. "What's the matter—you afraid to trust yourself with a real woman?" I countered with some hearty masculine ribaldry, vitiated, unfortunately, by my falling over a guy wire, and had to endure the humiliation of being assisted to my feet and brushed off. Norman wanted to hale me to the studio infirmary to have my shins dressed, and even spoke darkly of preventive tetanus shots, but I pooh-poohed his solicitude and left with assurances that we would meet again soon to resume our assay of Kinsey.

I was staying at the time with friends in Bel-Air, and they must have suspected I was pleasure-bent that evening, because while nothing in my speech or demeanor betokened exhilaration, I surprised my hostess discreetly removing some crystal epergnes from her foyer. True, I *had* borrowed her husband's brilliantine and inquired several times where people were wont to rumba nowadays; however, I happen to feel that the well-behaved guest does not burden his friends—and his wife's—with confidences, and I did not expatiate.

The section Audrey lived in was easily ten miles distant, south of Hollywood off Olympic Boulevard, and I consumed a good hour blundering around unfamiliar streets in my rented convertible, flashing its headlights up driveways and sending watchdogs into paroxysms. Just before eight o'clock, I drew up before a two-story house of peach-color stucco exhibiting a marked Spanish influence. Its entrance was flanked with dagger cacti, maguey plants, and similar lethal vegetation, so dimly lit that I lacerated my hands unmercifully groping for the bell. As the chimes within subsided, Audrey, her face transfigured with a smile of almost painful radiance, opened the door. She was wearing a black organza dress and some extremely becoming costume jewelry, and, to my uncritical eye, looked very chic, but for the second time that day I was oppressed by her size. The girl really loomed in the doorway.

"My fault for not giving you directions," she cooed, stemming my apologies. "Matter of fact, we didn't finish shooting till late, so I went ahead and had dinner with Mommy. Come in and meet her." Before I could find words to express my signal gaucherie with mothers, I was swept into a baronial hall that might have served as audience chamber for Queen Isabella. A gigantic hooded fireplace bearing the arms of Castile dominated the far end of the room; eight or nine thrones, council chairs, and pews upholstered in red damask and embossed with brass studs were ranged about the tiled floor; and wherever a visitor might want to drop his casque or mailed gloves there was a quartered-oak table or a *prie-dieu*. Seated by a lamp whose parchment-and-mica shade depicted the poop of a galleon was a prim-faced elderly woman in what I took to be a chasuble of flowered cotton. Somehow the workbasket in her lap seemed out of character. I expected her to be holding a mace.

"Do sit down, Mr. Parmalee," she said when Audrey had ceased bellowing my name into her ear. "I've heard so much about you." It occurred to me I was being confused with the transfer people, but instinct warned me to dummy up until I was besought to wrangle a trunk. While Audrey busied herself pouring out two ponies of Chartreuse, Mrs. Merridew embarked on a short review of the advantages of southern California—notably its abundance of flora and paucity of unions. She herself, she signified, was descended from one of the finest families in Georgia and had migrated hither at great personal sacrifice to further her daughter's career. She now feared, though, that an undesirable foreign element was creeping into the picture industry, exposure to which might have a malign effect on Audrey. "Honey, do your Goldwyn imitation," she begged her daughter. "I declare, Mr. Parmalee, it's better than a show." Alluring as was the prospect of a dialect lampoon, I felt the time had come to depart. The ladies exchanged kisses as protracted as though Audrey and I were setting off on a four-year whaling cruise, and in short order I was tooling my date toward a club celebrated for its jazz virtuosi. Audrey adored jazz; in fact, she said, giving me a coquettish nudge that almost capsized our vehicle, next to Easterners there was nothing she loved more than barrelhouse tempered with a couple of mild highballs.

As it developed, the star turn at the club was one of the great modern masters, the incomparable Jess Alexandria Stacy, of Cape Girardeau, Missouri. His keyboard was bewitched that night; never has there been such a rolling bass, such superb arpeggios. I was in a transport—destined, I should have known, to rank as the world's briefest. The moment Audrey's tongue touched bourbon, it began wagging in a key just resonant enough to drown out the music. Had I ever heard Carmen Cavallero play "The Flight of the Bumblebee"?

Yes, I admitted, we had been shipmates en route to Hawaii once, and for a whole blessed week—

Hawaii! She was ecstatic about the South Seas. Had I seen Esther Williams and Howard Keel in *Pagan Love Song*? The shots of Tahiti were ravishing. One day, she and Mommy were going to Tahiti, if it was the last thing they ever did. George Sanders had gone there in that picture about the artist who deserted his family and cut off his ear—she couldn't remember his name, but he had leprosy in the last reel. She understood they had found a new cure for leprosy; it was in the *Reader's Digest*, which she hoped I liked as much as she did, because it was practically her bible. As for artists, she had a particular kinship with them, her onetime girl friend having espoused a man who was in the paint business in Monrovia. Desperately trying to staunch her rhetoric and at the same time pay homage to Stacy, who was doing a transcendent version of "Back Home in Indiana," I made the fatal error of ordering double whiskeys. Under their influence, Audrey not only became more garrulous but beat time on her glass with a muddler. A party of cats in the next booth, who had been giving us frigid glances, started to mutter like the sans-culottes in a novel by Baroness Orczy. When Stacy stopped dead in the middle of "Riverboat Shuffle" and swung around ominously on his stool, I knew that jigwise, all was up.

"Judas priest!" I said, smiting my forehead. "I nearly forgot —Kid Ory's at the Beverly Cavern, with his whole ensemble! They're syncopation plus—let's go!" Luckily, Audrey's mood was still pliant. With a bright, detached smile, she fumbled together her gear and lurched after me.

In the next hour or two, we canvassed every snug on Beverly Boulevard from Figueroa Street to the Sunset Strip, an area comparable in size to Upper Assam. We were in grogshops where the patrons wore turtleneck sweaters and billycocks reminiscent of Chimmie Fadden, in juke joints, bodegas, rathskellers, and even sukiyaki parlors, but nowhere could we find a trace of the Kid and his golden horn. Despite my entreaties, Audrey insisted on pausing frequently for a chota peg, and finally, in a clangorous spot called the Dixieland, she took her stand and refused to continue. Nevertheless, she remained as articulate as ever, chattering away with such verve about her girlhood in the South and race relations there that the Negro bandsmen had to labor to make themselves audible.

At the conflux of Santa Monica and Wilshire boulevards, or hard by, there stands, as it has stood from time immemorial, a restaurant dedicated to serving the world's most succulent hot cakes. I speak of it wistfully—from a threshold acquaintance, as it were, for Audrey chose that point as a central and showy one in which to crumple. Happily, the lobby was crowded with people, many of whom I knew quite well and who were kind enough to avert their faces. The management also reflected admirable restraint by overlooking a philodendron snapped off at the base, and supplied me with native bearers to convey Audrey to the parking lot. On the way home, as I was pondering some means of delivering her short of a block and fall, she suddenly revived. Instead of husbanding her strength, however, she clamored that I must come home and let her prepare us hamburgers. In vain I pleaded that I was a vegetarian and a dyspeptic, that my presence in the house would compromise her, that I had an early appointment with my astrologer. Her insistence became so heated at last that I feared she might do me physical violence, and I pretended to submit. Actually, an easy solution had occurred to me.

"Let's have a bracer first," I whispered conspiratorially, herding her up the walk. "Where does Mommy hide the Chartreuse?" As she careered off into the dark in quest of it, I headed for the kitchen, figuring I could escape by the side door, but my evil star was in the ascendant, and I wound up in a cul-de-sac, a dismal cement patio fenced breast-high with woven paling. To swarm over it in my weakened condition without provoking a hue and cry was manifestly impossible. I was done for, trapped. I sank into a chair and, head in hands, reviled Norman Spindrift and all his issue from hell to breakfast. A few moments later, the odor of frying meat pervaded the air, and out bustled Audrey, sporting a bungalow apron. By some inexplicable process, she had known all along where I was; perhaps her beaux instinctively made for the patio, as eels seek out the Bahama Banks. From then on, the outlines began to shift and blur. I remember Audrey silhouetted against the eucalyptus tops, passionately declaiming fragments of Ella Wheeler Wilcox while I sat by in frozen despair. Through the torpor gradually enveloping me flashed a realization of the hopelessness of my position. I was enmeshed in a monstrous fairy tale, doomed to listen to this giantess until madness set me free. And then, out of the blue—or, rather, the Gray—came my reprieve. The voice of Mrs. Merridew, pure boll-weevil but more melodious to my ears than Galli-Curci's, cut across her daughter's. "Audrey!" it called from above. "It's five o'clock! You hush your bazoo and come to bed!"

A sob of gratitude constricted my larynx, and by the time it relaxed, I was roaring west on Pico Boulevard, jumping every light and singing "The Battle Hymn of the Republic." That I ran out of gas on Copa de Oro Road in Bel-Air and had to finish the journey on foot didn't upset me in the least. I bounced in just as the Japanese gardener was turning on the revolving sprinkler. He inclined his head gravely and I inclined back. We didn't exchange a word. As I always say, the deepest thoughts are those that are left unsaid.

Short Easterly Squall,
with Low Visibility
and Rising Gorge

C

I HAD A STRONG SENSATION of seesaw in rereading Mr. Maugham's agreeable book; what dear old Dr. Johnson in one of his prayers called "vacillation and vagrancy of mind." No wonder; perhaps a kind of telekinesis? For I first read the book last November, aboard my favorite S.S. *Media*, crossing the North Atlantic in what the chief officer's daily bulletins described as a long, very heavy westerly swell. The English edition was then just published and I had bought a copy (12s 6d) as viaticum. You know the tiffin routine aboard a British ship: after plenty of cold beef with mustard, and those huge baked Idahos buttered with red pepper, and a glass of ordinaire at a shilling, you totter up to the corridor of A deck. From your station amidship you see *Media*'s poop mightily soaring and sinking. You fall into your comfortable thwartship berth and in a few minutes—soothed by Mr. Maugham and perhaps a slab of treacle tart—you are off for such siesta as needs an ocean voyage to attain. About 5 P.M. you creep again into the corridor; and observe, through the open door to the after deck, how wildly she oscillates in the gigantic marching swells. . . . One of the things I used to sleep with, in our stormy little *Media,* was the idea of telling Maugham the various ways in which a set of Hazlitt has been one of my supreme frustrations. . . . Sometimes I went asleep with less luxury because Mr. Maugham (like Hazlitt, on whom he tutored himself too stringently) falls off-ear in his sentence-ends, apodoses. But as the ship's doctor said, he has the perfect negative charm: he delights you because he makes it so plain he doesn't care whether you like it or not. . . . How much, while passing unconscious aboard the plunging *Media,* I'd have enjoyed to argue with Mr. Maugham. . . . Mr. Maugham in these random essays seesaws like the *Media;* but no one has better earned the right to compose as he chooses.—*From a review by Christopher Morley of W. Somerset Maugham's* The Vagrant Mood *in the* Times.

WHAT ELFIN CHARM, what pawky and mettlesome humor, tessellate the pages of Oliver Cudlipp's new garland of whimsical papers, *From a Misanthrope's Inkwell!* The title, so gruff that the unwary may not descry the impudent grin lurking beneath the domino, is a wickedly disingenuous one, for if ever author were untainted by the cheap cynicism that characterizes your modernist, "avant-garde" scribbler, it is Cudlipp. Mellow, fantastical, *un feuilletoniste bien spirituel,* he wends his roguish way, gently puncturing our foibles with his unerring quill but never overstepping the bounds of good taste. If, occasionally, it is impossible to tell what he is driving at, do not be fooled into thinking him insipid. Pompous, attitudinizing, unreadable, yes, but never insipid.

Of all the improbable places to encounter Cudlipp's new book, you might suppose British North Borneo the most unlikely, yet there it was, or something very much akin to it, in the pirogue that was ferrying me upriver several years ago to visit my friend Ladysmith at his outstation. You know the *cafard* that overtakes one in those jungle waterways; you've lunched on a handful of stewed *bêche-de-mer*, mayhap, washing it down with a bottle of factitious Bols importuned from some remote Chinese merchant, and you lie there fretfully staring at the impenetrable wall of foliage rising sheer from the pinguid current. Ever and anon the stillness is rent by the scream of a pileated gibbon objurgating a hornbill, or something very much akin to it, but its stridor falls on heedless ear, for in fancy you are in England, peradventure at some transpontine hostel with a goodly company, quaffing the nut-brown October ale and roaring out a Rabelaisian stave. Decent enough though the Dyak paddlers of my craft were, they hadn't the same foci of reference as I, poor fellows; I doubt whether even one of them had ever heard of the *Areopagitica* or Otway's *Venice Preserved*, and time was beginning to hang somewhat heavy. I was all the more surprised, therefore, when the headman reached down one afternoon and proffered a volume I'd noticed floating about in the bilge the past four days.

"Hello, what's this?" I asked, scanning the title page. "Oliver Cudlipp's new tome, *From a Misanthrope's Inkwell?*"

"Him velly good book of whimsical papers," the headman assured me with emphasis. "You catchum plenty bellyraffs along him. Hot off the pless."

"But I say, look here," I expostulated. "The thing isn't scheduled to be published until three years from now. There's the date on the flyleaf, plain as day."

"Me no savvy copylight bobbery," he returned woodenly. "Me just simple Dyak boy, plitty crose to head-hunter." He directed a gob of betel juice expertly over his shoulder into the wake and took a fresh purchase on his sweep. "Borneo velly plimitive island, Tuan, allee same Manhattan," he grunted. "You askum you fliend."

Well, I knew better than to wax disputatious with an indigene who might slit my weasand at the drop of a turban, and, knocking the book against the gunwales to dislodge the leeches, I began savoring it at random. To say the contents absorbed me were to convey only the palest simulacrum of their puissance. I was transfixed, bound hand and foot, and what with the chant of the boatmen, the lap of the wavelets against our hull, and the rhythmic drip of the prose, I was sore put to it to distinguish between sleep and waking. Possessed of a beat at once staccato and sluggish, Cudlipp's style (fain would I refer to it as his *manière*, incorrigible Francophile that I am) defies analysis. It is mealy yet robustious, limpid as a mountain rill yet hopelessly opaque. When, *zum Beispiel*, he recounts the saga of his attempt to discourage a pair of vireos from nesting in an inscribed copy of Hall Caine's *The Deemster*—a contretemps, surely, that has arisen to vex every country dweller—he weaves a noose of drowsy enchantment about the reader such as methinks not even J. Donald Adams could equal. And have any of our *soi-disant* scriveners (a starveling crew by comparison, certes) ever limned frustration more graphically than he in the rueful chronicle wherein a neighborhood grimalkin evicts him from his own rose arbor? At least, that seems to be the theme, though the writing is so elliptical that at times one cannot be sure. I kept asking myself, the rest of the journey upriver, whether one could be sure of anything in Cudlipp's work, and after Ladysmith had leafed through it at my behest, I sued for his opinion.

He gave me a keen glance from under his tufted eyebrows and pulled contemplatively on his briar. "Take the mush out of your mouth, man," he suggested with the bluntness of those who have lived alone much in far places. "Exactly what d'ye want to know?" Ladysmith's an acerb duffer at times, and peradventure he was nettled at the sesquipedalian fashion in which I'd broached the matter.

"Well, everything," I confessed. "Frankly, I can't decide

whether the stuff is balderdash or not, but that's *nihil ad rem*. How in Tophet did this book, which won't be published until year after next, find its way into that pirogue?"

"You don't think the headman might have written it?"

"Oh, come now, Ladysmith," I objected.

"I wouldn't be too certain," he said thoughtfully. "Devious Johnnies, these Malays, as you'd know if you'd mucked about the archipelago as I have. Maybe the beggar found out you were influential and planted it, thinking you'd give him a leg up with the *Saturday Review*."

"But dad burn it, he couldn't have had a linotype and a bindery in his compound," I pointed out with ruthless logic.

"No?" said Ladysmith quietly. "Borneo's full of mysteries, laddie buck. I could tell you a weird tale." I pricked up my ears, but judging from the hush that ensued, broken only by the unmistakable crepitation of a hornbill excoriating a gibbon, my host must have fallen into a doze. After an interval, he rekindled his pipe. "See here," he said abruptly. "Maybe it hasn't any connection, but a rum thing happened to me a while ago. You knew I'd been a ship's surgeon?"

"I rather guessed it," I said. "I noticed a laryngoscope in your medical kit, the kind they use to auscultate—"

"Yes, yes," he cut me short testily. "Well, I've seen my share of salt water—nine years Chinaside with P. & O., Liverpool to Durban for the Union Castle people, pretty much everywhere. My last berth was transatlantic, one of those small Cunarders whose name escapes me for the moment—the *Miasma*, or something of the kind. We'd a literary cove aboard that trip—vital, tweedy sort of wallah, forever spouting Pepys and grousing to the bar steward because he didn't serve mulled sack or posset. Great trencherman, too; I used to watch him shovel in the victuals and pray to God his pepsin would hold out till we sighted Ambrose Channel. The deuce of it was that he had the cabin next to mine, and after cramming himself full of hell's own quantity of carbohydrates at lunch—which he insisted on calling tiffin, though we were well west of Suez—he'd stretch out in his bunk and lapse into these wild literary nightmares. You couldn't help overhearing 'em through the bulkhead. Full of eftsoons and quothas and all that rot."

"Could you make out what he was saying, *par hasard?*" I asked, enthralled.

"Only in a general way," admitted Ladysmith. "He seemed to be wrangling with somebody called Maugham about which one of them had a better right to imitate Hazlitt. Sounded pretty rancorous, though of course I couldn't hear Maugham's end of it. Who is he, anyway—some newcomer?"

"Oh, just one of those two-dimensional bores who make a fetish of being lucid," I said impatiently. "But do go on. Did you ever get to know the chap? What was his name?"

"I haven't the foggiest," returned Ladysmith. "It was a rough passage and all hands went horizontal, including my neighbor. On the return, I asked the purser and stewards who he was, but they'd forgotten him, and, oddly enough, there wasn't a trace of any such person in the passenger list." He emitted a mirthless chuckle. "It gave me rather a turn, I don't mind telling you. I'd always supposed I knew chalk from cheese, and yet here, under one's very nose, was a phantom writer—a literary Flying Dutchman, so to speak. Well, Ladysmith, thought I, you're potty; best join the civil service out East, where it'll never be noticed. And then, just off Land's End, the ship's librarian fetched around a book this passenger had given him, a collection of prankish tidbits called *Jiggery-Pokery.*"

"Half a guinea I know the rest," I burst out. "It was by Cudlipp here!"

"Don't ask me," said Ladysmith, with a shrug. "The title page was in ribbons and the spine was blurred, but it was the same sort of twaddle. What's more—and here's why it all came back just now—it was dated ahead, exactly like this thing. I checked with the publisher, who'd never heard of it. Wasn't expecting any such work for at least two years."

"Still," I pleaded, "he must have known who the author *was*."

"How could he, you bloody fool?" snapped Ladysmith. "He couldn't tell till he received the manuscript." He tossed the charred remnants of his briar to the white ants and arose. "Well, cheerio," he said shortly. "Too bad you'll be gone before I'm up in the morning, but that's Borneo. I'd watch my head going downriver, by the bye. Just between us, you're crowding your luck."

And there, through the eyes of one who almost knew Cudlipp and another who treasures him but affectionately recognizes his limitations, is the essence of that verbal enigma, that bard of ambiguity. Let the plaudits due him be withheld no longer; let him issue into the agora and be crowned with the laurel, the bay, and anything else that is handy. For these are piping times, and an he hang back, some Grub Street witling might make shift to gobble up his royalties. . . . By my halidom, I may do it myself, and cry pox on the Authors' League. They'll never catch up with me in Borneo.

When to the Sessions
of Sweet Silent Films . . .

ON A slumberous afternoon in the autumn of 1919, the shop-keepers along Weybosset Street in Providence, Rhode Island, were nonplused by a mysterious blinding flash. Simultaneously, they heard a sound like a gigantic champagne cork being sucked out of a bottle, and their windows bulged inward as though Dario Resta's Peugeot had passed, traveling at incalculable speed. Erupting from their bazaars, they saw a puny figure streaking in the direction of the Victory, the town's leading cinema. The first report, that anarchists had blown the cupola off the state capitol, swiftly yielded to a second, that a gopher mob had knocked over the vault of the Mercers' & Pursers' Trust Co. Before either rumor could be checked, a bystander appeared with a green baize bag dropped by the fugitive, establishing him as a sophomore at the Classical High School. Among its contents were a copy of Caesar's Gallic commentaries, a half-eaten jelly sandwich, and a newspaper advertisement announcing the première that afternoon at the Victory of Cecil B. DeMille's newest epic, *Male and Female*, starring Thomas Meighan, Gloria Swanson, and Lila Lee.

By the time the foregoing had been pieced together, of course, the sophomore in question—whose measurements coincided exactly with my own—was hanging out of a balcony seat at the Victory in a catatonic state, impervious to everything but the photoplay dancing on the screen. My absorption was fortunate, for at regular intervals the ushers circulated through the aisles, spraying the audience with an orange scent that practically ate away the mucous membrane. Whether this was intended to stimulate the libido or inhibit it, I never found out, but twenty years later, when I met Mr. DeMille in Hollywood, I could have sworn he exuded the same fragrance. The fact that we met in an orange grove, while relevant, did not materially alter my conviction.

Male and Female, as moviegoers of that epoch will recall, was based on James M. Barrie's *The Admirable Crichton*, a play that derided caste and sought to demonstrate how a family of *hochgeboren* snobs, marooned on a desert island, was salvaged physically and spiritually by its butler. That so special a problem could enthrall a youth living on a New England chicken farm might seem unlikely, but it did, and to such a degree that I saw the picture twice over again on the spot. The silken luxury of its settings, the worldliness and bon ton of the characters, and their harrowing privations held me spellbound. I was bewitched in particular by the butler as portrayed by Thomas Meighan. His devastating aplomb, the cool, quiet authority with which he administered his island kingdom and subdued the spitfire Lady Mary Lasenby, played by Miss Swanson, displaced every previous matinée idol from my heart. For weeks afterward, while toting mash to the hens or fumigating their perches, I would fall into noble attitudes and apostrophize the flock with lines like "One cannot tell what may be in a man, Milady. If all were to return to Nature tomorrow, the same man might not be master, nor the same man servant. Shall I serve the ices in the conservatory?" The consequences of this sort of lallygagging soon made themselves felt. There was a sharp decline in egg production, followed almost immediately by word from the Classical High School that I had achieved the lowest grade ever recorded in second-year Latin.

QUITE RECENTLY, through the good offices of the Museum of Modern Art, I was enabled to re-examine the masterwork that gave me so profound a catharsis. It was a reassuring experience; I discovered that although the world is topsy-turvy, DeMille still remains the same. His latest pictures display the same baroque pomp, the same good old five-cent philosophy, and the same lofty disregard for sense. *Male and Female* could be remade today with equal success at the box office. All I ask in return for the suggestion is that prior to its release I be given twenty-four hours' head start.

The film begins with a pious explanation that its title is derived from the passage in Genesis "Male and female created He them," and first introduces a scullery maid named Tweeny, in the person of Lila Lee. Tweeny is employed at fashionable Loam House, in London, where she nurses a violent, unreciprocated passion for its major-domo, Crichton. We now meet, in a series of keyhole shots, the various members of the Loam family as they appear to an impudent pageboy delivering their boots. They are, respectively, the Earl (Theodore Roberts), his silly-ass cousin Ernest (Raymond Hatton), and his daughters, Lady Mary and Lady Agatha. Miss Swanson, the former, reclines on a couch worthy of the Serpent of the Nile, having her nails and hair done by a pair of maids. This lovely sybarite is to learn, says an acid subtitle, that "hands are not only to be manicured but to work with, heads not only to dress but to think with, hearts not only to beat but to love with." Her sister, a languid wraith engaged in scrutinizing her cosmetic mask, fares no more kindly: "Lady Agatha, who is to find like most beauties that the condition of her face is less important than to learn to face conditions." There follows a piquant scene wherein Miss Swanson dons a peekaboo negligee, sinuously peels to enter a sunken marble tub, and sluices down in a shower containing a spigot marked "Toilet Water." Emerging, she finds a box of long-stemmed roses sent by an admirer named Lord Brocklehurst. The accompanying card read (as I thought), "My Lady of the Roses: I am coming over to show you something interesting for the slim white finger of your slim third hand," but this seemed so Surrealist in mood that I had the projectionist run it again. The actual phrase, "slim third finger of your slim white hand," is pretty humdrum by comparison.

Depicted next is the ritual of Lady Mary's breakfast, served by three underlings and presided over by Crichton. "The toast is spoiled," declares his mistress capriciously. "It's entirely too soft." Ever the flower of courtesy, Crichton pinks her neatly in the ego with a deadpan riposte: "Are you sure, Milady, that the toast is the only thing that is spoiled?" Leaving her to gnash her teeth on the soggy toast, he descends to the library, where Tweeny is dusting, and proceeds to read aloud, for no cogent reason, a dollop of poesy by William Ernest Henley beginning, "I was a King in Babylon and you were a Christian slave." The scullery maid, eyes swimming with adoration, furtively strokes his instep. "I wouldn't be nobody's slave, I wouldn't," she murmurs. "Unless maybe your slave." Lady Mary, who by a spooky coincidence has been reading the very same book earlier, now enters just in time to hear Crichton declaiming, "I saw, I took, I cast you by, I gently broke your pride." The delicious spectacle of varlets pretending to understand poetry evokes her patrician mirth, and, imperiously requisitioning the book, she goes to greet Lord Brocklehurst, her suitor.

Brocklehurst, by and large, is an inconsequential character in the drama—merely a lay figure dragged in to spice the budding romance between Lady Mary and Crichton. The plot, which has been betraying definite symptoms of rigor mortis, comes alive about teatime, when the Loams, frantic with ennui, determine to cruise to the South Seas in their yacht. As they animatedly begin studying maps, a confidante of Lady Mary's, Lady Eileen Duncraigie, drops in to consult her about a glandular dilemma. She is infatuated with her chauffeur—one of those typical crushes that followed in the wake of the internal-combustion engine—and wonders whether she stands any chance of happiness. Lady Mary smiles commiseratingly. Indicating a bird cage nearby, she poses a searching zoological parallel: "Would you put a jackdaw and a bird of paradise in the same cage? It's *kind to kind*, Eileen, and you and I can never change it." Well, sir, you know what happens to people who run off at the mouth like that. It's even money La Belle Swanson will be eating crow before the turn of the monsoon, and the cinematic bobbin shuttles madly back and forth as it starts weaving her comeuppance.

Dissolving to the Loam yacht at sea, we observe our principals leading the same unregenerate existence—squabbling endlessly and being coddled by Crichton, whose insteps, in turn, are being dogged by Tweeny. In a newspaper presumably flown to her by albatross, Lady Mary reads of her friend's marriage to her chauffeur. "I suppose," waggishly remarks Ernest, "that if one married a chauffeur, one would soon *tire* of him—get it?" Lady Mary haughtily rejoins that the whole affair is ridiculous—exactly as if she were to marry Crichton. The latter's face freezes as he overhears the slur, and when Thomas Meighan's face, already icy to begin with, froze, it looked like Christmas at Crawford Notch. "And there," explains a crunchy caption, "it might have ended had they not been blown by the Winds of Chance into uncharted Tropic Seas with Destiny smiling at the wheel." Which, draining away the schmaltz, is to say that the yacht runs aground, the crew obligingly perishes, and the Loams, plus their retinue, are washed up intact. The shot that gave one the old *frisson* in 1919, of course, was Meighan carrying Miss Swanson, more dead than alive and more naked than not, out of the surf. It is still gripping, and for those who are curious about its effect on Meighan—inasmuch as there is no clue to be found in his features—the succeeding title is helpful: "Suddenly, like mist melting before the sun, she was no longer a great lady to him, but just a woman, a very helpless and beautiful woman." Brother, they don't write subtitles like that any more. The fellows who dream up the scenarios nowadays are daffy enough, to be sure, but there's no *poetry* in them.

It takes approximately a reel and a half of celluloid and some of the most cumbersome foolery since the retirement of Louise Fazenda to reunite the shipwrecked party. The Earl, who has landed in a dressing gown and yachting cap, chewing the celebrated Theodore Roberts cigar, becomes embroiled in various comic misadventures, such as nestling against a turtle he mistakes for a boulder and disputing possession of a coconut with some chimpanzees. The mishmash of fauna on the island, by the way, would confound any naturalist past the age of twelve; I doubt whether Alfred Russel Wallace, either in the depths of the Malay Archipelago or malarial fever, ever saw apes and mountain goats, wild boars and leopards, sharing a Pacific atoll. When noses are finally counted, the survivors number seven—the four Loams, Crichton and Tweeny, and an unidentified young minister whose presence is never quite explained but whom DeMille was doubtless limbering up for one of his later Biblical productions. Crichton borrows the padre's watch crystal to light a fire, allots various chores to the group, and in short order manages to arouse Lady Mary's anger. When he proposes to use her gold lace stole as a fish net, she rebels openly and talks the others into seceding, but the revolt soon collapses. One by one, the insurgents sneak back to Crichton's fire and his kettle of seaweed broth, leaving her impenitent and alone. Then she too weakens, for, as the subtitle puts it, "You may resist hunger, you may resist cold, but the fear of the unseen can break the strongest will." The unseen in this case takes the form of a moth-eaten cheetah rented from Charlie Gay's lion farm in El Monte. As he noses through the undergrowth, Lady Mary's nerve cracks and she scurries to Crichton for protection. Ultimately, after much digging of her toe awkwardly in the hot sand, or what used to be known as the Charlie Ray school of acting, she knocks under and ponies up the gold lace stole. The sequence, or the round, or whatever it is, ends with both breathing hard but not the least bit winded—considerably more, goodness knows, than can be said for the spectator.

"Under the whiplash of necessity," the narrative continues sonorously, "they come to find that the wilderness is cruel only to the drone, that her grassy slopes may clothe the ragged, her wild boar feed the hungry, her wild goats slake their thirst." Two years, we discover, have wrought substantial changes in the castaways. They have fashioned themselves a nobby compound, domesticated everything in sight but the chiggers, and dwell contentedly under a benevolent despotism set up by Crichton. Lady Mary and Lady Agatha, in play suits of woven bark and in Robinson Crusoe hats, skip over the savannas hunting wild fowl with bow and arrow; the Earl, still chewing the same cigar stump, hauls lobster pots on the lagoon; Ernest and the anonymous divine milk goats in a corral; Tweeny, whose status nothing apparently can alter, stirs a caldron of poi in the kitchen; and Crichton, garbed in a tunic resembling a Roman centurion's made of palm fronds, labors in his study on a Boob McNutt contraption designed to ignite a rescue flare on the cliffs. His new eminence is illustrated at mealtime that evening, when he is revealed dining in splendid isolation, fanned by a punkah that is operated by Lady Mary. Henley's poems, providentially saved from the wreck, are propped up before him, and he is rereading "I was a King in Babylon," the eternal references to which were beginning to give me a dull pain in the base of my scullery. It presently develops that the greedy old Earl has eaten some figs earmarked for Crichton's dessert, and Lady Mary hurries to pick more. Learning she has gone to "the drinking place of the leopards," Crichton hastens after her and transfixes one of the beasts as it attacks. She gratefully flings herself into his arms, and confesses her belief that he is the reincarnation of a king in Babylon. "Then you were a Christian slave," he says with sudden understanding, turning her face up to his. The action thereupon pauses for what is unquestionably the snazziest flashback that has ever emerged from silver nitrate. Meighan, duked out as a Semitic tyrant on the order of Ashurbanipal, receives from a vassal a tigerish, scantily clad slave girl—i.e., Miss Swanson—who repays his tentative caresses by biting him in the wrist. With a cruel sneer, he promises to tame her, and she is borne off snarling defiance in the classic tradition. In due time, she re-enters on a palanquin powered by Nubians, clothed in sequins and wearing on her head a triumph of the taxidermist's art, a stuffed white peacock. "Bring forth the sacred lions of Ishtar," Meighan commands, gesturing toward an arena installed meanwhile by the studio carpenters. "Choose thine own fate. Yield to me willingly or thou shalt know the fitting cage built for thee, O Tiger Woman." Secure in her long-term contract, Miss Swanson proudly elevates her chin. "Through lives and lives you shall pay, O King," she predicts, and advances into the pit. As the episode concludes, we are back on the island, with Crichton telling Lady Mary, in mettlesome spondees, "I know I've paid through lives and lives, but I loved you then as I love you now." A Zbyszko hammer lock, and at long last their lips, parched with rhetoric, meet in a lingering kiss.

24

The note of implied finality, however, is only a ruse; if the fable is to come full circle, its characters must show the effect of their sojourn away from civilization. Just as the pair are being united by the preacher, a ship appears on the horizon. Lady Mary tries to dissuade her chieftain from signaling for help, but he knows the code and gallantly bows to it. "Babylon has fallen and Crichton must play the game," he announces, gently unyoking her arms and yoking the metaphors.

Transported back to England in an agile dissolve, master and servant promptly revert to type. Lady Mary agrees to wed Lord Brocklehurst, though she reveals her heartbreak to Lady Eileen, whose marriage to her chauffeur has spelled social obloquy. Crichton retaliates by proposing to Tweeny, and, in a penultimate scene, we see them, between kisses, operating an Australian sheep farm. For the tag, or washup, DeMille chose a bittersweet dying fall. On the lawn of a vast country house, amid drifting petals, Lady Mary toys with her parasol and dreams of what might have been. The title reads, "You may break, you may shatter, the vase if you will, but the scent of the roses will hang around her still. Thus does the great sacrifice shed its fragrance over a lifetime." Enter a beflanneled Brocklehurst, who stands regarding her with doglike devotion. "I understand, my dear, why you postponed our marriage," he declares, manfully sweeping up the loose exposition. "You loved Crichton, the admirable Crichton. I'll be waiting for you at the judgment day." He raises her hand to his lips, Lady Mary's eyes under her picture hat fill with tears, and, to use a very apt technical term, we squeeze.

I SUSPECT that a lot of people in my generation, the kind of romantics who blubber at the sight of a Maxfield Parrish print or a Jordan roadster, would not have withstood my sentimental excursion as gracefully as I did, and would have wound up fractured at the Jumble Shop, harmonizing "The Japanese Sandman." Matter of fact, I ran into a couple of these romantics *at* the Jumble Shop, strangely enough, right after seeing *Male and Female*. We got to talking, and darned if they hadn't seen it too as kids. Well, we had a bite of supper, took in the ice show at the Hotel New Yorker, and then, armed with plenty of ratchets, started back to the Museum about midnight so I could screen the picture for them. Luckily, their car hit a hydrant en route and I managed to slip away unnoticed. If I hadn't kept my wits about me, though, the whole day might have ended with much worse than eyestrain. As a middle-aged movie fan, I've learned one lesson: Lay off that nostalgia, cousin. It's lethal.

No Starch in the Dhoti,
S'il Vous Plaît

Up until recently, I had always believed that nobody on earth could deliver a throwaway line with quite the sang-froid of a certain comedian I worked for in Hollywood during the thirties. You probably don't recall the chap, but his hallmark was a big black mustache, a cigar, and a loping gait, and his three brothers, also in the act, impersonated with varying degrees of success a mute, an Italian, and a clean-cut boy. My respect for Julio (to cloak his identity partially) stemmed from a number of pearls that fell from his lips during our association, notably one inspired by an argument over dietary customs. We were having dinner at an off-Broadway hotel, in the noisiest locale imaginable outside the annual fair at Nizhnii Novgorod. There were at least a dozen people in the party—lawyers, producers, agents, brokers, astrologers, tipsters, and various assorted sycophants—for, like all celebrated theatrical personages, my man liked to travel with a retinue. The dining room was jammed, some paid-up ghoul from Local 802 was interpreting the "Habanera" on an electric organ over the uproar, and, just to insure dyspepsia, a pair of adagio dancers were flinging themselves with abandon in and out of our food. I was seated next to Julio, who was discoursing learnedly to me on his favorite subject, anatomical deviations among showgirls. Halfway through the meal, we abruptly became aware of a dispute across the table between several of our companions.

"It is *not* just religious!" one was declaring hotly. "They knew a damn sight more about hygiene than you think in those Biblical days!"

"That still don't answer my question!" shouted the man he had addressed. "If they allow veal and mutton and beef, why do they forbid pork?"

"Because it's unclean, you dummy," the other rasped. "I'm trying to tell you—the pig is an unclean animal!"

"What's that?" demanded Julio, his voice slicing through the altercation. "The pig an unclean animal?" He rose from his chair and repeated the charge to be certain everyone within fifty feet was listening. "The pig an unclean animal? Why, the pig is the cleanest animal there is—except my father, of course." And dropped like a falcon back into his chow mein.

As I say, I'd gone along for years considering Julio preeminent in tossing off this kind of grenade, and then one Sunday a few weeks ago, in the *Times* Magazine, I stumbled across an item that leaves no doubt he has been deposed. The new champ is Robert Trumbull, the former Indian correspondent of the paper and a most affable bird with whom I once spent an afternoon crawling around the Qutb Minar, outside New Delhi. In the course of an article called "Portrait of a Symbol Named Nehru," Mr. Trumbull had the following to say: "Nehru is accused of having a congenital distaste for Americans because of their all too frequent habit of bragging and of being patronizing when in unfamiliar surroundings. It is said that in the luxurious and gracious house of his father, the late Pandit Motilal Nehru—who sent his laundry to Paris—the young Jawaharlal's British nurse used to make caustic remarks to the impressionable boy about the table manners of his father's American guests."

It was, of course, the utter nonchalance of the phrase "who sent his laundry to Paris" that knocked me galley-west. Obviously, Trumbull wasn't referring to one isolated occasion; he meant that the Pandit made a practice of consigning his laundry to the post, the way one used to under the academic elms. But this was no callow sophomore shipping his wash home to save money. A man willful and wealthy enough to have it shuttled from one hemisphere to another could hardly have been prompted by considerations of thrift. He must have been a consummate perfectionist, a fussbudget who wanted every last pleat in order, and, remembering my own Homeric wrangles with laundrymen just around the corner, I blenched at the complications his overseas dispatch must have entailed. Conducted long before there was any air service between India and Europe, it would have involved posting the stuff by sea— a minimum of three weeks in each direction, in addition to the time it took for processing. Each trip would have created problems of customs examination, valuation, duty (unless Nehru senior got friends to take it through for him, which was improbable; most people detest transporting laundry across the world, even their own). The old gentleman had evidently had a limitless wardrobe, to be able to dispense with portions of it for three months at a time.

The major headache, as I saw it, though, would have been coping with the *blanchisseur* himself. How did Pandit Motilal get any service or redress out of him at such long range? There were the countless vexations that always arise: the missing sock, the half-pulverized button, the insistence on petrifying everything with starch despite the most detailed instructions.

29

The more I thought about it, the clearer it became that he must have been enmeshed in an unending correspondence with the laundry owner. I suggest, accordingly, that while the exact nature of his letters can only be guessed at, it might be useful —or, by the same token, useless—to reconstruct a few, together with the replies they evoked. Even if they accomplish nothing else, they should help widen the breach between East and West.

ALLAHABAD,
UNITED PROVINCES,
JUNE 7, 1903

Pleurniche et Cie.,
124, Avenue de la Grande Armée, Paris.
MY DEAR M. PLEURNICHE:

You may be interested to learn—though I doubt that anything would stir you out of your vegetable torpor—that your pompous, florid, and illiterate scrawl of the 27th arrived here with insufficient postage, forcing me to disgorge one rupee three annas to the mailman. How symbolic of your character, how magnificently consistent! Not content with impugning the quality of the cambric in my drawers, you contrive to make me *pay* for the insult. That transcends mere nastiness, you know. If an international award for odium is ever projected, have no fear of the outcome as far as India is concerned. You can rely on my support.

And à propos of symbols, there is something approaching genius in the one that graces your letterhead, the golden fleece. Could any trademark be more apt for a type who charges six francs to wash a cummerbund? I realize that appealing to your sense of logic is like whistling an aria to the deaf, but I paid half that for it originally, and the Muslim who sold it to me was the worst thief in the bazaar. Enlighten me, my dear fellow, since I have never been a tradesman myself—what passes through your head when you mulct a customer in this outra-

geous fashion? Is it glee? Triumph? Self-approbation at the
cunning with which you have swindled your betters? I ask altogether without malice, solely from a desire to fathom the dark
intricacies of the human mind.

To revert now to the subject of the drawers. It will do you
no good to bombinate endlessly about sleazy material, de-
terioration from pounding on stones, etc. That they were immersed in an acid bath powerful enough to corrode a zinc
plate, that they were wrenched through a mangle with utmost
ferocity, that they were deliberately spattered with grease and
kicked about the floor of your establishment, and, finally, that a
white-hot iron was appliquéd on their seat—the whole sordid
tale of maltreatment is writ there for anybody to see. The
motive, however, is far less apparent, and I have speculated
for hours on why I should be the target of vandalism. Only one
explanation fits the facts. Quite clearly, for all your extortionate
rates, you underpay your workmen, and one of them, seeking
to revenge himself, wreaked his spite on my undergarment.
While I sympathize with the poor rascal's plight, I wish it understood that I hold you responsible to the very last sou. I therefore deduct from the enclosed draft nine francs fifty, which will
hardly compensate me for the damage to my raiment and my
nerves, and remain, with the most transitory assurances of my
regard,

Sincerely yours,
PANDIT MOTILAL NEHRU

PARIS,
JULY 18, 1903

Pandit Motilal Nehru,
Allahabad, U.P., India.
DEAR PANDIT MOTILAL:

I am desolated beyond words at the pique I sense between
the lines in your recent letter, and I affirm to you on my wife's
honor that in the six generations the family has conducted this

business, yours is the first complaint we have ever received. Were I to list the illustrious clients we have satisfied—Robespierre, the Duc d'Enghien, Saint-Saëns, Coquelin, Mérimée, Bouguereau, and Dr. Pasteur, to name but a handful—it would read like a roll call of the immortals. Only yesterday, Marcel Proust, an author you will hear more of one of these days, called at our *établissement* (establishment) to felicitate us in person. The work we do for him is peculiarly exacting; due to his penchant for making notes on his cuffs, we must observe the greatest discretion in selecting which to launder. In fine, our function is as much editorial as sanitary, and he stated unreservedly that he holds our literary judgment in the highest esteem. I ask you, could a firm with traditions like these stoop to the pettifoggery you imply?

You can be sure, however, that if our staff has been guilty of any oversight, it will not be repeated. Between ourselves, we have been zealously weeding out a Socialist element among the employees, malcontents who seek to inflame them with vicious nonsense about an eleven-hour day and compulsory ventilation. Our firm refusal to compromise one iota has borne fruit; we now have a hard core of loyal and spiritless drudges, many of them so lackluster that they do not even pause for lunch, which means a substantial time saving and consequently much speedier service for the customer. As you see, my dear Pandit Motilal, efficiency and devotion to our clientele dominate every waking thought at Pleurniche.

As regards your last consignment, all seems to be in order; I ask leave, though, to beg one trifling favor that will help us execute your work more rapidly in future. Would you request whoever mails the laundry to make certain it contains no living organisms? When the current order was unpacked, a small yellow-black serpent, scarcely larger than a pencil but quite dynamic, wriggled out of one of your *dhotis* and spread terror in the workroom. We succeeded in decapitating it after a modicum of trouble and bore it to the Jardin d'Acclimatation, where the curator identified it as a krait, the most lethal of your indigenous snakes. Mind you, I personally thought M. Ratisbon an alarmist—the little émigré impressed me as a rather cunning fellow, vivacious, intelligent, and capable of transformation into a household pet if one had leisure. Unfortunately, we have none, so fervent is our desire to accelerate your shipments, and you will aid us materially by a hint in the right quarter, if you will. Accept, I implore of you, my salutations the most distinguished.

> Yours cordially,
> OCTAVE-HIPPOLYTE PLEURNICHE

ALLAHABAD, U.P.,
SEPTEMBER 11, 1903

DEAR M. PLEURNICHE:

If I were a hothead, I might be tempted to horsewhip a Yahoo who has the effrontery to set himself up as a patron of letters; if a humanitarian, to garrote him and earn the gratitude of the miserable wretches under his heel. As I am neither, but simply an idealist fatuous enough to believe he is entitled to what he pays for, I have a favor to ask of you, in turn. Spare me, I pray, your turgid rhetoric and bootlicking protestations, and be equally sparing of the bleach you use on my shirts. After a single baptism in your vats, my sky-blue *jibbahs* faded to a ghastly greenish-white and the fabric evaporates under one's touch. Merciful God, whence springs this compulsion to eliminate every trace of color from my dress? Have you now become arbiters of fashion as well as littérateurs?

In your anxiety to ingratiate yourselves, incidentally, you have exposed me to as repugnant an experience as I can remember. Five or six days ago, a verminous individual named Champignon arrived here from Pondichéry, asserting that he was

33

your nephew, delegated by you to expedite my household laundry problems. The blend of unction and cheek he displayed, reminiscent of a process server, should have warned me to beware, but, tenderhearted ninny that I am, I obeyed our Brahmin laws of hospitality and permitted him to remain the night. Needless to say, he distinguished himself. After a show of gluttony to dismay Falstaff, he proceeded to regale the dinner table with a disquisition on the art of love, bolstering it with quotations from the Kamasutra so coarse that one of the ladies present fainted dead away. Somewhat later, I surprised him in the kitchen tickling a female servant, and when I demurred, he rudely advised me to stick to my rope trick and stay out of matters that did not concern me. He was gone before daylight, accompanied by a Jaipur enamel necklace of incalculable value and all our spoons. I felt it was a trivial price to be rid of him. Nevertheless, I question your wisdom, from a commercial standpoint, in employing such emissaries. Is it not safer to rob the customer in the old humdrum fashion, a franc here and a franc there, than to stake everything on a youth's judgment and risk possible disaster? I subscribe myself, as always,

Your well-wisher,

PANDIT MOTILAL NEHRU

PARIS,

OCTOBER 25, 1903

DEAR PANDIT MOTILAL:

We trust that you have received the bundle shipped five weeks since and that our work continues to gratify. It is also pleasing to learn that our relative M. Champignon called on you and managed to be of assistance. If there is any further way he can serve you, do not hesitate to notify him.

I enclose herewith a cutting which possibly needs a brief explanation. As you see, it is a newspaper advertisement embodying your photograph and a text woven out of laudatory remarks culled from your letters to us. Knowing you would gladly concur, I took the liberty of altering a word or two in places to clarify the meaning and underline the regard you hold us in. This dramatic license, so to speak, in no way vitiates the sense of what you wrote; it is quite usual in theatrical advertising to touch up critical opinion, and to judge from comment I have already heard, you will enjoy publicity throughout the continent of Europe for years to come. Believe us, dear Pandit, your eternal debtor, and allow me to remain

Yours fraternally,
OCTAVE-HIPPOLYTE PLEURNICHE

ALLAHABAD,
NOVEMBER 14, 1903

DEAR M. PLEURNICHE:

The barristers I retained immediately on perusing your letter—Messrs. Bulstrode & Hawfinch, of Covent Garden, a firm you will hear more of one of these days—have cautioned me not to communicate with you henceforth, but the urge to speak one final word is irresistible. After all, when their suit for a million francs breaks over you like a thunderclap, when the bailiffs seize your business and you are reduced to sleeping along the *quais* and subsisting on the carrot greens you pick up around Les Halles, you may mistakenly attribute your predicament to my malignity, to voodoo, djinns, etc. Nothing of the sort, my dear chap. Using me to publicize your filthy little concern is only a secondary factor in your downfall. What doomed you from the start was the bumbling incompetence, the ingrained slovenliness, that characterizes everyone in your calling. A man too indolent to replace the snaps he tears from a waistcoat or expunge the rust he sprinkles on a brand-new Kashmiri shawl is obviously capable of any infamy, and it ill becomes him to snivel when retribution overtakes him in the end.

Adieu then, *mon brave,* and try to exhibit in the dock at least the dignity you have failed to heretofore. With every good wish and the certainty that nothing I have said has made the slightest possible impression on a brain addled by steam, I am,

Compassionately,

PANDIT MOTILAL NEHRU

De Gustibus Ain't
What Dey Used to Be

A GIRL and the four walls she lives in can get mighty tired of each other. Especially in mid-winter. Well, here are twenty-five transfusions which, with a minimum investment of time and money, will repay sparkling dividends. They're as effective as the dozen roses someone once sent you just for fun, as easy as a birthday telephone call. Most of them don't even demand that you roll up your sleeves.

1. Invest in eight small white pots of ivy to range on your window sills. 2. *Paint* a gaily fringed rug on a wooden floor. 3. Rent an original picture from a painting rental library. (Between $2 and $35 will let you live with a masterpiece for two months.) 4. Put a bowl of glittering goldfish on your coffee table. 5. Partition a room with fish-net running on a ceiling track. 6. Get a kitten. 7. Cover your throw pillows with polka-dot cotton—perhaps white dots on black, black dots on white—variously sized and

spaced. 8. Get a mobile to grace your room with motion—or better, make one yourself. 9. Slip cover your couch in dark denim—navy, brown or charcoal, maybe—depending on your color scheme. 10. If your living room walls are plain—on a Sunday, wallpaper just one wall. 11. Give houseroom to a *tree* in a big wooden tub. 12. Paste golden notary seals in an all-over design on your white window shades. 13. Wallpaper the insides of your cabinets and drawers with a flower print. 14. Have a favorite drawing photostated up as big as they'll make it; then hang it on your wall. 15. Forget polishing forever and spray all your metal surfaces with a new plastic preservative. 16. Buy a new shower curtain—and make it SILLY. 17. Make a new table cloth out of irresistible cotton yard goods. 18. Draw outline pictures of your kitchen utensils on the wall right where each should hang. 19. Dye your mother's white damask table cloths in brilliant shades. If they're huge, cut the surplus up into squares and hem them for napkins. 20. Put silk fringe along the bottoms of window shades. 21. Get yards of fake leopard skin to throw over your studio couch. 22. Make a cork bulletin board. 23. Cover your lampshades in wallpaper to match your papered walls. 24. Find some cutlery boxes to keep your jewelry lucid in the drawers. 25. Invest in flowered china or glass doorknobs.

. . . And if you're still yearning for a change: Spend an evening by candlelight.

—Glamour.

SCENE: *A one-room apartment in Manhattan occupied by April Monkhood, a young career woman. At some time prior to rise, April and her four walls have tired of each other, and she has called in Fussfeld, a neighborhood decorator, to give the premises the twenty-five transfusions recommended above. Fussfeld, a lineal descendant of Brigadier General Sir Harvey Fussfeld-Gorgas, the genius who pacified the Sudan, has attacked the assignment with the same zeal that characterized his famous relative. He has placed at stage center a magnificent specimen of Bechtel's flowering crab, the boughs of which are so massive that it has been necessary to stay them with cables and turnbuckles. This has perforce complicated the problem of the fish-net partitions on their ceiling tracks, but, fortunately, most of these have ripped off and now depend from the branches, supplying a romantic effect akin to that of Spanish moss. What with the hodgepodge of damask, yard goods, fake leopard skin, floral wallpaper, silk fringe, and notary seals, it is difficult at first to distinguish any animate object. Finally, though, the eye picks out a rather scrawny kitten, licking its lips by an overturned goldfish bowl. A moment later, April Monkhood enters from the kitchenette, practically on all fours. She is a vivacious brownette in knee-hugging poltroons, with a retroussé nose which she wears in a horsetail. Behind her comes Fussfeld, a small, haggard gentleman with a monocle he affects for chic. However, since he is constantly losing it in the décor and scrabbling about for it, he fails to achieve any impressive degree of sang-froid.*

FUSSFELD (*dubiously*): I'm not so sure it's advisable, dusting spangles over the gas stove like that. The pilot light—

APRIL: Now, Mr. Feldpot, don't be an old fuss— I mean stop worrying, will you? It's gay, it's chintzy. It's a whiff of Mardi Gras and the storied Vieux Carré of New Orleans.

FUSSFELD (*with a shrug*): Listen, if *you* want to run down a fire escape in your nightgown, that's your privilege. (*Looking around*) Well, does the job suit you O.K.?

APRIL: Mad about it, my dear—simply transported. Of course, it doesn't quite have a feeling of being lived in . . .

FUSSFELD: I'd sprinkle around a few periodicals, or a can of salted peanuts or so. Anyway, a place gets more homey after your friends drop around.

APRIL: Golly, I can't wait to have my housewarming. Can you imagine when people step off the dumbwaiter and see this room by candlelight?

FUSSFELD (*faintly*): You—er—you're hoisting them up here?

APRIL: How else? We'll be using the stairs outside to eat on.

FUSSFELD: M-m-m. I'm trying to visualize it.

APRIL: I thought of Basque place-mats, two on each stair, and sweet little favors made of putty. Don't you think that would be amusing?

FUSSFELD: Oh, great, great. (*Produces a statement.*) I got everything itemized here except what you owe the paper-hanger. When he gets out of Bloomingdale, he'll send you a separate bill.

APRIL (*frowning*): Sixteen hundred and ninety-three dollars. Frankly, it's a bit more than I expected.

FUSSFELD: Well, after all, you can't pick up this kind of stuff for a song. Those notary seals, for instance. We used nine dozen at fifty cents apiece. The guy at the stationery store had to witness each one.

APRIL: I know, but you list four hundred dollars for structural work.

FUSSFELD: We had to raise the ceiling to squeeze in the tree. The plumber was here three days changing the pipes around.

APRIL (*gaily tossing aside the bill*): Ah, well, it's only money. I'll mail you a check shortly.

FUSSFELD: No hurry—any time in the next forty-eight hours. (*Carelessly*) You still work for the same concern, don't you?

APRIL: Certainly. Why?

FUSSFELD: In case I have to garnishee your pay. (*A knock at the door. April crosses to it, admits Cyprian Voles. The associate editor of a pharmaceutical trade journal, he is a rabbity, diffident young man with vague literary aspirations. He is at present compiling* The Pleasures of Shag, *an anthology of essays relative to smoking, which will contain excerpts from Barrie's* My Lady Nicotine, *Machen's* The Anatomy of Tobacco, *etc., and which will be remaindered within thirty days of publication.*)

CYPRIAN: Am I too early? You said six-thirty.

APRIL: Of course not, dear. Cyprian, this is my decorative-relations counsel, Mr. Fussfeld—Mr. Voles.

FUSSFELD: Likewise. Well, I got to be running along, Miss Monkhood. About that check—

APRIL: Just as soon as my ship comes in.

FUSSFELD: I'll be studying the maritime news. (*Exits. Cyprian, meanwhile, has backed into a mobile of fish and chips suspended overhead and is desperately fighting to disengage it from his hat.*)

APRIL (*thirsting for approval*): Isn't the flat delectable? Have you ever in your whole life seen anything so cozy?

CYPRIAN: Yes, it—it's stunning. It's really *you*—it captures the inner essence—that is, the outer inwardness—

APRIL: You don't think it's overdone, do you?

CYPRIAN: Overdone? Why, it's stark! You couldn't omit one detail without damaging the whole composition.

APRIL (*hugging him*): You old sorcerer. You know just the words to thaw a woman's heart. Now, I've an inspiration. Instead of going out for dinner, let's have powdered snails and a bottle of Old Rabbinical under the crab.

CYPRIAN (*fingering his collar*): Er—to tell you the truth, I— I find it a little close in here. You see, I fell into a grain elevator one time when I was small—

APRIL: Nonsense, it'll be heaps of fun. I loathe those big, expensive restaurants. Sit ye doon while I mix us an apéritif. (*She thrusts him backward onto the studio couch, almost decapitating him with a guy wire, then whisks a bottle from a cabinet.*) Who do you suppose called me today? My husband, of all people.

CYPRIAN: Hanh? You never told me you were married.

APRIL: Oh, Sensualdo and I've been separated for years. He's a monster—an absolute fiend.

CYPRIAN: Is he a Mexican?

APRIL: Uh-uh—Peruvian. One of those insanely jealous types, always opening your mail and accusing you of carrying on with his friends. He tried to stab a man I was having a coke with. That's what broke up our marriage.

CYPRIAN: W-where is he now?

APRIL: Right here in New York. His lawyers are trumping up evidence for a divorce— What's the matter?

CYPRIAN (*he has risen and sways dangerously*): I feel faint ... spots before the eyes ...

APRIL: Lie down. I'll get you some water—

CYPRIAN (*panting*): No, no. I've got to get out of here. The walls are closing in. (*He becomes entangled in a pile of mill-end remnants and flounders hopelessly. Simultaneously, a peremptory knock at door.*)

VOICE (*offscene*): Open up there!

CYPRIAN (*in an agonized whisper*): Who's *that*?

APRIL: I don't know, unless—

ANOTHER VOICE (*offscene*): Open the door, you tramp, else we break eet down!

APRIL (*biting her lip*): Damnation. It's Sensualdo. (*Grabbing Cyprian's arm*) Quick, into the bathroom—no, wait a second, stand over there! (*She snatches a handful of notary seals from a shelf, and, moistening them, begins pasting them at random on his face.*)

CYPRIAN (*struggling*): What are you doing?

APRIL: Sh-h-h, never mind—help me! Stick them on your clothes—anywhere! (*Pandemonium at the door as Sensualdo attempts to kick in the panels. April, in the meantime, has found a heavy iron ring—conveniently included in the props by the stage manager—and now arranges it to dangle from Cyprian's outstretched hand.*) There. Now lean forward and try to look like a hitching post. That's perfect—don't budge! (*She runs to the door, yanks it open. Sensualdo, an overwrought Latin in the world's most expensive vicuña coat, erupts in, flanked by two private detectives.*)

SENSUALDO (*roaring*): Where is thees animal which he is defiling my home? (*He and his aides halt in stupefaction as they behold the apartment.*)

APRIL: Get out! How dare you barge in without a warrant? Help! Police!

42

FIRST SHAMUS (*ignoring her*): Holy cow! What kind of a joint is this?

SECOND DITTO: It's a thrift shop. Look at that statue with a ring in its hand.

FIRST SHAMUS (*to Sensualdo*): Hey, Bright Eyes, we didn't hire out to break in no store. I'm takin' a powder.

SENSUALDO: Eet's a trick! Search in the closets, the bathroom—

SECOND SHAMUS: And lay in the workhouse ninety days? No sirree. Come on, Havemeyer. (*The pair exit. Sensualdo, his hood engorged with venom, turns on April.*)

SENSUALDO: You leetle devil. One day you go too far.

APRIL (*tremulously*): Oh, darling, don't—you mustn't. I'm so vulnerable when you look at me like that.

SENSUALDO (*seizing her roughly*): Do not play pelota weeth my heart, woman. You mean you are still caring for me?

APRIL: Passionately, joyously. With every fiber of my being. Take me, hold me, fold me. (*Her eyeballs capsize.*) To kiss anyone else is like a mustache without salt.

SENSUALDO: Ah-h-h, *Madre de Dios*, how you set my blood on fire anew. Let me take you out of all thees—to a hilltop in Cuzco, to the eternal snows of the Andes—

APRIL (*simply*): Geography don't matter, sugar. With you I could be happy in a hallway. (*They depart, absorbed in each other. Cyprian holds his pose a few seconds, and then, straightening, tiptoes after them as warily as the goldfish bowl on his foot permits. His face at the moment is inscrutable, but, broadly speaking, he has the look of a man hellbent on completing an anthology on the joys of the weed.*)

CURTAIN

I Am Not Now, Nor Have I
Ever Been, a Matrix
of Lean Meat

I AWOKE with a violent, shuddering start, so abruptly that I felt
the sudden ache behind the eyeballs one experiences after bolt-
ing an ice-cream soda or ascending too recklessly from the
ocean floor. The house was utterly still; except for the tumult
of the creek in the pasture, swollen with melting snow, a silence
as awesome as that of Fatehpur Sikri, the abandoned citadel
of the Moguls, shrouded the farm. Almost instantly, I was filled
with an immense inquietude, an anxiety of such proportions
that I quailed. The radium dial of the alarm clock read two-
thirty: the exact moment, I realized with a tremor, that I had

become involved the night before in the Affair of the Boneless Veal Steaks. The Boneless Veal Steaks—it had the same prosaic yet grisly implications as the Five Orange Pips or the Adventure of the Engineer's Thumb. Propped up on one elbow and staring into the velvet dark, I reviewed as coherently as I could the events of the preceding night.

I had awakened around two and, after thrashing about in my kip like a dying tautog, had lit and smoked the cork tip of a cigarette until I was nauseated. I thereupon woke up my wife, who apparently thought she could shirk her responsibilities by sleeping, and filed a brief résumé of the disasters—financial, political, and emotional—threatening us. When she began upbraiding me, in the altogether illogical way women do, I did not succumb to justifiable anger but pacifically withdrew to the kitchen for a snack. As I was extricating a turkey wing from the tangle of leftovers in the icebox (amazing how badly the average housewife organizes her realm; no man would tolerate such inefficiency in business), my attention was drawn by a limp package labeled "Gilbert's Frozen Boneless Veal Steaks." Stapled to the exterior was a printed appeal that had the lugubrious intimacy of a Freudian case history. "Dear Chef," it said. "I've lost my character. I used to have sinews, then I met a butcher at Gilbert's. He robbed me of my powers of resistance by cutting out some of the things that hold me together. I am a matrix of lean meat with my trimmings ground and worked back into me. Please be kind. Pick me up with a pancake turner or a spatula, don't grab me by the edges with a fork. Because of all I've been through I'm more fragile than others you've known. Please be gentle lest you tear me apart. Tillie the Tender."

The revelation that food had become articulate at long last, that henceforth I was changed from consumer to father confessor, so unmanned me that I let go the turkey wing; with a loud "Mrkgnao" she obviously had learned from reading

Ulysses, the cat straightway pounced on it. I must have been in a real stupor, because I just stood there gawking at her, my brain in a turmoil. What floored me, actually, wasn't that the veal had found a way to communicate—a more or less inevitable development, once you accepted the basic premise of Elsie, the Borden cow—but rather its smarmy and masochistic pitch. Here, for the first time in human experience, a supposedly inanimate object, a cutlet, had broken through the barrier and revealed itself as a creature with feelings and desires. Did it signalize its liberation with ecstasy, cry out some exultant word of deliverance, or even underplay it with a quiet request like "Mr. Watson, come here. I want you"? No; the whole message reeked of self-pity, of invalidism, of humbug. It was a sniveling, eunuchoid plea for special privilege, a milepost of Pecksniffery. It was disgusting.

In the same instant, however, I saw both the futility of moral indignation and an augury of things to come. Before long, the other victuals in the icebox, their tongues loosened by some refrigerative hocus-pocus as yet unknown to science, would undoubtedly emulate Tillie and demand similar coddling. Two courses presented themselves; I could either scream the house down and prepare it for the contingency, or I could bear the brunt singlehanded—i.e., get back into bed and let things take their course. The latter plainly being the coward's way, I adopted it at once. Between various distractions, I neglected to check the icebox the next morning, but now, as I lay there sleepless, I knew that every second of delay was calamitous. With the stealth of a Comanche, I swung my feet over the side of the bed and stood up on a standard apricot poodle who happened to be dozing there. He emitted a needle-sharp yelp.

"Shut up, damn you," I hissed through my teeth, immediately tempering it with a placatory "Good boy, good boy." The brute subsided, or pretended to, until I closed the bedroom door behind me; then, convinced I was sneaking off on a coon hunt or some other excursion without him, he started excitedly clawing the panels. I permitted him to follow and, when we were well out of earshot of his mistress, gave him a kick in the belly to teach him obedience. The moment I opened the refrigerator door, I sensed mischief was afoot. Clipped to an earthenware bowl of rice pudding was a note scrawled in a shaky, nearly illegible hand. "Dear Chef," it said breathlessly. "You're living in a fool's paradise. You wouldn't believe some of the things that go on in this box—the calumny, the envy, the trickery. They're all against me because I have raisins. Ish ka bibble—I had raisins when that Nova Scotia salmon in the upper tier was a fingerling in the Bay of Fundy. But don't take my word, just look around for yourself. Nuf sed. A Friend."

A quick scrutiny of the various compartments revealed that something was indeed very much awry. Two bunches of celery had worked their way out of the freezer, where they normally lay, and stood jammed in a cluster of milk bottles. A mayonnaise jar had been emptied of its rightful contents and was half-filled with goose fat, hinting at the possibility of foul play. It wasn't any one single factor—the shreds of icy vapor or the saucer of frozen gravy, as bleak as Lake Baikal—but the interior was filled with a premonitory hush of the sort that precedes a cyclone or a jail break. All of a sudden, as I racked my wits for some clandestine method of eliciting the true state of affairs, the perfect solution hit me—my tape recorder. I could secrete it in the adjacent kitchen cabinet, run the microphone inside disguised as a potato knish, and overnight astound the world with its first documentary on talking groceries. The thought of the millions I was scheduled to make in royalties, the *brouhaha* in the press and the acclaim of learned societies, and the chagrin of my enemies when I was elevated to a niche beside that of Steinmetz so dizzied me that I had to drink a split of Dr. Dadirrian's Zoolak to recover. True, I felt a bit anthropophagous as I swallowed it, and I half expected a gurgled Levantine outcry, but nothing more dramatic than a slight attack of double vision ensued, and within minutes I had the mechanism hooked up and ready to function.

"Now, then," I ordered the poodle, flicking on the switch, "back to the hay we go. Better be up bright and early before someone finds this and misinterprets it."

"Applesauce," he retorted. "It's your recorder, isn't it?"

"Sure," I said, "but you know how silly peop— *What did you say?*" Of course, he dried up then, not another word out of him, and you'd have thought the cat had his tongue.

I got to bed pretty perplexed about the whole thing and, what with fear lest I oversleep and worry at the quantity of current the machine was using, fell into a wretched slumber that terminated around daylight. Hastening to the kitchen, I downed some black coffee, and rewound the spool of tape to get the playback. The first few revolutions were unproductive of anything but conspiratorial whispers and an occasional word too jumbled to decipher. Then, all at once, I heard a low-pitched voice in the background, oily and yet pompous, stiff with disdain.

"Beggars on horseback," it was saying contemptuously. "Strictly keeping up appearances. I spotted him and the Missis right away the day they came into the delicatessen. She was wearing an old Persian-lamb coat, remodeled. 'Something in the way of a cocktail snack, Greengrass,' she says, yawning like she's Mrs. T. Markoe Robertson. 'I'll take a two-ounce jar of that domestic caviar.' Then she turns to her husband, which he's nervously jingling the change in his pants, and she says, 'Dear, don't you think it would be amusing to have a slice or two of Novy for our guests?' Well, the poor *shmendrick* turned all different colors when the boss weighed me on the scales. Five cents more and he'd have had to walk home in the rain like a Hemingway hero."

"Listen," rejoined a grumpy bass voice that unmistakably

proceeded from a forsaken bottle of horseradish. "Stick around as long as I have and nothing these people do will surprise you. Why, one time we had a rack of lamb in here seven weeks. The plumber had to cut it out with a blowtorch."

A mincing, rather overbred voice, of the sort usually associated with Harvard beets, chimed agreement. "There's one thing that doesn't get stale here, though," it said. "Club soda. How long can he last on that liquid diet of his?"

"Forever, if he don't fall down and cut himself," the lox replied with a coarse guffaw.

"Can't you make less noise, please?" put in a hateful, meaching soprano. "I haven't closed an eye. I'm just a bundle of nerves ever since my operation—"

"Pssst, there goes Tillie again," warned the horseradish. "Pipe down or she'll write him another note. The little sneak repeats everything you say." A hubbub of maledictions and recriminations broke out, the upshot of which I never heard. Quivering with fury, I stripped the tape off the reel, ran into the living room, and flung it on the embers in the hearth. Specks of assorted hues swam before my eyes; it was unendurable that I should have nourished such vipers in my bosom. Drastic steps were indicated, and I was the boy who could take them. As I flew back to the refrigerator, bent on evicting the whole kit and caboodle without mercy, I caromed off my wife, huddled in a plain wrapper, for all the world like a copy of *Lady Chatterley's Lover*, and gaping at the recorder.

"Wh-what happened?" she stammered. "What are you doing with that microphone in the icebox?"

WELL, I learned one lesson from the episode; suavity is lost on women. There isn't a blessed one, from the Colonel's Lady to Judy O'Grady, capable of dealing with abstract ideas, and if you try a civilized, worldly approach, it just antagonizes them. Can you imagine a person getting so huffy that she barricades herself in a henhouse and refuses to breakfast with her own husband? I made a meal off a few odds and ends—a grapefruit and a couple of eggs—but I can't say much for their dialogue. You need someone you can really talk to.

CLOUDLAND REVISITED:

Roll On, Thou Deep and Dark Scenario, Roll

ℭ

ONE AUGUST MORNING during the third summer of the First World War, Manuel Da Costa, a Portuguese eel fisherman at Bullock's Cove, near Narragansett Bay, was calking a dory drawn up beside his shack when he witnessed a remarkable exploit. From around a nearby boathouse appeared a bumpkin named Piggy Westervelt, with a head indistinguishable from an Edam cheese, lugging a bicycle pump and a coil of rubber hose. Behind him, with dragging footsteps, because of the quantities of scrap iron stuffed into his boots, came another stripling, indistinguishable from the present writer at the age of twelve, encased in a diving helmet that was improvised from a metal lard pail. As Da Costa watched with fascinated attention, Piggy ceremoniously conducted me to the water's edge, helped me kneel, and started securing the hose to my casque.

"Can you breathe in there all right?" he called out anxiously. There was some basis for his concern, since, in the zeal of creation, we had neglected to supply a hinge for my visor, and between lack of oxygen and the reek of hot lard my eyes were beginning to extrude like muscat grapes. I signaled Piggy to hurry up and start pumping, but he became unaccountably angry. "How many hands do you think I got?" he bawled. "If you don't like the way I'm doing it, get somebody else!" Realizing my life hung on a lunatic's caprice, I adopted the only rational attitude, that of the sacrificial ox, and shallowed my breathing. Finally, just as the old mitral valve was about to close forever, a few puffs of fetid air straggled through the tube and I shakily prepared to submerge. My objective was an ancient weedy hull thirty feet offshore, where the infamous Edward Teach, popularly known as Blackbeard, was reputed to have foundered with a cargo of bullion and plate. Neither of us had the remotest idea what bullion and plate were, but they sounded eminently useful. I was also to keep a sharp lookout for ambergris, lumps of which were constantly being picked up by wide-awake boys and found to be worth forty thousand dollars. The prospects, viewed from whatever angle, were pretty rosy.

They began to dim the second I disappeared below the surface. By that time, the hose had sprung half a dozen leaks, and Piggy, in a frenzy of misdirected co-operation, had pumped my helmet full of water. Had I not been awash in the pail, I might have been able to squirm out of my boots, but as it was, I was firmly anchored in the ooze and a definite candidate for Davy Jones's locker when an unexpected savior turned up in the person of Manuel Da Costa. Quickly sculling overhead, he captured the hose with a boat hook, dragged me inboard, and pounded the water out of my lungs. The first sight I saw, as I lay gasping in the scuppers, was Manuel towering over me like the Colossus of Rhodes, arms compressed and lips akimbo. His salutation finished me forever as an undersea explorer. "Who the hell do you think you are?" he demanded, outraged. "Captain Nemo?"

That a Rhode Island fisherman should invoke anyone so recherché as the hero of Jules Verne's submarine saga may seem extraordinary, but actually there was every justification for it. All through the preceding fortnight, a movie version of *Twenty Thousand Leagues Under the Sea* had been playing to packed houses at a local peepshow, engendering almost as much excitement as the Black Tom explosion. Everyone who saw it was dumfounded—less, I suspect, by its subaqueous marvels than by its hallucinatory plot and characters—but nobody besides Piggy and me, fortunately, was barmy enough to emulate it. In general, I experienced no untoward effects from my adventure. It did, however, prejudice me unreasonably against salt water, and for years I never mentioned the ocean floor save with a sneer.

SOME WEEKS AGO, rummaging through the film library of the Museum of Modern Art, I discovered among its goodies a print of the very production of *Twenty Thousand Leagues* that had mesmerized me in 1916, and, by ceaseless nagging, bedeviled the indulgent custodians into screening it for me. Within twenty minutes, I realized that I was watching one of the really great cinema nightmares, a *cauchemar* beside which *King Kong, The Tiger Man,* and *The Cat People* were as staid as so many quilting bees. True, it did not have the sublime irrelevance of *The Sex Maniac,* a masterpiece of Krafft-Ebing symbolism I saw in Los Angeles whose laboratory monkeyshines climaxed in a scene where two Picassoesque giantesses, armed with baseball bats, beat each other to pulp in a cellar. On the other hand, it more than equaled the all-time stowage record set by D. W. Griffith's *Intolerance,* managing to combine in one picture three unrelated plots—*Twenty Thousand Leagues,*

The Mysterious Island, and *Five Weeks in a Balloon*—and a sanguinary tale of betrayal and murder in a native Indian state that must have fallen into the developing fluid by mistake. To make the whole thing even more perplexing, not one member of the cast was identified—much as if all the actors in the picture had been slain on its completion and all references to them expunged. I daresay that if Stuart Paton, its director, were functioning today, the votaries of the Surrealist film who sibilate around the Little Carnegie and the Fifth Avenue Playhouse would be weaving garlands for his hair. That man could make a cryptogram out of Mother Goose.

The premise of *Twenty Thousand Leagues,* in a series of quick nutshells, is that the Navy, dismayed by reports of a gigantic sea serpent preying on our merchant marine, dispatches an expedition to exterminate it. Included in the party are Professor Aronnax, a French scientist with luxuriant crêpe hair and heavy eye makeup who looks like a phrenologist out of the funny papers; his daughter, a kittenish ingénue all corkscrew curls and maidenly simpers; and the latter's heartbeat, a broth of a boy identified as Ned Land, Prince of Harpooners. Their quarry proves, of course, to be the submarine *Nautilus,* commanded by the redoubtable Captain Nemo, which sinks their vessel and takes them prisoner. Nemo is Melville's Captain Ahab with French dressing, as bizarre a mariner as ever trod on a weevil. He has a profile like Garibaldi's, set off by a white goatee; wears a Santa Claus suit and a turban made out of a huck towel; and smokes a churchwarden pipe. Most submarine commanders, as a rule, busy themselves checking gauges and twiddling the periscope, but Nemo spends all his time smiting his forehead and vowing revenge, though on whom it is not made clear. The décor of the *Nautilus,* obviously inspired by a Turkish cozy corner, is pure early Matisse; Oriental rugs, hassocks, and mother-of-pearl taborets abound, and in one shot I thought I detected a parlor floor lamp with a fringed shade, which must have been a problem in dirty

weather. In all justice, however, Paton's conception of a submarine interior was no more florid than Jules Verne's. Among
the ship's accouterments, I find on consulting the great ro-
mancer, he lists a library containing twelve thousand volumes,
a dining room with oak sideboards, and a thirty-foot drawing
room full of Old Masters, tapestry, and sculpture.

Apparently, the front office figured that so straightforward
a narrative would never be credible, because complications now
really begin piling up. "About this time," a subtitle announces,
"Lieutenant Bond and four Union Army scouts, frustrated in an
attempt to destroy their balloon, are carried out to sea." A long
and murky sequence full of lightning, falling sandbags, and
disheveled character actors occupies the next few minutes, the
upshot being that the cloud-borne quintet is stranded on a
remote key called Mysterious Island. One of its more mysterious aspects is an unchaperoned young person in a leopard-
skin sarong, who dwells in the trees and mutters gibberish to
herself. The castaways find this tropical Ophelia in a pit they
have dug to ward off prowling beasts, and Lieutenant Bond,
who obviously has been out of touch with women since he was
weaned, loses his heart to her. To achieve greater obscurity,
the foregoing is intercut with limitless footage of Captain Nemo
and his hostages goggling at the wonders of the deep through
a window in the side of the submarine. What they see is approximately what anybody might who has quaffed too much
sacramental wine and is peering into a home aquarium, but,
after all, tedium is a relative matter. When you come right
down to it, a closeup of scup feeding around a coral arch is no
more static than one of Robert Taylor.

At this juncture, a completely new element enters the plot
to further befuddle it, in the form of one Charles Denver, "a
retired ocean trader in a distant land." Twelve years earlier,
a flashback reveals, Denver had got a skinful of lager and tried
to ravish an Indian maharani called Princess Daaker. The lady
had thereupon plunged a dagger into her thorax, and Denver,

possibly finding the furniture too heavy, had stolen her eight-year-old daughter. We see him now in a mood of remorse approaching that of Macbeth, drunkenly clawing his collar and reviling the phantoms who plague him—one of them, by the way, a rather engaging Mephistopheles of the sort depicted in advertisements for quick-drying varnish. To avoid losing his mind, the trader boards his yacht and sets off for Mysterious Island, a very peculiar choice indeed, for if ever there was a convocation of loonies anywhere, it is there. Captain Nemo is fluthering around in the lagoon, wrestling with an inflated rubber octopus; Lieutenant Bond and the leopard girl (who, it presently emerges, is Princess Daaker's daughter, left there to die) are spooning on the cliffs; and, just to enliven things, one of Bond's scouts is planning to supplant him as leader and abduct the maiden.

Arriving at the island, Denver puts on a pippin of a costume, consisting of a deerstalker cap, a Prince Albert coat, and hip boots, and goes ashore to seek the girl he marooned. He has just vanished into the saw grass, declaiming away like Dion Boucicault, when the screen suddenly blacks out, or at least it did the day I saw the picture. I sprang up buoyantly, hoping that perhaps the film had caught fire and provided a solution for everybody's dilemma, but it had merely slipped off the sprocket. By the time it was readjusted, I, too, had slipped off, consumed a flagon or two, and was back in my chair waiting alertly for the payoff. I soon realized my blunder. I should have stayed in the rathskeller and had the projectionist phone it to me.

Denver becomes lost in the jungle very shortly, and when he fails to return to the yacht, two of the crew go in search of him. They meet Lieutenant Bond's scout, who has meanwhile made indecent overtures to the leopard girl and been declared a pariah by his fellows. The trio rescue Denver, but, for reasons that defy analysis, get plastered and plot to seize the yacht and sail away with the girl.

During all this katzenjammer, divers from the *Nautilus* have been reconnoitering around the craft to learn the identity of its owner, which presumably is emblazoned on its keel, inasmuch as one of them hastens to Nemo at top speed to announce with a flourish, "I have the honor to report that the yacht is owned by Charles Denver." The Captain forthwith stages a display of vindictive triumph that would have left Boris Thomashefsky, the great Yiddish tragedian, sick with envy; Denver, he apprises his companions, is the man against whom he has sworn undying vengeance. In the meantime (everything in *Twenty Thousand Leagues* happens in the meantime; the characters don't even sneeze consecutively), the villains kidnap the girl, are pursued to the yacht by Bond, and engage him in a fight to the death. At the psychological moment, a torpedo from the *Nautilus* blows up the whole shebang, extraneous characters are eliminated, and, as the couple are hauled aboard the submarine, the big dramatic twist unfolds: Nemo is Prince Daaker and the girl his daughter. Any moviemaker with elementary decency would have recognized this as the saturation point and quit, but not the producer of *Twenty Thousand Leagues.* The picture bumbles on into a fantastically long-winded flashback of Nemo reviewing the whole Indian episode and relentlessly chewing the scenery to bits, and culminates with his demise and a strong suspicion in the onlooker that he has talked himself to death. His undersea burial, it must be admitted, has an authentic grisly charm. The efforts of the funeral party, clad in sober diving habit, to dig a grave in the ocean bed finally meet with defeat, and, pettishly tossing the coffin into a clump of sea anemones, they stagger off. It seemed to me a bit disrespectful not to blow "Taps" over the deceased, but I suppose nobody had a watertight bugle.

AN HOUR after quitting the Museum, I was convalescing on a bench in Central Park when a brandy-nosed individual approached me with a remarkable tale of woe. He was, he declared, a by-blow of Prince Felix Youssoupoff, the assassin of Rasputin, and had been reared by Transylvanian gypsies. Successively a circus aerialist, a mosaic worker, a diamond cutter, and a gigolo, he had fought (or at least argued) with Wingate's Raiders, crossed Outer Mongolia on foot, spent two years in a Buddhist monastery, helped organize the Indonesian resistance, and become one of the financial titans of Lombard Street. A woman, he confided huskily, had been his undoing—a woman so illustrious that the mere mention of her name made Cabinets totter. His present financial embarrassment, however, was a purely temporary phase. Seversky had imported him to the States to design a new helicopter, and if I could advance him a dime to phone the designer that he had arrived, I would be amply reimbursed. As he vanished into oblivion cheerily jingling my two nickels, the old lady sharing my bench put down her knitting with a snort.

"Tommyrot!" she snapped. "Hunh, you must be a simpleton. That's the most preposterous balderdash I ever heard of."

"I *am* a simpleton, Madam," I returned with dignity, "but you don't know beans about balderdash. Let me tell you a movie I just saw." No sooner had I started to recapitulate it than her face turned ashen, and without a word of explanation she bolted into the shrubbery. An old screwbox, obviously. Oh, well, you can't account for anything nowadays. Some of the stuff that goes on, it's right out of a novel by Jules Verne.

The Saucier's Apprentice

CB

THE LAST PLACE I would have expected to run into Marcel Ribo-flavin, *sous-inspecteur* of the Police Judiciaire—which is to say, the Sûreté—was the Sunday-morning bird market in Paris, but then Marcel's vagaries have long since ceased to surprise me. Stoop to tie your shoelace in Baton Rouge or Bombay, in Dublin or Dar es Salaam, and like as not you will find Marcel confronting you with an owlish eye and nibbling a meditative praline. Where he gets all those meditative pralines from—or why, since they attract a veritable canopy of flies—the Lord only knows; nonetheless, there he is in rusty bourgeois black, patiently following up some infinitesimal clue, or like as not just nibbling a praline. I was standing in the hurly-burly of the bird market three Sundays ago, lost in admiration of two little doves in georgette blouses who would have rounded out any boy's aviary, when an unmistakable voice sounded in my ear.

"Doucement, mon vieux," it warned. "We old roosters must be cautious. Don't try to outwit your arteries."

Startled, I turned to behold Marcel, an indulgent smirk on his face, wagging his forefinger at me. It was quite apparent what he was thinking, and I hastened to disabuse him. "The fact is," I explained, "the smaller of that pair—the helpless-looking one—reminds me of a teacher of mine at grammar school, a Miss Floggerty. She had taffy-colored hair, as I recall—"

"Bien sûr, bien sûr," he said sympathetically. "I, too, have those symptoms of senility. Tragic but inescapable. Come, let us link arms and stroll through the complex of alleys fringing the Quartier Latin." As we linked arms and strolled, genially updating each other on our activities since our last meeting, I noticed a strangely familiar magazine protruding from my friend's coat pocket.

"You have symptoms of gentility also," I remarked. "Since when have you taken to reading *Harper's Bazaar?* Or do your investigations extend into the gilded salons of the *haute couture?*"

Marcel's face, or at least that portion of it visible through the flies, suddenly became cryptic. "In my post, one is called on to unravel many tangled skeins," he said evasively. "By the way, this café we are nearing is reputed to have the worst anisette in Paris. Shall we try it?" We did, and it was unspeakable. After a moment, Marcel withdrew a praline from a recess in his clothing and nibbled it meditatively. I am not overly intuitive, but I have learned that when sub-inspectors of the Sûreté with dickty fashion magazines protruding from their pockets invite one to share an apéritif, curious stories ofttimes unfold, and so it proved.

"As you are doubtless aware," began Marcel, drawing on his praline, *"Harper's Bazaar* not only prognosticates the mode but frequently publishes news of consuming interest—you will pardon the play on words—to gourmets. Such was the arresting article you see here." He spread out the periodical and indicated a piece entitled "Sauces from the Source," by Rosamund Frost. At first glance, it did not seem particularly cataclysmic. Maxim's, the celebrated Paris restaurant, had confected five basic frozen sauces calculated to tease the American palate. It was the secrecy attending their manufacture, however, and the abnormal precautions adopted to guard the creators, that riveted my attention. "Seat of the production," wrote Miss Frost, conspiratorially turning up the collar of her typewriter, "is Seabrook Farms in New Jersey, the well-known purveyors of frozen fruit and vegetables. But because M. and Madame Vaudable, owners of the Paris Maxim's, have a deep distrust of American cooking methods, they have evolved their own system of preparation. For each large batch of sauces, a head chef, an assistant, and several *sauciers* are flown over from Paris, to be held virtually incommunicado in New Jersey until the batch is finished. They are then flown home before they have had any chance to be contaminated by such ill practices as thickening with flour."

I lifted my eyes slowly to Marcel's, the question I was almost afraid to put into words muted to a whisper. "You mean . . ." I asked.

"Precisely," he said, dislodging a grain of sugar from his denture. "Scarcely a month after this information appeared, the chief of our Bureau Culinaire, the section specializing in food outrages, sent for me in a state of pronounced agitation. A few nights earlier, faint but indisputable traces of flour had been detected in a pipkin of sauce béarnaise served at Maxim's."

"It could have been pure coincidence," I objected. "A harassed scullion, a sudden avalanche of orders—"

"In France," Marcel said with wintry dignity, "accidents occur in the bedroom, not the kitchen. No, it was all too plain that this was a deliberate, predetermined *coup de main*, a perfidious assault on the very citadel of our national cuisine. The victim of the atrocity, it appeared, was a distinguished artist of the Comédie-Française and one of its foremost tragedians, Isidor Bassinet. Providentially, Bassinet realized the implications of his discovery in time to avert a panic that might easily have wrought havoc among the clientele. Summoning the maître d'hôtel, he cuttingly suggested that the sauce was more suitable for calking a boat, tweaked the man's nose, and retired. The headwaiter, of course, relayed the gibe to the chef, who instituted a probe forthwith and immediately gave us the alert."

"I hesitate to denigrate an actor," I said, hesitating almost a full second, "but might not Bassinet himself have insinuated flour into the sauce as the pretext for a histrionic outburst?"

"We did not discount the possibility," said Marcel. "A clandestine search was made of his rooms that yielded naught incriminating gravywise; his erotic photomurals, his collection of whips, and the jar of candied hashish by his bedside could have belonged to any floorwalker in the Bon Marché. The longer I pondered the problem, the more convinced I became it was an inside job. Someone on the kitchen force—whether a madman or a cold, diabolic intelligence I was not yet prepared to say—had engineered the deed, and I knew that, encouraged by success, he would strike again. My theory was vindicated all too swiftly. Two evenings later, Alexander Satyriasis, the Greek shipping magnate, was dining at Maxim's with his wife and his mistress. The occasion was their silver wedding anniversary, and Satyriasis, an epicurean, had left no spit unturned to insure a gastronomical triumph. The hors d'oeuvres, the soup, the roast—all were transcendent. Then, as the trio expectantly attacked the salad, Paradise crumbled about their ears. Under their forks lay the ultimate annihilation, the final obscenity—a canned pear stuffed with cream cheese and walnuts, garnished with cole slaw and Russian dressing."

"Good God!" I exclaimed. "At the Fig 'n Thistle, yes; at the

Mumble Shop and a thousand Stygian tearooms, yes; but in the Rue Royale—"

Marcel repressed an involuntary shudder. "It was appalling," he admitted. "When I got there, the table was cordoned off and Satyriasis had not yet recovered consciousness. He came around eventually, but, *entre nous*, the man will never be the same. I instantly fell to work and grilled the entire personnel, from the head sommelier down to the doorman. Nobody would even hazard a guess at the origin of the salads; apparently they had been slipped onto the service tray while the waiter's back was turned, and beyond that not a vestige of a clue. Those were dark days, I can tell you," Marcel went on somberly. "The knowledge that we were powerless to combat him exhilarated our mysterious adversary, spurring him on to new and more gruesome excesses. Under the management's very nose, patrons were assailed with baked grapefruit topped with maraschino cherries, fried clams encapsulated in deep fat, mashed potatoes pullulating with marshmallow whip. The nadir of bestiality was reached one night when cards were surreptitiously pinned to the menu inviting diners to have their tea leaves read by a gypsy palmist."

"Forgive me for underscoring the obvious," I said. "Surely it must have occurred to you that a woman, and patently an American, was at the bottom of all this?"

"Naturally," said Marcel with a shade of impatience. "The crucial question, though, was where was she and how was she effecting her depredations? Five of the restaurant's employees, as you saw from the magazine account, had been flown to New Jersey and held there incommunicado. Plainly, one of their number—younger and more impressionable than the rest—had evaded his custodians and succumbed to some harpy who had lured the fatuous boy to a drive-in like those Howard Monsoon places that line your roads, and there, befuddled by viscous malted drinks and chicken-in-the-basket, he had been persuaded to betray his birthright. In all likelihood, I reasoned, the seductress had followed him to Paris to gloat over her handiwork; perhaps, if I could ferret out the cat's-paw, he might lead me to her. Acting on my presentiment, I at once attached myself to the kitchen in the guise of an assistant pastry chef and proceeded to elicit what I could about the quintet who had been overseas."

"And your hypothesis bore fruit?"

"In a fashion I never anticipated," replied Marcel. "Four of them were prosaic, stodgy types, family men whose world revolved around their thimbleful of Pernod and their game of bowls. The youngest, however, was an altogether different piece of work. A mere novice entrusted with handling condiments, he was a shy, secretive lad with long eyelashes and a curiously girlish aspect. Whenever the badinage among his mates grew ribald, he flushed deeply and made himself scarce, and once or twice I surprised him examining his complexion in a compact. The conviction that our little colleague was a masquerader emboldened me to experiment. Utilizing the test that had unmasked Huckleberry Finn, I casually asked the youth to thread a needle. As I expected, he brought the thread to the needle instead of vice versa. Then I shied an egg beater at him without warning—that is, without warning that I was shying an egg beater at him—and, sure enough, he automatically spread the knees under his apron to form a lap. The evidence was too damning to be ignored. That night, when my suspect let himself into his modest furnished room in the Saint-Germain-des-Prés quarter, stripped off his mess jacket, and disclosed a brassière, I emerged from an armoire and sprang the trap."

"You might have waited a moment or two for confirmation," I remonstrated.

"As a reader of *Harper's Bazaar*, I am reasonably *au courant* with the subject," said Marcel tartly. "Besides, I had all the proof necessary to stamp the creature as the perpetrator of the

crimes. Simmering on the gas stove was a dish of salmon cro-
quettes flanked by carrots and peas, and, in the oven beneath, a
graham-cracker pie. Overcome by remorse, yet grateful that
the suspense had ended, the fair culprit dissolved in tears. Her
name, she confessed, was Gristede Feigenspan, and she was a
feature writer for *Effluvia*, a periodical circulated gratis by
supermarkets in your country. To dramatize the pre-eminence
of American cookery, her editors had abducted the youngest
member of the French contingent, had substituted Gristede,
and were planning to publicize her exploits under the title 'I
Was a Fake Saucier at Maxim's.'"

I drew a long breath. "A singular tale," I commented. "I take
it she paid the inevitable price for her audacity?"

"That," said Marcel, with an enigmatic smile, "is a matter of
opinion." He hoisted himself cumbrously to his feet as a dynamic young woman in black jodhpurs, with a bag slung over
her shoulder, gravitated toward our table. "I don't think you
know my wife," he said. "Gristede, allow me to present an old
copain from the States—a journalist, like yourself."

"Too, too fantastic," she trilled, extending her hand. "How
long are you staying in Paris? You must come to dinner."

"I—er—I'm just en route to Beirut," I stammered. "I mean I'm
off to a fiesta in Trieste—"

"Don't be an Airdale," she said forcefully. "We'll give you a
real home-cooked meal. Hasn't Marcel told you about my
noodles Yankee Doodle, smothered in peanut butter and mayonnaise?"

I looked at Marcel, but his face, flies and all, had turned to
stone. That's the trouble with these garrulous French detectives—they're unpredictable. One moment they wring their dos-
siers inside out for you, and then—*pouf!*—they shut up like a
clam.

Whereas, the Former
Premises Being Kaput—

CP

I was backed into a corner at a party last week with a couple named either Swineforth or Twyeffort—between the melee and their tutti-frutti delivery, I never found out which—and was nearing the point where you scream to equalize the pressure when my wife hewed her way through the crush and, much to my surprise, greeted the pair as though they really existed.

"You remember them, don't you?" she shouted into my ear trumpet as they flapped away to eviscerate someone else. "They lived in the studio across from us in the Aragon. He was the treasurer of the tenants' committee." I naturally gave her the benefit of the doubt and assumed she was talking gibberish, but after a while their faces took on a horrid familiarity, and the whole episode, encrusted with lichen, came back to me. It fair gives you a turn, the way you can expunge the past. I daresay I pass the place—the new building, that is—almost every time I get down to the Village, yet I can't seem to associate myself with that corner. I only remember the one the Swineforths (or Twyefforts) backed me into.

The Aragon, as we knew it, was a five-story affair of mellowed brick with a cool marble foyer and a walled garden containing a fountain, as gracious a dwelling as ever adorned the Washington Square area. Contrary to the widespread belief that it was a historic old family mansion, it dated back only to 1927, when the three brownstones composing it were remodeled and given a common façade. Its residents were also rather routine—statisticians and wool factors, a heavy concentration of affluent elderly widows, and the usual complement of walking dead that one meets in any New York apartment elevator. The most glamorous tenant, but so rarely visible during waking hours that few knew he lived there, was Archie Carmine, the celebrated Broadway producer. Archie, a legend in his own lifetime, is a pale, unshaven wraith of a man whose patent-leather eyes have the glitter of a fer-de-lance's and whose reputation is no less lethal. Though admittedly a genius, he devours whomever he loves at the moment, and it is a canon around Sardi's that any traffic with him is a passport to a nervous breakdown. Novels have been written about Archie's perfidy; playwrights and actors quit rooms at the mere rumor of his approach, scenic designers turn lilac at his name. My own relationship with him was ideal, never having been sullied by business, and I always enjoyed his tirades against the critics and the decline of the theater when he glided into the lobby of the Aragon, his fangs still dripping from some midnight conference.

For about a year, there was disquieting talk that our building was up for sale, that it was going to be converted into a waxworks, that New York University had leased it to accommodate courses in square dancing, that Trans-Jordan was eying the site for a legation, et cetera. Something obviously was cooking, because every other month the name of a different landlord would appear on the rent bill—strange corporations like the Sword of Damocles Holding Company and Samjo Realty Associates. It was manifest that the property was being traded daily at Longchamps by dapper, aromatic men in sharkskin and effulgent neckties, and life suddenly became precarious. One morning, the suspense ended. We were notified that the Moloch Management Company had acquired the premises and that we were to vacate on the double, as demolition was to begin shortly. The same day, the newspapers carried an interview with Alex Moloch, head of the organization, describing the skyscraper he intended to erect on the plot and the four or five adjoining it. To conform to the rich artistic tradition of the neighborhood, he declared, the ground floor would contain exhibition halls where local painters could show their work. A jar of free tuning forks would be available at all times in the lobby for composers, and any sculptor leasing one of the top-floor studios—the rents of which were to start at five hundred dollars a month—would receive a spatula and fifty pounds of clay. Without actually bracketing himself with Lorenzo de' Medici, Moloch grew quite lyrical as he visualized the role he and the edifice would play in New York's cultural life.

That evening, a dozen of us at the Aragon, who had never exchanged more than nods and grunts, assembled and pledged ourselves to resist. Archie Carmine sent word by the doorman that unavoidable business had summoned him to the Coast but that he was in the fray to the finish. The meeting was, for the most part, consumed in parliamentary wrangling; most of those present, apparently, had never had any audience beyond their husbands or wives, and, once on their feet, strayed off into irrelevancies as windy as a Senate filibuster. At length, however, a measure of cohesion obtained, and we appointed a chairman, a vibrant, knifelike accountant with a Rand School manner, named Fessenden. Swineforth (or Twyeffort) was elected treasurer, not for his financial acumen but because his wife's mink coat inspired confidence. Then a per-capita levy to hire an attorney was imposed, and a publicity junto chosen to awaken sympathy for our plight, and we adjourned in an orgy of self-congratulation. The Moloch Management crowd was practically on the run, we jubilantly assured each other. It just proved that a few spunky people could trounce a big, soulless corporation if they stuck together.

Unfortunately, the opposition refused to be awed. Deriding our tocsin in the press to the effect that the city's most historic landmark was about to be razed, our new landlord called us a bunch of plutocrats hypocritically bent on preserving cheap rents. He drew an affecting portrait of himself as an altruist whose sole aim was to provide adequate housing. "Ever since I was a poor East Side boy, I have carried a dream in my heart," he went on, and disclosed how, as an urchin, he used to haunt Washington Square and envision the mammoth structure, designed to shelter the common man, that he would build on our corner. This arrant humbug evoked a counterblast from us, of course, and for weeks thereafter the newspapers boiled with recriminations and pontifical statements by architects, civic planners, and all kinds of busybodies. Meanwhile, in the background, the legal battle was under way. Our respective lawyers bombarded each other with writs and stays, hearings were constantly being scheduled, and almost daily some fresh ukase full of judicial argle-bargle found its way under our doors.

At three o'clock one winter morning, I was wrenched out of bed by a series of peremptory rings on our doorbell. Arming myself with a Balinese kris, I cautiously slid back the bolt. The scourge of Broadway, Archie Carmine, confronted me, wrapped in a polo coat and swaying like a Lombardy poplar. His face was cadaverous, even for him, and when he spoke he exuded a wave of cognac that nearly felled me.

"Crisake, are you in bed *already*?" he demanded with indignation. "What are you, a farmer or something?" I started to protest the intrusion, but he cut me short. "Look, cousin, better not waste any time sleeping," he said darkly. "A hell of a situation's come up here. You know what I heard when I got home just now? Some bastard's planning to tear this building down!"

As gently as I could, I reminded him that everyone, including myself, had known about it for months. "And while we're on it," I added, keeping my shoulder braced against the door, "I wish you'd pony up your end of the legal fee to Swineforth and get him off my neck. Every time I see him, he asks me where you are, why you're avoiding him—"

"Oh, he thinks I'm not good for it, does he?" Archie roared. "Why, I'll break his bloody arm! Where is he, the little mope? Which apartment is he in? What does he look like?"

It took the guile of Machiavelli (who happened to be sleeping in our foyer) to calm Archie down and persuade him to retire, but before he left he vowed to appear at the next tenants' meeting with an abysmally simple program for saving the house. He had it all worked out, every last detail, and he would outline it so that even chowderheads like us could comprehend it. As I had anticipated, he failed to turn up, either then or at subsequent meetings, and, whatever his reasons, he showed rare judgment. Each gathering was, if possible, more tedious than the last. Fessenden, our chairman, began fancying himself another Gladstone, and delivered long, rambling speeches that made one's teeth ache with boredom. The schemes to publicize our cause grew steadily loonier: a tag day, a parade, proposals to bomb Moloch's offices or chain ourselves like suffragettes to the hydrant outside the Aragon. As the months wore on, an air of doom invaded the building. One by one, doormen and elevator operators disappeared, until only a frowzy alcoholic was left to tend the furnace, distribute the mail, and police the lobby. A number of the tenants, deciding that the conclusion was foregone, moved out, and finally, inescapably, the court handed down the fiat that sealed our destiny. The thirty-day eviction notice did not shilly-shally. Anyone found on the premises one hour later would be taken by the scruff of his neck and dropped, together with his chattels, into the Washington Square fountain. It was all over but the snuffling and the thud of the wreckers' crowbars.

Of the thirteen souls who assembled in Fessenden's apartment for the wake, at least six were old ladies in jet chokers and bombazine. The rest were idealists like me, lured by a rumor that the money in the kitty was to be apportioned among us. It proved baseless; in fact, as Swineforth's report incontrovertibly showed, we each owed twenty-two dollars for stamps and mimeographing. Fessenden had just embarked on a punishing valedictory when the doorbell pealed. My wife tiptoed out, and reappeared in a moment with a nonplused expression. Behind her stalked Archie Carmine, clad in pajamas and a rumpled blue moiré dressing gown and bearing a highball. Someone must have recognized him, for an excited buzz spread through the room. For such a mythical figure to appear, and, moreover, *en déshabillé*, was a sensation, and Archie, always the showman, exploited it to the utmost. Magnanimously signaling to Fessenden to proceed, he thrust his glass into a pocket, sat down, and fell into an attitude of deep meditation, like Rodin's "Thinker."

"Gassed," my wife confided tersely in my ear. "Absolutely loaded. He'll erupt in about ten minutes."

Her prediction was conservative; Fessenden had barely managed to restore ennui before Archie raised his hand.

"Pardon me, friend," he said with what he supposed was courtly elegance. "Give us the floor a second, will you?" He rose unsteadily and took up a position at stage center, in front of the fireplace. "Folks, I've been following this discussion closely, and if I may say so, it's a lot of pazooza. You're tackling the problem all wrong. You want to save the building, do you? Well, I'll tell you how to do it." He lowered his voice dramatically. "Call up Bernie Baruch."

"Baruch?" Swineforth repeated, openmouthed. "But it's too late! We've been ordered to move. They've torn the ivy off the walls—"

"It's never too late, Buster," Archie interrupted. "The only thing that'll work now is drag. You need a really important figure to go to bat for you, and he's the gee who can do it. Yes, sir, I'll make book on him. If anybody in the world can save the Aragon, he can."

"Sure, but how do we approach him?" Fessenden demurred. "After all, he's our elder statesman, one of the most distinguished men in the country."

"Duck soup," said Archie airily. "I just call up Billy Rose, he gives Bernie a bell, and we're in like a burglar."

There was an electric pause; then a confused babble filled the room. "Did you hear that?" the old ladies queried each other feverishly. "Bernard Baruch is going to help us! . . . Yes, yes, it's all decided. . . . That man is a close friend of his. . . . No, dear, not an invalid, he's a big theatrical producer. . . . He's with Klaw & Erlanger—you know, the Shubert people. . . . My numerologist *told* me there'd be a dark stranger with a miracle. . . . I don't understand—do we pay our rent to Mr. Baruch now?"

Fessenden, his eyes dilated with excitement, beat on a table for silence. "Wait a minute, *please!*" he besought everyone. "Let's observe the rules of order! Mr. Carmine has generously offered to intercede in our behalf. Do I hear any objections?"

"Objections!" someone exclaimed. "Why, we ought to present him with a medal. It's a marvelous idea, an inspiration!"

One of the ladies, a portly beldam with a blue marcel and harlequin glasses, waved importunately. "May I ask the chair a question?" she called out. "I think the basic idea is splendid, but, Mr. Carmine, are you sure that Bernard Baruch is the right person for us to appeal to?"

"Who?" Archie inquired, staring at her as though his ears had deceived him. She repeated the name, and simultaneously the avalanche, so long overdue, descended. Like a small British car turning in its own wheelbase, Archie executed a characteristic switch. "Baruch?" he snarled. "Are you bughouse? What makes you think a man of Baruch's caliber would bother with a lot of pipsqueaks like you? Brother, I've heard some dillies in my day, but that's the payoff. Baruch! Ho-ho—what a yock this'll give the mob at Sardi's!"

In the ensuing hush, no louder than that which pervades any Egyptian tomb, my wife and I dropped on all fours and crept out. Whether Archie escaped intact, we never learned, though instinct tells me he must have. The last we knew, he was living on a seventy-foot ketch off Coral Gables with an auxiliary engine and a Cuban strip teaser. The owner, I understand—or maybe it was her husband—was suing him for eleven months' rent. I'll give him a tip: he hasn't a Chinaman's chance of collecting. As I told our own landlord last month, you can't get blood out of a stone.

My Heart's in the Highlands, and My Neckband, Too

⊂⊐

MAYBE I'm hypersensitive, but has anybody else noticed how deucedly artless and aboveboard the copy in those Hathaway shirt advertisements is becoming? I mean the ones where the man in the eye patch is engaged in fingering an oboe or hybridizing orchids or riffling through the poems of Gerard Manley Hopkins—pastimes indicative of a patrician taste and, it is tacit, the sort of thing you might develop a flair for if you were similarly attired. The accompanying letterpress, couched in a breezy yet decorous vein, has always avoided shrillness or ballyhoo; it recognizes you quite accurately for what you are, a connoisseur of the finer things—or at least an embryonic one—and merely offers a setting worthy of the jewel. Recently, how-

74

ever, an almost neurotic punctilio has invaded the text. The Hathaway people seem so intent on demonstrating their candor, their utter lack of guile, that they have begun calling attention to nonexistent defects in their product. The last ad I caught showed their Polyphemus against the background of some native Indian state that looked like Jaipur, to judge by the pink architecture and the colorful procession of elephants behind him. He was dressed in pukka garb—sola topee and a swagger blouse—and the caption said, in part,

> This shirt is made of India Madras, which Hathaway imports from India. [As distinguished, one assumes, from India Madras imported from Cedar Rapids.] This is the real stuff, woven by Indian cottagers on their handlooms. . . . The natural dyestuffs used by these Indian cottagers aren't completely color-fast—they fade a little, with washing and sunshine. This gives the shirts a look of good breeding and maturity which no mass-produced fabric can ever aspire to.

The old verbal alchemy, in short, is at work. By an adroit shift of logic, Hathaway has in one breath affirmed its probity and established the canon that it's smart to be weatherbeaten. Confidentially, I plan to bleach everything I own in lye—India lye, of course—including my underthings. Nobody's going to call *me* a parvenu.

For pure winsomeness, though, the apogee in consumer courtship was the advertisement a year or so ago that genuflected to one of the folks who supply Hathaway with its raw material. Under a photograph of an alert cock sparrow of a man surrounded by heaps of cloth was the legend "Hathaway salutes a great Scotsman" and the following panegyric:

> James White of Auchterarder is one of the most unforgettable characters we have ever met. Proud, kindly, adventurous, warm-hearted—and perhaps a little dour by American standards. We got to know him in the ordinary way of business—he makes

fabrics for Hathaway shirts. But our admiration for Jimmy White goes far beyond our mercantile relations. He is a GREAT MAN. To begin with, he is one of the shrewdest fishermen on earth, equally wise in the ways of trout and salmon. He is also one of the most brilliant designers of shirtings alive today. His craftsmanship is a magnificent anachronism. For many years he refused to sell his cloth to America. He finally gave in when we trudged five miles to his mill in a heavy rainstorm; he liked that.

THAT MR. WHITE is a paragon among weavers, an alloy of the Chevalier Bayard, Balthasar Gobelin, and Izaak Walton, I do not doubt, though what earthly relevance his knack for circumventing fish has to his fabrics is obscure. The thing that cries out for clarification (well, maybe that's too strong; "whimpers" would be closer) is the nature of the tactics Hathaway used to cajole him. Who conceived the idea of the pilgrimage in the rain and made it, and why did it melt the intractable Caledonian? I can't answer these questions, but it so happens that I have here a small proscenium arch, a clump of heather, a safari animated by similar motives—and, what is more, an irresistible urge to weave a playlet. Start the looms, laddie.

SCENE, *a typical Highland glen not a hundred miles from Auchtertochty—in fact, two and a half miles from Auchtertochty. It has been raining steadily for months prior to the rise of the curtain, so that a fearful smog shrouds the glen, but in the weak light filtering through the boscage there is visible an ancient stone footbridge and, huddled beneath it, a quartet clad in rough shooting clothes—Norfolk jackets, gaiters, and waterproofs. They are Finucane, Disbrow, and Ermatinger, executives of an American shirt corporation, and Kluckhorn, an advertising man. The morale of the group is at a very low ebb. Kluckhorn, employing a jet lighter, is trying to ignite a pile of wet leaves and brush, and the resulting smoke has thrown his companions into paroxysms of coughing. After a moment, Disbrow, with a stifled oath, rises and kicks apart the smudge.*

KLUCKHORN (*aggrievedly*): Hey, that's a hell of a thing to do! It was just starting to catch on!

DISBROW: Aw, go jump in the loch. You may be the fair-haired boy of American advertising, but you're a square when it comes to woodcraft.

KLUCKHORN: Is that so? Why, you big tub of lard, I forgot more—

FINUCANE (*stepping between them*): Oh, dry up, both of you. We've got enough headaches without you two bickering.

ERMATINGER: Damn right. If you ask me, we were fools to ever leave the hotel. Why couldn't that Scotch genius of yours have come over there to see us?

KLUCKHORN: Because he's dour, that's why. Because he don't want any part of you or your shirts.

DISBROW: So we walk five miles in a cloudburst to beg a few crummy bolts of material from a man that hates our guts. That's logical.

KLUCKHORN: He doesn't hate your guts. He doesn't even know you're alive.

FINUCANE: Says you. Didn't I cable him we were planing over from London just to huddle with him?

KLUCKHORN (*patiently*): Look, fellows, I'm not underestimating your importance, but it's time you realized who we're dealing with. Jock Smeed of Auchtertochty isn't any fly-by-night weaver. He's a world figure, like Chou En-lai or— or Musa Dagh.

ERMATINGER: Yeah, yeah, we heard all that before—he's an authority on salmon. Well, so am I, Nova Scotia and every other kind, but if customers want to see me, they don't have to scramble on their belly through a marsh.

DISBROW: Check. We might as well face it—we're on a wild-goose chase. Even if we find this joker, there's no guarantee he'll cough up the goods. Let's get back to the goddam hotel.

KLUCKHORN: Now, hold on one second. Men, I've got a surprise for you. I didn't want to spill it, but you forced my hand. (*Impressively*) At this exact moment, the four of us are practically within spitting distance of Jock Smeed!

OMNES: What? . . . Where is he? . . . What the hell are we waiting for?

KLUCKHORN: Easy, easy—just listen to me. Remember that pub we stopped at—the Moral Quagmire? Well, I had a brain wave and I slipped the barmaid a couple of farthings. She told me that our man takes every Tuesday off to fish, right here in this very glade.

ERMATINGER (*cunningly*): Meaning that we could bump into him accidentally on purpose, give him the old banana oil, and convince him to allot us some cloth?

KLUCKHORN: Bull's-eye. But we've got to play it smart, mind you. We mustn't excite his suspicion. Woo him, tickle his vanity.

FINUCANE: Not such a bum idea. The only knock is—when will he show? I'm starving.

KLUCKHORN: I thought of that, too. Hand me my knapsack there. (*He burrows into it, extracts a haggis.*)

ERMATINGER: What's *that*, for God's sake?

KLUCKHORN: A sheep's stomach. It's got the liver and lights chopped up inside, mixed with suet and oatmeal.

DISBROW (*with a shudder*): I'd rather die.

KLUCKHORN: Go on, try a piece. Didn't you ever read *Rob Roy*?

DISBROW: Yep, and I read *Dracula*, too, but I still prefer water.

FINUCANE (*suddenly*): Sh-h-h! Someone's coming . . . Up there, by that rock . . .

ERMATINGER: It's a woman—no, a man and a woman. Holy cow, they're handcuffed together!

KLUCKHORN: Jeez, maybe we're in the wrong glen. (*A young couple, numb with exhaustion, totter in. The woman is a ravishing ash blonde with a classic profile, her companion a Canadian rancher whose features are not unfamiliar to Scotland Yard. Both are considerably the worse for wear.*)

WOMAN (*breathlessly*): Is this the road to Inveraray?

KLUCKHORN: I couldn't say. We're strangers here ourselves.

MAN: Oh, bother. I say, forgive me, but by any chance have you gentlemen ever heard of an organization called the Thirty-nine Steps?

KLUCKHORN: Not that I recall. Is it a lodge of some sort?

MAN: That's putting it mildly. Anyhow, if you run into a man the tip of whose little finger is missing, tell him I'm looking for him, won't you? Thanks awfully. (*He whisks his fellow captive out.*)

FINUCANE (*suspiciously*): I've seen that pair before.

DISBROW: So have I. I can't think where.

KLUCKHORN: Ah, probably tourists from the Edinburgh Festival—the moors are lousy with 'em. Listen, boys—just so we don't queer the pitch with Smeed, I better be spokesman for the party. You see, whenever Sir Harry Lauder used to come to Buffalo, my grandfather and I—

ERMATINGER: Pss-st, dummy up! There's a guy wading down the brook—

KLUCKHORN (*jubilantly*): That's him, all right—it couldn't be anybody else! Now, remember—cagey. (*A leathery little Scotsman, attired in hip boots and with a creel slung from his back, enters flicking a trout rod. All toothy good will, Kluckhorn advances humming "A Wee Deoch an Doris."*) Good afternoon to you, sir. How are they biting?

MAN: With their mouths.

KLUCKHORN (*convulsed*): Hot ziggety, that's a good one! J must jot it down.

MAN: Do. There's just room enough on your forehead.

79

KLUCKHORN: I beg pardon? . . . Oh, yes—yes, of course. Are you from Auchtertochty, by any chance?

MAN: Aye.

KLUCKHORN (*slyly*): Would you be engaged in the textile industry there, I wonder?

MAN: Aye.

KLUCKHORN: But you're equally wise in the ways of trout and salmon, aren't you? (*The other shrugs modestly.*) Well, I'll be jiggered! You must be that brilliant designer of shirtings, Jock Smeed!

MAN: Aye.

KLUCKHORN (*twinkling*): And you're pretty dour, I can see that.

SMEED: You can, eh? Then perhaps you can see into this creel I have here.

KLUCKHORN: Why, no. What *is* in it?

SMEED: Orders. Big, whopping orders from Cluett Peabody, the Manhattan Shirt Company, and Wilson Brothers. (*Producing a thick sheaf of paper*) You should have seen the ones that got away.

DISBROW (*derisively, to Kluckhorn*): Well, spokesman, what's the matter? The cat got your tongue?

KLUCKHORN: I— I was just figuring out my next move.

DISBROW: I'll give you a tip—cash in your annuities. (*Confronting the designer*) Smeed, I'm a man of few words. Stranglecraft will take your entire output. We'll give you twice as much as your highest present bid.

SMEED: Uh-uh—three times. Plus a nice worldwide advertising campaign in five colors testifying how proud, kindly, adventurous, and warmhearted I am.

FINUCANE: You're a cheap, cold-blooded skinflint and I rue the day we ever crossed the Firth of Forth.

SMEED (*sympathetically*): So do I. What an appalling thing commerce is, scarring this bonnie land with its heaps of slag and setting every man against his neighbor. Ah, weel, we shan't see the end of it in our lifetime, I'll wager. (*He seats himself, dexterously carves off a chunk of haggis with his jackknife, and starts chewing it with relish. As Disbrow, Finucane, and Ermatinger exeunt and Kluckhorn, his face richer by several tics and his hair gone silver, lopes after them—*)

CURTAIN

CLOUDLAND REVISITED:

Vintage Swine

SOME HOLLYWOOD FLACK, in a burst of inspiration, dubbed him the Man You Love to Hate. He was a short man, almost squat, with a vulpine smirk that told you, the moment his image flashed upon the screen, that no wife or bank roll must be left unguarded. The clean-shaven bullethead, the glittering monocle, and the ramrod back (kept rigid by a corset, it was whispered) were as familiar and as dear to the moviegoing public as the Pickford curls or Eugene O'Brien's pompadour. No matter what the background of the picture was—an English drawing room, a compartment on the Orient Express, the legation quarter of Peiping—he always wore tight-fitting military tunics, flaunted an ivory cigarette holder, and kissed ladies' hands profusely, betraying them in the next breath with utter impartiality. For sheer menace, he made even topnotch vipers

like Lew Cody, Ivan Lebedeff, and Rockliffe Fellowes seem
rank stumblebums by comparison. He was the ace of cads, a
man without a single redeeming feature, the embodiment of
Prussian Junkerism, and the greatest heavy of the silent film,
and his name, of course, was Erich von Stroheim.

I first saw him in a tempestuous drama, presented by Carl
Laemmle in 1919, called *Blind Husbands*, which von Stroheim,
with cyclonic energy, had adapted into a photoplay, and directed, from *The Pinnacle*, a novel he had also written. Actually, I must have seen him three years earlier as the Second
Pharisee in the Judean movement of *Intolerance*, wearing a
fright wig and a gaudy toga and heckling the Nazarene, but
there was so much Biblical flapdoodle flying around that I was
too confused to peg him.

The picture that definitely canonized von Stroheim for me,
though, was *Foolish Wives*, a gripping exposé of the swindlers
who were popularly supposed to prey on rich Americans in
Monte Carlo. In this 1922 chef-d'oeuvre, he impersonated a
spurious Russian noble named Ladislaw Sergius Von Karamzin, as ornery a skunk as ever flicked a riding crop against a
boot. Everything about him seemed to me touched with enchantment: his stiff-necked swagger, his cynical contempt for
the women he misused, and, above all, his dandyism—the monogrammed cigarettes, the dressing gowns with silk lapels, the
musk he sprayed himself with to heighten his allure. For six
months afterward, I exhibited a maddening tendency to click
my heels and murmur *"Bitte?"* along with a twitch as though a
monocle were screwed into my eye. The mannerisms finally
abated, but not until the Dean of Brown University had taken
me aside and confided that if I wanted to transfer to Heidel-
berg, the faculty would not stand in my way.

Not long ago, the Museum of Modern Art graciously permitted me to run its copy of *Foolish Wives*, on condition that if
I became overstimulated or mushy, I would not pick the veneer
off the chairs or kiss the projectionist. Such fears, it presently

turned out, were baseless. The showing roused me to neither vandalism nor affection; in fact, it begot such lassitude that I had to be given artificial respiration and sent home in a wheelbarrow. Ordinarily, I would incline to put the blame on my faulty metabolism, but this time I knew what the trouble was. A certain satanic *Schweinhund* hadn't blitzed me as he used to thirty years ago.

Foolish Wives upsets precedent by first investigating the seamy side of Monte Carlo instead of its glamour. We fade in on a milieu brimful of plot—the tenebrous hovel of an aged counterfeiter named Ventucci. A visit from his principal client, Count Karamzin, establishes that the latter is using Ventucci's green goods to support an opulent villa as a front for his stratagems. During their colloquy, the Count's jaded appetite is whetted by his host's nineteen-year-old daughter, a poor daft creature fondling a rag doll. The old man stiffens. "She is my only treasure," he snaps at von Stroheim, unsheathing a stiletto. "If anyone should harm her . . ." Leaving this promissory note to be honored at whatever point von Stroheim has run his gamut, the action shifts to an exclusive hotel near the casino. Here we meet an overripe young matron with a face like a matzoth pancake, all bee-stung lips and mascara, the wife of an American millionaire called (*sic*) Howard Hughes, and played by a sluggish Mittel-europan identified in the cast of characters only as Miss Dupont. Von Stroheim ogles the lady, who seems complaisant, gets himself presented to her, and, baiting his hook with a sermon about the pitfalls of Monte Carlo, offers to introduce her to his cousins the Princesses Olga and Vera Petchnikoff. He furthermore assures her, brazenly squinting down her bodice, that they—and, of course, he— would be enraptured to act as her social sponsors. Mrs. Hughes, understandably, is *bouleversée*, and, consenting to accompany him to a water carnival several nights thence, lumbers away to loosen her stays and recover her wits. Whether she has any of either is debatable; both her figure and her deportment are so flabby that one cannot work up much moral indignation against von Stroheim. The man is earning a very hard dollar.

Disclosed next is the Villa Amorosa, the seaside lair of the Count and his confederates, Princess Olga (Maude George) and Princess Vera (Mae Busch). For my money, Mae Busch never possessed the spidery, ghoulish fascination of that consummate she-devil Jetta Goudal, but she ranked high as a delineator of adventuresses and Eurasian spies. At any rate, the two lady tricksters, far from being von Stroheim's cousins, live in what appears to be a languid state of concubinage, switching about in negligees and exchanging feline gibes. Over breakfast, the three agree on the *modus operandi* standard among movie blackmailers, whereby the Princesses are to divert Mr. Hughes while von Stroheim compromises his wife. Ventucci, meanwhile, bustles into focus in the crisp, matter-of-fact fashion of a milkman, trailed by his daughter and bringing a satchel of fresh queer just off the press. He gives off ominous rumblings when the Count behaves familiarly with the girl, but nothing more consequential than glowering results. The same is true of the water carnival that evening. Mr. Hughes, a silver-haired, phlegmatic wowser, whose civilian name escaped me in the credits, betrays mild pique at the sight of his wife paddling around the studio tank and pelting von Stroheim with artificial roses but, after a few heavy sarcasms, relapses into coma. Had the the tempo not quickened in the ensuing scene, the picture might have ended right there for me. What with the whir of the projector and the weight of my eyelids, it took every bit of buckram I had, plus frequent pulls at a Benzedrine inhaler, to keep from sliding into the abyss.

Whittled down to essentials, the purport of the scene is that the Count takes Mrs. Hughes on an afternoon excursion, pretends to get lost in a thunderstorm, and steers her to a sinister house of assignation run by a crone called Mother Gervaise. The sole function of this unsavory character, as far as I could tell, was to persuade the young matron to doff her wet shimmy, so that von Stroheim, who has made a great show of turning his back, can stealthily appraise her in a pocket mirror—as neat a sample of voyeurism, I may add, as any ever reported by Wilhelm Stekel. After endless chin music calculated to allay her trepidation, von Stroheim has just maneuvered his sweetmeat into the horizontal when a wild-eyed anchorite reels in, ululating for shelter. Who this holy man is the picture never explains, but his scowls put a quietus on the high jinks, and Mrs. Hughes regains her hotel next morning shopworn but chaste. Inexplicably enough, the Count does not use the incident to shake down her husband—indeed, he has Princess Vera affirm that Mrs. Hughes spent the night with her—and the whole affair mystifyingly trails off with nobody the wiser, least of all the audience.

Up to now, the element of gambling has been so ruthlessly slighted in the story that the locale might as well have been a Scottish tabernacle or the annual dance festival at Jacob's Pillow. Suddenly, however, Lady Luck rears her head beside that of Sex. In addition to his other *chinoiserie*, von Stroheim has been shacking up with a bedraggled maiden named Malishka, a servant at the villa, whom he has glibly promised to wed as soon as the Bolsheviki are deposed. To still her importunities, the Count cooks up a pitiable tale of insolvency and borrows her life savings, which he loses at roulette. Mrs. Hughes, who is also having a flutter at the wheel, observes his despair and lends him her pile of counters—a gesture that abruptly changes his luck. Strong though the temptation is to pocket his winnings, he craftily relinquishes them to his benefactress, and then, a few hours later, lures her to the Villa Amorosa with a plea that his life and honor are at stake. The rendezvous takes place in a tower room. Outside the door, Malishka crouches in a fever of jealousy, and this time generates sparks in a quite literal sense. Infuriated by her lover's endearments to Mrs. Hughes prior to easing her of ninety thousand francs, the maid locks the pair in and sets fire to the stairs. They take refuge on an exterior balcony, from which they shout appeals for help, but the other guests at the villa are absorbed in being fleeced at baccarat by the Princesses and fail to respond. Hughes, meanwhile, has become increasingly worried about his wife's absence, pantomiming his solicitude by sitting on the edge of his bed and thoughtfully scratching his chin. Eventually, the Monte Carlo Fire Department, which has been snoozing under the bulldog edition of *Le Petit Monégasque*, bestirs itself, and, dashing to the scene, spreads a net under the balcony. Von Stroheim gallantly knees his companion aside and jumps first. Mrs. Hughes follows, almost hurtling through the roof of the limousine in which her husband has just driven up. Apart from the indignity of the *pompiers'* catching a glimpse of her bloomers, though, she sustains no perceptible damage, and the episode peters out, like all those preceding it, with Morpheus, the patron saint of the scenario, drowsily sharpening his quill for the next sequence.

Low as were the price of film and the salaries of actors in 1922, Mr. Laemmle and his aides must nevertheless have decided at this point in *Foolish Wives* that the consumer's patience was finite, and ordered the curtain down. The last reel, therefore, begins with Hughes' discovery, in his wife's corsage (while hunting for his pipe or a pair of shoe trees, I got the impression), of the note by which the Count had enticed her to his villa. He seeks out von Stroheim, knocks him down, and exposes his activities to the police. The Princesses are apprehended on the verge of flight, and unmasked as a couple of actresses named Maude George and Mae Busch, and now all that early scaffolding about Ventucci and his fey daughter comes in handy. Von Stroheim, in a stormy Dostoevskian finish, sneaks back to the coiner's hovel, ravishes the girl, is disemboweled by her father, and winds up being stuffed into a cistern. The concluding shot shows the Hugheses reunited—if two pieces of strudel can be said to be en rapport—lying in bed and reading, from a volume entitled *Foolish Wives*, the passage

"And thus it happened that disillusionment came finally to a foolish wife who found in her husband that nobility she had sought for in—a counterfeit."

THE VEHICLE creaks and possibly should have been left to molder in the carriage loft, yet it confirmed one opinion I had treasured for three decades. Whatever von Stroheim's shortcomings were as an artist, he was consistent. When he set out to limn a louse, he put his back into it. He never palliated his villainy, never helped old ladies across the street to show that he was a sweet kid *au fond* or prated about his Oedipus complex like the Percy boys who portray heavies today. I remember Grover Jones, a scenarist of long experience, once coaching me in Hollywood in the proper method of characterizing the menace in a horse opera. "The minute he pulls in on the Overland Stage," expounded Jones, "he should dismount and kick the nearest dog." Von Stroheim not only kicked the dog; he kicked the owner and the S.P.C.A. for good measure. With the things he has on his conscience, I don't suppose the man ever sleeps a wink. But after all, nobody needs a whole lot of sleep to keep going. You can always drop off for a jiffy—especially if there's a projector and a can of old film around.

Long Time No Sheepskin

MR. ISLAMIC, my news dealer on lower Sixth Avenue, is a man on whose bilious face a Plutonic scowl is deeply etched and who looks as though he had just leaked out of Gustave Doré's inkwell. Since Mr. Islamic's calling requires him to rise at 4:30 A.M.—a circumstance that, Thoreau and Samuel Smiles to the contrary, does not sweeten the disposition—his eyes are usually bloodshot and puffy, his beard blue-black, and his temper venomous. By the time I drop in at ten for my paper, he has managed to accumulate such fury over the small irritations of the morning that the greeting cards swirl around his shop like snowflakes. One day several weeks ago, I found him disentangling a hillock of paper clips and staples he had inadvertently spilled on the floor. My entrance afforded him an ideal opportunity to vent his wrath.

"What's the matter, don't you ever call for merchandise you order?" he shouted. "Five months I'm waiting for you to pick up that magazine you told me to get!" It took superhuman restraint not to answer him in kind, but I exercised it and meekly accepted the copy of the *Journal of Heredity* he shoved at me. The outburst, coupled with the dollar and fifty cents I handed him, evidently had an analgesic effect on Islamic, for he picked up the magazine and examined the photograph of a bumper crop of sorghum on the cover. "A farm paper, eh?" he growled. "You a farmer?"

"Well—er—not exclusively," I said, blushing. "Of course, we grow our own cereals in Bucks—I have a field of winter oatmeal, I think it is—"

Islamic, however, had turned a deaf ear to my pastorale and was scanning the table of contents in some perplexity. " 'Mutilation Patterns and Hereditary (?) Cannibalism in Mice,' " he read laboriously. " 'Induced Tetraploidy in Muskmelons.' Say," he said, fixing me with a Cyclops eye, "what kind of a magazine *is* this?" I snatched back the periodical and fled, but not so precipitately that I missed hearing him mutter under his breath, "Cannibalism in mice. Jeez, no wonder a woman ain't safe on the streets."

Islamic's bewilderment, frankly, would beset any lay reader of the *Journal of Heredity*; to grasp the nuances of an article like "A Rare Dominant Chlorophyll Mutant in Durum Wheat" or "Wild Type Plumage Pattern in the Fowl," one would have to be Gregor Johann Mendel or at least a member of the American Genetic Association, which publishes it. The issue, however, contained one article, "The Score of the Colleges," that nobody should have any trouble comprehending. It appears that geneticists, who disturb as easily as a covey of teal, have become increasingly disturbed in the past thirty-five years by the alarmingly low rate of reproduction among college graduates. In the *Journal's* own words, "A number of surveys fully justify the conclusion that graduation from college constitutes partial sterilization. In 1927 Dr. John Phillips announced that the average Harvard graduate was only half replacing himself. Following that, the alumni and alumnae of a number of universities have been polled as to their reproductive performance. In almost every instance, these surveys have revealed fecundity below replacement." The five pages of appended tables incontestably support this somber verdict. Except for the alumni of a few institutions like Brigham Young University and Providence College, who are spawning as intensively as ever, the average college graduate gets less prolific by the year. At Wellesley, for instance, members of the class of 1925 bore 1.4 bambinos apiece, as opposed to their sisters in 1921, who racked up 1.5; at Tufts 1.7, as against 1.8; and at Pratt Institute, where the emphasis on the arts might be expected to foster a certain reckless exuberance, the average has declined even more steeply. All in all, a pretty dismal picture. The one discernible ray of hope is that among graduates of the last ten years fertility does seem to be waxing. Says the *Journal*, owlishly twirling its editorial mustache, "Mark Twain's comment that all the talk about the weather had never led to any action seems to apply in this area too, if by 'action' we mean planning and an organized and functioning program to increase the birth rate of the intelligent. But there is some indication that the talk itself—even in the absence of any program—may be having some effect. If the recent increase in the fecundity of college graduates can be attributed to the discussion of this matter which has been going on for so many years, then it would seem that a big increase in such conversation is needed."

That talk about the subject is on the increase and may be having a marked effect indeed is a conclusion I myself reached the other afternoon at a refined shebeen in the East Fifties. Immersed in the last canto of *Don Juan* over a quiet sundowner, I had paid no special attention to the two young matrons at the table next to mine. One of them, I was vaguely aware, was a lush blonde with honey-colored hair, clad in a wool dress of forest green edged in rickrack, gunmetal stockings, black suède pumps, and a nutria jacket. The other, a rather smoldering brunette, wore a pin-checked tweed suit with poodle scatter pins on the lapel, brown oxfords, a cocoa-colored riding hat, three-quarter-length tan gloves, and an American-broadtail stole. The light in the bar was too dim to determine whether their lingerie had come from Bendel's or Bonwit's, but everything proclaimed them to be women not visibly harassed by the specter of want. By the third round of Gibsons (my third), their whispers had become so audible that they drowned out Byron's strophes, and I was compelled to listen.

"But didn't he have credentials or something?" the brunette was objecting. "I mean, if anybody rang my bell and asked me such intimate questions—"

"Oh, don't be a pill, Valerie," said the blonde impatiently. "It was just one of those surveys—you know, like a census. He wanted to know how long Turk and I'd been out of college, and were we—well, *simpatico*, and goodge like that. Then he told me about the birth rate declining at Vassar."

"How did he know you'd gone there?" queried Valerie.

"Why, I told him, silly," said her friend. "It was a scientific poll, wasn't it?" She giggled. "You'll never dream what he said about Harvard men." She leaned over and whispered into the other's ear. Valerie stiffened.

"I don't believe it!" she said. "Whitney went there, and he certainly isn't. At—at least, I don't think so."

"Well, don't be too sure," the blonde returned. "It happens to all college graduates, but apparently it's like an epidemic at Harvard."

"What else did he tell you?" Valerie pressed her. "Did he have any figures on Bryn Mawr?"

"I don't remember," her companion said. "We had a drink or two and I got a little fuzzy." She smiled reminiscently. "He was kind of cute, though."

"So I gather," said Valerie. "Are you seeing him again?"

"Well," said the blonde, gathering her effects, "you never

know. Look, darling, you pay the check—I've got to run. I'm meeting Turk at the Biltmore."

"I thought he was in Oswego," said Valerie.

"He—er—he took an early plane back," her friend replied. "Bye now—I'll call you." As she cleared off and Valerie extracted her compact, I noticed that another person had been attending the duologue—a crop-haired gentleman in a tartan waistcoat at the farther adjoining table. The sidelong glance he was directing at Valerie was so brazen that I was momentarily tempted to alert her to her peril, but I was avid to learn how the canto came out, and, removing the muddler I had used as a bookmark, I gave myself up to it.

A scant ten seconds later, I heard a man's voice lifted in urgent apology. "Good heavens, I'm sorry!" it was saying. "Here, use my handkerchief." The crop-haired eavesdropper, or eavescropper, so to speak, was on his feet, sponging Valerie's purse and making a great show of remorse. "Idiotic of me to spill that. You must let me replace your pocketbook—"

"Nonsense," Valerie assured him brightly. "There, you can barely see it. It's just a cheap bag anyway." She paused an eye flick, and added inconsequentially, "An anniversary present."

"I know," said the *caballero*, nimbly accepting the gambit. "They give the expensive ones to their secretaries, don't they?" Far from drawing the rebuff I expected, the gibe seemed to delight Valerie; she emitted an appreciative tinkle and, by some tortuous logic I could not quite fathom, coyly consented to let him replenish her glass. The velocity with which their acquaintance grew, in fact, astounded me. In less than three minutes, I learned indirectly that the poacher was named Hemphill, shared Valerie's passion for Alec Guinness and small-boat sailing, and summered, by sheerest coincidence, at Nantucket, an island she had once circumnavigated.

"Listen, I hope you won't mind!" exclaimed Hemphill with a

boyish twinkle that made me positively ill. "You know what I was thinking when I was sitting there before? What a becoming hat that is."

"This old thing?" said Valerie, flattered. "Why, it's just an old riding hat; I haven't worn it in years. Do you really like it?"

"You never ought to wear anything else," he assured her fervently. Before either of us could triangulate the Freudian implication of the remark, he rushed on to amplify it. "I can't *stand* those fussy hats most women wear, all veils and gingerbread. My wife, for instance—I've begged her for years to buy a hat like yours, but she just doesn't know what I mean."

"Married people get that way," Valerie agreed. "They develop the weirdest blind spots. If I could only persuade my husband to wear colorful ties—say like the one you have on—"

"That's very interesting," said Hemphill. "I wonder how widespread that yearning for color in the mate is among women. You see, in my profession—I'm a statistician—we like to keep tabs on these things."

"How exciting!" said Valerie. "I've always been fascinated by statistics. Those darling little soldiers of different sizes."

"Oh, it's pretty humdrum for the most part," chuckled Hemphill. "But every so often you get a project that's rewarding. Like this survey we're conducting on the reproductive pattern in college graduates."

"Now, isn't that simply uncanny!" Valerie exclaimed. "Someone was just mentioning that to me. I mean—er—someone who was approached in connection with it."

"Really?" said Hemphill, with a crocodile smile. "Well, it's absolutely terrific, the dope we've uncovered. I'd love to tell you more about it. Look here, do you know this marvelous little French place on East Sixty-third they call Le Rognon?"

"Thank you, but I don't think I could tonight," said Valerie hastily. "I sort of promised my godmother—"

"Their specialty's *moules marinière*, and Cosette makes the chocolate soufflé herself," Hemphill continued, as though he

had not heard her. "Afterward we could drop in at Le Down-
beat for their late jam session."

"We-ell," said Valerie, chewing her underlip thoughtfully,
"it *is* sort of scientific, in a way; perhaps I might be able to
manage one quick Pernod. You don't suppose they have a
phone here, do you?"

"No," said Hemphill, springing up, "but Le Drugstore,
around the corner, has one that communicates with all parts of
the world. Waiter!"

They made an attractive couple as they went out, leaving
me with an unfinished canto and a flea in my ear. One of these
mornings, I must pick up a *Journal of Heredity* at Islamic's and
see what the final score of the colleges is. It ought to be a banner year for a lot more than sorghum.

The Swirling Cape and
the Low Bow

If I live to be a hundred years old (a possibility that must have actuarial circles sick with fear), I doubt that I shall ever forget the winter of 1932. It needs no cup of lime-flower tea, macaroon or other Proustian accouterments to help me recall that that was the year I worked on a revue called *Sherry Flip*. It was also the year Rudy Vallee crooned his way to fame in a voice as seductive as mineral oil, the year Douglas MacArthur brilliantly routed the bonus marchers at Anacostia Flats, and the year those sparkling philosophers, Father Coughlin and Howard Scott, bedazzled the lunatic fringe, but all these calamities were trifling compared to *Sherry Flip*. Speaking dispassionately, I would say that the people responsible for that show—and I was as culpable as anyone--set the American theater back a hundred years.

The producer of *Sherry Flip* was a *bon vivant* named Avery Mapes, a onetime yacht broker riding out the depression on a cask of Courvoisier, and its creators were three: Lazlo Firkusny, a Budapest composer, a lyric writer named Lytton Swazey, and myself. Swazey, after years of grinding out special material for those willowy pianists who chant in cocktail bars at nightfall, had teamed up with Firkusny, who wrote popular airs under the pseudonym of Leonard Frayne. Together they confected a valiseful of show tunes, and it was on these, and half a dozen sketches I wrung out of a dry sponge I carried in my head, that the revue was based.

From the first week of rehearsals, it was obvious that the Furies had marked us down. The leading lady fell out with the composer, branded him a Hungarian meat ball, and went into nervous collapse. The comedians, who had made their reputation in burlesque, took a very dim view of my sketches, referring to me disdainfully as Percy Bysshe Shelley. They abandoned the material agreed on and began improvising routines in which they flimflammed a Polack from Scranton with a wallet stuffed with tissue paper, gave impersonations of humorous tramps, and spawned *double-entendres* that made the brain reel. Once embarked, no protestations, no appeals, could curb them; they girded themselves with grotesque rubber feet and boutonnières that spurted water, pursued squealing showgirls into the boxes and thwacked their bottoms with rolled-up newspapers. Their behavior totally unnerved Wigmore, our director, a brilliant man around an Ibsen revival but a newcomer to the revue theatre. The poor man fluttered about in a continual wax, pathetically wringing his hands like Zazu Pitts and endeavoring to assert his authority. In the dance division, there was a similar lack of co-ordination. The production numbers, two portentous ballets of the type informally known in dance circles as "Fire in a Whorehouse," had got away out of hand. Muscle-bound youths stamped about bearing dryads

97

who whinnied in ecstasy, shoals of coryphees fled helter-skelter across the stage, and the choreographer, wild-eyed with exhaustion, sat slumped in the apron, dreaming up new flights of symbolism. It was a holocaust.

We opened in Boston on the eve of Thanksgiving, a season associated from time immemorial with turkeys, and our *première*, I am told, is still spoken of along the Charles. The house curtain did not rise on *Sherry Flip* in the conventional fashion; instead, it billowed out and sank down over the orchestra, perceptibly muffling the overture. The musicians fiddled with might and main underneath, but Firkusny's score was too fragile and lilting to overcome the handicap. The comedy, on the other hand, was exceedingly robust, so much so that the police stepped in the next day and excised four sketches.

The tone of the reviews, by and large, was vengeful. One of the critics felt that we ought to be hunted down with dogs. Another, singling me out as the chief malefactor, stated he would be appeased by nothing short of my heart's blood. For the first time in its twenty-seven years of publication, *Variety* was guilty of a glaring omission. It forgot to review the show at all.

Two nights later, I was emerging from the stage door after a post-mortem when I heard my name called. Turning, I beheld one of our showgirls, a gazelle whose lavish *poitrine* was the despair of the wardrobe mistress and the lodestar of every male in the cast. She was accompanied by a vital, leathery taxpayer with protuberant eyes, opulently clad in a black astrakhan coat sporting a mink collar. His face was screwed around an unlit Partagas which he was savagely chewing into submission.

"My friend would like to know you," said the winsome balloon smuggler. "Meet Georgie Jessel."

"Hello, kid," said her escort hoarsely, seizing me in a paralyzing handclasp. "I've just been out front watching the performance. Does the name of George Armstrong Custer suggest anything to you?"

"Well—er—yes," I said innocently. "Isn't it usually identified with some massacre or other?"

"Indeed it is," he affirmed. "And as I sat there tonight, the walls of the theater receded and it seemed to me that I was back on the Little Big Horn. My friend," he said, his voice solemn, "the handwriting on the wall reads '*Mene mene tekel upharsin.*' Your goose is cooked, the scuppers are awash. Get out of town while there's still time."

"D-don't you see any hope at all?" I asked, trembling.

"Only for the Shuberts," he said inexorably. "They can always flood the auditorium and rent it out to hockey teams. As for yourself, go back to that job at the slaughterhouse. It's not glamorous work, but I can tell from your sketches that you have a career there. *Zei gezünt.*" He wrapped a proprietary arm around his date and swept her off to a hot bird and a cold bottle at Locke-Ober's. Desolate, I watched them go; then, hailing a jitney, I sped to Back Bay and boarded the midnight to New York.

Considering that I spent most of the ensuing decade in Hollywood writing scenarios, an occupation akin to stuffing kapok in mattresses, it was strange that I should not have encountered Jessel. The fact was, however, that he went there infrequently, for his services were not avidly sought by the movie satraps. He held them in rather low regard and his tongue was much too unruly to disguise his contempt. On one occasion, for example, he waspishly interrupted a panegyric someone was delivering about several production geniuses. "Overrated," he snapped. "They could put butter on the film and sell it." Jessel's intimates begged him to be more politic, pointing out that other actors were being given parts he might have had, but the poniard flashed automatically out of the sheath. Typical was the evening he was taken to dine at the home of an M-G-M big wheel who was considering him for a role. Throughout dinner, Jessel was a model of tact and affability. After the walnuts and wine, the party adjourned to the rumpus room for a game of poker. All went well until the host's nine-year-old son, a particularly objectionable lad, entered and began kibitzing. Jessel gnawed his cheroot to ribbons in an effort to contain himself. At length he turned on the producer. "Listen," he rasped. "Why don't you sling that punk across the bridge of your nose and tote him off to bed?" The name of Jessel, needless to add, was conspicuously absent from the cast of characters when the picture was released.

In the amnesty and repatriation that followed the accession of Zanuck I of the Skouras dynasty to the throne of Twentieth Century-Fox, Jessel suddenly confounded the wiseacres and bobbed up as one of the very clan he had derided for years. Whether he became a movie producer through hunger or sheer contrariness is uncertain, but he vanished from Times Square and the lush pastrami beds of the West Forties knew him not. It was whispered along the grapevine that the man was now a Zoroastrian and a food faddist, subsisting entirely on dates, bran, and blintzes made of soybeans, and engaged between times on projects clearly beyond mortal skill, such as translating the prose of Louella Parsons into English. Some even asserted that the real Jessel had succumbed a year before to steam poisoning in a Finnish bath, and that his studio was employing a double to impersonate him.

None of this kit-kit, happily, was true. A few weeks ago, lunching with a friend in the Twentieth Century-Fox commissary, I heard a familiar raucous voice upraised several tables away. "Sure I like Grossinger's," it was saying, "but let me warn you—if you go up there, be sure and wear sunglasses. You can get snow blindness from the sour cream." It was Jessel, right enough, and nothing had changed but his attire. He was clad in white sharkskin and a chocolate-colored shirt with pale-blue collar and cuffs, wore a coconut-fiber straw encircled by a pug-gree band, and rotated the inevitable perfecto in his cheek. Our eyes met at the same instant.

"Percy B. Shelley!" he gasped, springing toward me. No Siberian exiles could have exchanged more emotional salutations. "What happened to that revue of yours in Boston? Is it still open?" I revealed that it had closed just prior to its nineteenth anniversary, and he shook his head. "Oh, well, we all have flops," he commiserated. "Say, who's this interesting-looking fellow you're with?"

"Excuse me," I apologized. "Mr. Jessel—John Keats."

"A pleasure, Keats," said Jessel. "I've read your *Ode on a Grecian Urn*. There's a great picture in it; tell your agent to call me. Well," he said, taking me by the arm, "come on, I have to get back to my office. We can talk there."

"But I haven't had my dessert," I protested.

"Quiet," he said under his breath. "You don't want to be seen eating with starvelings—it's bad for you socially in Hollywood." To save Keats's feelings, I told him that since he was jobless, a nonentity, and furthermore strongly suspected of being un-American, he could be of no earthly use to me, and ran after Jessel. Our chance meeting had thrown him into a reminiscent mood; his rhetoric as he expatiated on the early thirties grew more florid by the moment.

"Halcyon days, by Jove," he declaimed. "Gad, I was a picaresque fellow then, another Benvenuto Cellini. It was the day of the swirling cape and the low bow. What madcap escapades, what deeds of high emprise! Albeit my purse was empty, I was ever ready for a duel or a bout with the flagons. One look from Milady's eyes——"

"À propos of that," I put in, "whatever became of the pouter pigeon who introduced us?"

"She married into the peerage," said Jessel impressively. "The Turkish peerage. I sent them a box of halvah for the wedding." His face took on a faraway expression. "What a dainty waist that creature had!" he marveled. "You could span it with your two hands. I spent the winter of '32 spanning it. Here we are." The anteroom of his suite was a smoke-filled chamber resembling a vaudeville booking office. A handful of callers—a lush blonde, a small, ulcerous agent, an insurance canvasser, and a carefully unobtrusive citizen who looked like a dice hustler—greeted Jessel effusively. When they had been disposed of, I rejoined him in his inner sanctum. The memorabilia accumulated in an extensive career as monologist and toastmaster overflowed the walls and furniture; testimonial letters from presidents, banquet scenes, signed cigarette boxes, and posters lay jumbled on his desk amid movie scripts, clippings, and a mountainous correspondence. He was shouting into a phone as I entered.

"How can I open the Santa Anita track that Friday?" he bellowed in anguish. "I have to dedicate a new playground in Tel Aviv the next day! Yes, and emcee the Lambs' Gambol in New York two days after! I tell you, you're killing me, you're ruining my stomach—say no more, Harry, I'll be there." He waved me into a chair, picked up a script, and began intoning over it. "M-m-m. 'Lucy, your eyes are like sesame seeds tonight, sesame and lilies. Anybody who says different is a liar.' 'Oh, Ruskin, don't, don't. What if my husband should come in from his destroyer?' No, that's too bald. The writer's using a javelin instead of a needle." He blue-penciled the speech, and tossing aside the script, swung toward me.

"Why do I do it?" he demanded. "Why does a gifted Thespian, a mummer in the great tradition of Burbage, Macready, and Booth, hock out his brains here for a lousy twenty-five hundred a week when he could be holding audiences spellbound with his magic? I should be playing Strindberg and Shaw in the different world capitals, not vegetating in this cactus-covered suburb!" He smote his breast, taking care not to muss his pocket

handkerchief. "When I remember those early days in the theater—the freedom, the bonhomie, the comradeship of those
roaches in the dressing rooms! A man could live on nothing at
all; I used to pay off my Chinese laundryman in lichee nuts.
Today I've got a mansion overlooking the Pacific, with a library of the world's most expensive classics, a retinue of serv-
ants, a cellar of the finest French wines, brandies, and cordials,
every luxury money can buy—and yet I'm like a bird in a gilded
cage. Sometimes I'm tempted to kick over the whole shebang.
If it wasn't for the crushing weight of responsibility, the whole
studio on my shoulders——"

"Let someone else carry the load," I advised. "Get away from
the artificiality and hypocrisy of Hollywood. Go down to Palm
Springs."

"No, it's too primitive, too remote," he said uneasily. "Sometimes it takes the *Hollywood Reporter* a whole day to reach
there. Wait a minute, though," he exclaimed. "You gave me an
idea. Have you ever been in Catalina? A Garden of Eden—a
little fragment of Paradise in an emerald sea! How soon can you
be back here?"

"I *am* here," I replied, "and what's more, I've seen Catalina.
I went over there in 1938——"

"Look, I haven't got time to listen to travelogues, I'm a busy
man," Jessel broke in. "Get some pajamas and a toothbrush, and
meet me in an hour at Woloshin's delicatessen. I'll phone down
to San Pedro for a boat, we'll pick up a cargo of lox and
bagels, and I'll guarantee you a cruise that'll make Magellan
look like a farmer."

Naturally, I had no intention of abetting any such hare-
brained scheme, and I said so. I was still saying so about mid-
afternoon as Jessel propelled me down a wharf at San Pedro
toward a luxurious motor cruiser, all mahogany and brass,
moored alongside it. My companion's innate flair for pagean-
try had impelled him to outfit us both with yachting caps and

binoculars, and he was as salty as one of Joseph C. Lincoln's down-East skippers. The captain of the vessel, a stout foxy-nose in brown gabardine whom I would have cast more accurately as a defaulting bank cashier, welcomed us aboard and begged our indulgence. The starboard Diesel had broken down, but we should be under way within a few minutes. "Take your time, Captain Applejack," said Jessel negligently, stretching out in a chair under the awning. "The others haven't showed up anyway."

"What others?" I asked apprehensively.

"Oh, just some people I invited along to keep us company," he returned. "I figured we might as well play pinochle to while away the trip. How long can you look at the ocean, for God's sake? When you've seen one wave, you've seen 'em all." Before I could invent some plausible excuse to disembark, like a ruptured appendix, our fellow passengers appeared in a peach-colored convertible, clad, to a man, in nylon windbreakers, Bermuda shorts, and berets. They all proved to be either former studio heads who were now agents or former agents who had just become studio heads, and their conversation was so cryptic that it might as well have been in Pawnee. The occasional monosyllables I caught, however, indicated that they were highly suspicious of each other and were only undertaking the voyage as a mark of esteem for Jessel. How profound this was I shortly discovered. One of them deserted the card table at which the rest sat engrossed in the pasteboards and joined me at the rail.

"A great guy, Georgie," he observed emotionally. "Salt of the earth. You and I'll be lucky to have him read over us when our time comes." I did not quite grasp his meaning and begged for elucidation. "The eulogy," he said impatiently. "Haven't you ever heard him give an address at a burial? Jeez, he'll make you bawl like a baby. I've heard him speak at all kinds of dinners and affairs, but take it from me, nobody can top that boy at a funeral." He was launching into a hushed account of Jessel's eloquence at the interment of some picture notable when the captain reappeared with a long countenance. The engine was hopelessly out of commission, and to further confound our plans, an unexpected tidal wave had submerged Catalina and swallowed it up in the depths of the Pacific. The news acted like digitalis on Jessel, whose mood had been growing progressively more somber at the thought of putting to sea.

"Good riddance," he commented exultantly, as we drove back into Los Angeles. "As a matter of fact, I was opposed to the trip from the start—I only agreed to humor you. Now we can have a good juicy steak and go to the fights." The prospect of watching a number of third-rate pugs maul each other into insensibility in a drafty armory full of cigar smoke was an exhilarating one. Unluckily, I had a prior engagement to dine with two other old friends in the movie colony, Doc Johnson and Jamie Boswell, who were collaborating on a Biblical film at Paramount, and I did not feel I could let them down. The mention of their names drew immediate approbation from Jessel. "A topflight comedy team," he declared. "Strictly with the boffs. Keep this under your hat, but I'm planning a musical about Disraeli, with Yvonne de Carlo as Queen Victoria, and I'd love to have those boys write it. Tell their agent to call me."

"Right," I said, as we drew up before the Hollywood hotel where I was bivouacked. "Well, it's been a treat seeing you again, old man. By the way, please don't bother to drive me out to the airport when I leave, will you?"

"Of course not," he said warmly. "Now remember, any time you're having a banquet, a christening, a wedding anniversary, or a shower, don't forget Jessel. I've got speeches for all occasions, grave or licentious as the case may be. I can tug at the heartstrings, I can tickle the risibilities, and, if the caterer needs an extra man, I can even carry chairs. *Lox vobiscum*, and give my regards to Broadway." His custom-built wig slid away from the curb and was lost in the stream of traffic. On the sidewalk two urchins were turning handsprings, and somehow they provided a note of poetic justice. After all, nobody could follow Jessel but acrobats.

Genuflection in the Sun

I AM NOT A TEETOTALER and enjoy a good snort as well as the next one, but for sheer delight and ecstasy in the region of the tonsils none of them can even begin to compare with that strange combination of syrup, ice cream and carbonated water skillfully proportioned and compounded by some Master Dispenser at my favorite Liggett fountain.

I can see him now, this delicate and brilliant chemist, his head tilted forward slightly as his ear reaches for my order— "All black, please."

"All black!" Already his hand has whisked a large-sized tumbler whose narrowed round bottom was scientifically designed to aid the magical blending of all the weird component parts of the soda. Under the chocolate syrup faucet it goes. See how the rich, dark brown goo covers a third of the bottom of the glass, clinging lovingly to the side.

Now a splash of cream and the first of a series of wonderful amalgams has taken place. The dark chocolate is lighter in tone, more fluid, better prepared for the life infusion that follows—the fizzer.

Here is surely the secret of this nectar for the Gods of America, the genius touch of this unknown benefactor of mankind. The Master Dispenser is all concentration now, for this is a solemn moment, the aerating of the milk and chocolate mixture with the wire-thin stream of vital and living fizz. It hisses into the glass as he turns it carefully to all points of the compass. Under the impulse of this injection, the liquid suddenly begins to bubble and boil and heave, seething with a new and inner life of its own. Whereas a moment ago it was somber and viscous, now it is light, merry, purposeful, and gay.

Plop! Into its joyously heaving bosom is dropped a rounded gobbet of smooth, rich ice cream.

Now the Master Dispenser approaches the climax. Infected by his own artistry, he swings the glass and turns on the soda faucet, his eye keen to the task of producing perfection. As the charged water joins the composition, great, luscious brown bubbles begin to rise in the glass. Higher and Higher under the watchful gaze of the Super Dispenser. Not yet . . . not yet . . . NOW! A corona of pure aerated chocolate flavor stands an inch high above the glass, a crown of sweet nothing, too superb in texture and flavor for words. A spoon, two straws, and there it is vibrant, pulsating—ready. . . .

Ah, Ye Gods of Gluttony! That first taste, the mouthful of froth, the sweet of the chocolate, the brisk tang of the soda, the ecstasy of the now-you-have-it, now-you-haven't, which sends you on for fulfillment into the first bite of ice cream irrigated with the lovely fluid of the soda.

Rich though these rewards be, they are nothing to the grand finale, the climax of enjoyment, when with froth gone, ice cream gone, you discard the straws, lift the glass, tilt back your head and subject your tonsils to the first superb shock of the pure Ichor of the soda, syrup, bubble water, water, melted ice cream, all blended into one Ambrosia of flavor, action and chill.

What is there to match it? Where is it to be found? Who, oh, who, is the great, great man who thought it all up for the likes of you and me?—*From a Liggett menu.*

Two MILES south of Corona del Mar, I saw looming up ahead the Piggy-Wig Drive-In they had told me in Balboa to watch for. Narrowly missing a Hupmobile driven by an old harpy in curlers, who interpreted my left-hand signal as an invitation to sleep with her, I swerved off the Coast Highway and pulled up alongside it. A heavy miasma of frying lard and barbecued ribs drifted across the wheel of asphalt radiating from the structure; somewhere inside, the sepulchral voice of Patti Page sniveled a plaint about a doggie in a window. Three lackluster carhops, manifestly chosen for their resemblance to porkers, were seated under a bong tree made of papier-mâché, and as one languidly rose and undulated toward me, I noticed a curled pink celluloid tail protruding from her scientifically designed narrowed round bottom, which bobbled as she moved.

"Villa Jacaranda?" she repeated, swallowing a yawn. "What is it—a motel?" I explained I was looking for the residence of Willard Inchcape, the writer. "I wouldn't know, I'm sure," she returned with disdain. "There's some bohemians up that dirt road there. They all sculp or weave or something."

I thanked her and, resisting an impulse to order a slice of quince to see whether it came with a runcible spoon, a form of cutlery that has always pricked my curiosity, drove on. The road straggled into the foothills past a cluster of aggressive ranch-style homes—each equipped with an incinerator adapted for those murders in which southern California seems to excel —and terminated at a high wall of whitewashed brick. Over the massive gate was a chemically aged plastic shingle bearing the legend "Villa Jacaranda" in Carborundum Old Style. I pushed the gate open and stepped down into a garden choked with poinsettias. Their foliage was so lush that it veiled the outlines of the house beyond, but in a patch of greensward at

109

the far end there was visible a woman laboring at a sculptor's table. As I approached, she turned and I beheld a portly matron of fifty-odd in a green smock, with an uncompromising henna bob and Hashimura Togo spectacles.

"Mrs. Inchcape?" I asked. "I phoned from Los Angeles."

"Oh, yes," she said energetically. "You're the man who wanted to talk to Willard. Come in." She laid her graving tool on the stand, a gesture that automatically drew my eye to the object she was modeling. It was the head of a Scotch collie, carved from a block of castile soap with such fidelity to nature that I had no difficulty repressing a start.

"Aha," I commented with a portentous frown, aware that she was watching me closely. "Er—is that an actual portrait or more of an idealized conception, as it were?"

"Half and half," said Mrs. Inchcape. "I based it on our Timmy. He passed on several years ago."

"You don't say," I murmured, attempting to mingle respect for her bereavement with a note of philosophic fatalism.

"Yes, he's buried right where you're standing." I jerked sidewise, remorseful at having desecrated a tomb. "Do you like it?"

I cocked my head and nodded emphatically. "You certainly got him down cold," I said. Then, conscious of the ambiguity of my critique, I added hurriedly, "What I mean is you sure got him dead to rights." I felt the perspiration start on my forehead. "Of course, I never knew Timmy—"

"You bet you didn't," said Mrs. Inchcape. "If he were alive, you'd never be in this garden. He'd have torn you limb from limb."

"Well, well," I said, feigning admiration for her pet's loyalty. "I guess his death was a real loss."

"I can't imagine to whom," she returned. "He bit everybody, right up to the man who chloroformed him. But I suppose you're one of those people who get sentimental about animals."

It impressed me as singular that she should be immortalizing a beast she abhorred, but I decided not to pry. "Is Mr. Inchcape home?" I asked, looking around. "I wouldn't like to disturb him if he's working."

"Don't get fidgety, he'll be along in a minute," she said, motioning toward a bench. "Sit down while I clean up this mess. Did you ever hear of Daniel Chester French?"

"The sculptor?"

"Well, I certainly don't mean Daniel Chester French the upholsterer," she said with asperity. "The one who did the statue of 'Memory' at the Metropolitan. I studied with him for two years, and let me tell you, young man, there wasn't a mean bone in his body." I tried to recall anything discreditable I had ever heard about French, and failed. "Your ears remind me of his. The way they're articulated to the head."

"Gee," I said, feeling it was incumbent on me to exhibit some sign of elation. "I've never been told that before. You—ah— It must have been a great privilege to know Mr. French."

"That depends on how you look at it," said Mrs. Inchcape acidly. She lapsed into a tight-lipped silence, dusting chips of soap from the stand and casting me an occasional suspicious glance.

Suddenly a man's voice, tremulous with excitement, resounded through the shrubbery. "Rowena!" it called. "Where are you—in the patio?" Her hail of response, easily audible in Mazatlán, flushed up my quarry, a leathery old gentleman with an Armagnac nose, a black velvet tam, and a smoking jacket. In one hand he clenched a Tyrolean porcelain pipe fluttering a pair of green tassels and in the other a typewritten sheet that bristled with interlineations. "Just listen to this, honey bun!" he crowed. "It's the copy for Mother Stentorian's Fish Kebabs, and if I do say so, it's a sockdolager. I couldn't get the exact poetic throb at first—"

"This geezer here's waiting for you," said his wife laconically.

"Well, he's got a stomach—let him hear it, too!" said Inchcape jovially. He rotated toward me. "You the party called me about my ice-cream-soda tribute?"

"I am, sir," I said, extending my hand, "and I've come to tell you it's the finest thing since Baudelaire's *Flowers of Evil.* I just wanted to pay my respects to a great poet."

"Thank you, son, thank you," he replied, his face suffused with pleasure. "But if you think that was good, get ready for a real treat." He adjusted a pince-nez secured to his lapel by a silver chain, cleared his throat, and began declaiming in a rich, fruity baritone: " 'Up from the silent, sunless depths of the seven seas into Mother Stentorian's spotless antiseptic kitchens come the hake, the scrod, the plaice, the fluke, the cream of the finny tribe, briny-fresh and jam-packed with succulent vitamins, to tickle the gourmet palate. Man alive, watch these yum-dingers, these dorsal dainties, tumble from the nets in silver iridescence, splendid largess from Nature's treasure-trove, yearning to sputter in butter and ravish the jaded esophagus! Here in this hygienic temple of the culinary art, under the watchful yet kindly eye of Mother Stentorian, they are por-tioned into appetizing mouth-size chunks, sprinkled with mace, dill, rape, capsicum, and rose leaves, and precooked on skew-ers over aromatic fires of specially processed driftwood im-ported from faraway Armenia.' "

"Jiminetty," I ejaculated as he paused for breath. "That's in-spired, Mr. Inchcape! You can almost taste the crisp, savory—"

"Wait, you haven't heard anything yet," he broke in. "I'm just warming up. Then each individual kebab, its delectable goodness sealed in, is wrapped in gleaming chlorophane—cello-phane from which all harmful chlorophyll has been extracted—by deft-fingered, full-bosomed girls pledged to change their uniforms every hour. Now comes the most vital phase in the preparation of Mother Stentorian's Matchless Fish Kebabs. Science has discovered that these fishy shasliks—or, more prop-erly, fishliks—acquire a mysterious added tang when impreg-nated with the folk songs of Asia Minor. Consequently, before your personalized package of kebabs is handi-packed, it is locked into a special tone chamber—a musical autoclave, so to speak—where it is saturated with rollicking airs like "The Well-Tufted Ottoman," "Sohrab and Rustum Were Lovers," and "Sister, Shake That Amphigouri." Why deny yourself any longer the color and enchantment of the Near East you've always secretly hungered for? Simply perfume your house with the odor of cold mutton fat, heat up a box of Mother Stentorian's Genuine Fish Kebabs, and become part of the world's most ancient culture. As you squat on your hams greedily engorging these zestful tidbits, you, too, will be at one with Shadrach, Meshach, and Abednego, with Nineveh and Tyre.' "

Mrs. Inchcape was the first to break the silence when her husband had concluded. "Will he be staying for lunch?" she demanded, nodding in my direction.

"Why, I can't really say," hesitated Inchcape, obviously derailed. "We haven't had a chance—"

"No, no, thank you," I said hastily. "I'm bound for La Jolla. I'll be leaving very soon."

"Then I'll just make a soybean *pizza* for two," Mrs. Inchcape announced, departing. "Come when I call you, now. It's no good cold."

The bard looked so stricken that first aid was indicated at once. "Mr. Inchcape," I said, "this may sound insincere, but when you were reading that, you brought a lump to my throat. It's tremendous. Absolutely symphonic."

"You think it jells, do you?" he asked eagerly.

"Good heavens, man, it sings!" I said. "They'll be quoting you in advertising circles for years to come. The lyricism—the imagery! It's a downright classic, I promise you."

"Oh, shucks, it's only a pastiche," said Inchcape, buffing his nails on his sleeve. "I mean with a theme as limited as kebabs you don't have the scope, naturally. Now, the ice-cream soda—there I had material to work with. I employed a kind of a cosmic approach, if you noticed."

"It struck me right away," I confessed. "First the syrup, then the cream, then the fizz. Like architecture."

"Each symbolizing a step in the universal creative process," he pointed out. "Fire, earth, and water, all uniting to produce bliss everlasting, or, in the wider sense, the Promethean spark."

"And the whole compounded by a Master Dispenser," I recalled. "Yes, the mystical analogy was perfect. Did you ever get any figures from Liggett's? Were there many conversions?"

"You mean abstainers who took up ice-cream soda as a result?" queried Inchcape. "Frankly, it *was* rather impressive; in fact, for a while they considered having prayers with the sandwiches, but the customers balked." He shrugged. "Ah, well, between you and me, I was shooting at the aesthetic angle more than the religious."

"You hit the bull's-eye, in any case," I declared. "Tell me, how did you happen to get into inspirational writing?"

He pondered for a moment before replying. "Well, it was sort of a call," he said reflectively. "I had my own business up in Hollywood, a few doors from Grauman's Egyptian, on the Boulevard. We eternalized baby shoes—you know, dipped them in bronze for ashtrays and souvenirs. The work was creative, but somehow I felt I wasn't realizing my potentialities. Then one day I came across a copy of Elbert Hubbard's magazine, *The Philistine*, and his style reacted on me like a long, cold drink of sauerkraut juice. Right there, I made up my mind to follow in the footsteps of the Sage of East Aurora, and I never deviated one hair from my resolve. Which I'm thankful to say that Rowena—that's Mrs. Inchcape—has always been my shield and my buckler, urging me on and giving unselfishly of her artistic judgment. She's a very gifted woman, as you can see for yourself."

"And a very gracious one," I agreed. "Well, I must be moving on, Mr. Inchcape. Much obliged for the preview of Mother Stentorian's Fish Kebabs. I'll be on the lookout for them."

"Yes, I hear they're quite tasty," he said. "Sure you won't stay and take potluck with us? Rowena can fix you a mock omelet or some toasted dates or something."

"No, thanks a million," I said, backing through the poinsettias. "Well, goodbye, sir, and long may you flourish." I got into my rented convertible, switched on a commercial for atomic laxatives, and drove down to the coast road. As I passed the Piggy-Wig Drive-In, I saw two persons costumed as an owl and a pussycat dancing hand in hand on the edge of the asphalt. At least, I thought I saw them, but it may have been only a mirage. That southern California sunlight can be pretty tricky at times.

The Wickedest Woman
in Larchmont

IF YOU WERE BORN anywhere near the beginning of the century and had access at any time during the winter of 1914–15 to thirty-five cents in cash, the chances are that after a legitimate deduction for nonpareils you blew in the balance on a movie called *A Fool There Was*. What gave the picture significance, assuming that it had any, was neither its story, which was paltry, nor its acting, which was aboriginal, but a pyrogenic half pint by the name of Theda Bara, who immortalized the vamp just as Little Egypt, at the World's Fair in 1893, had the hoochie-coochie. My own discovery of Miss Bara dates back to the sixth grade at grammar school and was due to a boy named Raymond Bugbee, a detestable bully who sat at the desk behind mine. Bugbee was a fiend incarnate, a hulking, evil-faced youth related on both sides of his family to Torquemada and dedicated to making my life insupportable. He had perfected a technique of catapulting BB shot through his teeth with such force that some of them are still imbedded in my poll, causing a sensation like *tic douloureux* when it rains. Day after day, under threat of the most ghastly reprisals if I squealed, I was pinched, gouged, and nicked with paper clips, spitballs, and rubber bands. Too wispy to stand up to my oppressor, I took refuge in a subdued blubbering, which soon abraded the teacher's nerves and earned me the reputation of being refractory. One day, Bugbee finally overreached himself. Attaching a steel pen point to the welt of his shoe, he jabbed it upward into my posterior. I rose into the air caterwauling and, in the attendant ruckus, was condemned to stay after school and clap erasers. Late that afternoon, as I was numbly toiling away in a cloud of chalk dust, I accidentally got my first intimation of Miss Bara from a couple of teachers excitedly discussing her.

"If you rearrange the letters in her name, they spell 'Arab Death,'" one of them was saying, with a delicious shudder. "I've never seen an actress kiss the way she does. She just sort of glues herself onto a man and drains the strength out of him."

"I know—isn't it revolting?" sighed the other rapturously. "Let's go see her again tonight!" Needless to add, I was in the theater before either of them, and my reaction was no less fervent. For a full month afterward, I gave myself up to fantasies in which I lay with my head pillowed in the seductress's lap, intoxicated by coal-black eyes smoldering with belladonna. At her bidding, I eschewed family, social position, my brilliant career—a rather hazy combination of African explorer and private sleuth—to follow her to the ends of the earth. I saw myself, oblivious of everything but the nectar of her lips, being cashiered for cheating at cards (I was also a major in the Horse Dragoons), descending to drugs, and ultimately winding up as a beachcomber in the South Seas, with a saintly, ascetic face

117

like H. B. Warner's. Between Bugbee's persecutions that winter and the moral quicksands I floundered into as a result of *A Fool There Was*, it's a wonder I ever lived through to Arbor Day.

A WEEK or so ago, seeking to ascertain whether my inflammability to Miss Bara had lessened over the years, I had a retrospective look at her early triumph. Unfortunately, I could not duplicate the original conditions under which I had seen her, since the Museum of Modern Art projection room is roach-free and lacks those powerful candy-vending machines on the chairs that kicked like a Colt .45. Nonetheless, I managed to glean a fairly comprehensive idea of what used to accelerate the juices in 1915, and anyone who'd like a taste is welcome to step up to the tureen and skim off a cupful.

Produced by William Fox and based on the play by Porter Emerson Browne, *A Fool There Was* maunders through a good sixth of its footage establishing a whole spiral nebula of minor characters before it centers down on its two luminaries, the Vampire and the Fool. As succinctly as I can put it, the supporting players are the latter's wife Kate, an ambulatory laundry bag played by Mabel Frenyear; their daughter, an implacably arch young hoyden of nine, unidentified; Kate's sister (May Allison); her beau, a corpulent slob, also anonymous; and a headlong butler seemingly afflicted with locomotor ataxia. All these inhabit a depressing chalet in Larchmont, where, as far as I could discover, they do nothing but shake hands effusively. A tremendous amount of handshaking, by the way, distinguished the flicks in their infancy; no director worth his whipcord breeches would have dreamed of beginning a plot before everybody had exchanged greetings like a French wedding party entering a café. In any case, the orgy of salutation has just begun to die down when John Schuyler, the Fool, arrives by yacht to join his kin, and the handshaking starts all over again. Schuyler (Edward José), a florid, beefy lawyer in a high Belmont collar, is hardly what you would envision as passion's plaything, but I imagine it took stamina to be a leading man for Theda Bara—someone she could get her teeth into, so to speak. We now ricochet to the Vampire and her current victim, Parmalee (Victor Benoit), strolling on a grassy sward nearby. The siren, in billowing draperies and a period hat, carries almost as much sail as the Golden Hind, making it a bit difficult to assess her charms; however, they seem to have unmanned the young ne'er-do-well with her to the point where he is unable to light the Zira he is fumbling with. Their affair, it appears, has burned itself out, and Parmalee, wallowing in self-pity, is being given the mitten. Midway through his reproaches, a chauffeur-driven Simplex, sparkling with brass, pulls alongside, Miss Bara shoves him impatiently into it, and the pair whisk offscreen. These turgid formalities completed, the picture settles down to business, and high time. In another moment, I myself would have been shaking hands and manumitting the projectionist to the ball game I was keeping him from.

In a telegram from the President (Woodrow Wilson presumably chose his envoys in an extremely haphazard manner), Schuyler is ordered to England on some delicate mission, such as fixing the impost on crumpets, and makes ready to leave. He expects to be accompanied by Kate and his daughter, but just prior to sailing, his sister-in-law clumsily falls out of the tonneau of her speedster, and Kate remains behind to nurse her. The Vampire reads of Schuyler's appointment, and decides to cross on the same vessel and enmesh him in her toils. As she enters the pier, an aged derelict accosts her, observing mournfully, "See what you have made of me—and still you prosper, you hellcat." Meanwhile, Parmalee, learning of her desertion from a Japanese servant whose eyelids are taped back with two pieces of court plaster, smashes all the bric-a-brac and ferns in their love nest, tears down the portieres, and hastens to intercept her. The derelict waylays him at the gangplank. "I might have known you'd follow her, Parmalee," he croaks. "Our predecessor, Van Diemen, rots in prison for her." The plea to desist from his folly falls on deaf ears; Parmalee sequesters his Circe on the promenade deck and, clapping a pistol to his temple, declares his intention of destroying himself if she abandons him. She smilingly flicks it aside with a rose and a line of dialogue that is unquestionably one of the most hallowed in dramaturgy: "Kiss me, my fool." Willful boy that he is, however, Parmalee must have his own way and shoots himself dead. The gesture, sad to say, is wasted, exciting only desultory interest. The body is hustled off the ship, a steward briskly mops up the deck, and by the time the *Gigantic* has cleared Sandy Hook, Theda and her new conquest are making googly eyes and preparing to fracture the Seventh Commandment by sending their laundry to the same *blanchisseuse* in Paris.

A time lapse of two months, and in a hideaway on the Italian Riviera choked with rubber plants and jardinieres, the lovers play amorous tag like Dido and Aeneas, and nibble languidly on each other's ears. Although everything seems to be leeches and cream, a distinct undercurrent of tension is discernible between them; Schuyler dreams betimes of Suburbia, his dusky cook who used to make such good flapjacks, and when Theda jealously tears up a letter from his wife, acrimony ensues. Soon after, while registering at a hotel, Schuyler is recognized by acquaintances, who, much to his anguish, recoil as from an adder. Back in Westchester, Kate has learned of his peccadilloes through a gossip sheet. She confronts Schuyler's law partner and, with typical feminine chauvinism, lambastes the innocent fellow: "You men shield each other's sins, but if the woman were at fault, how quick you'd be to condemn her!" Mrs. Schuyler's behavior, in fact, does little to ingratiate her. Not content with barging into a busy law office and disrupting its routine, she then runs home and poisons a child's mind against its father. "Mama," inquires her daughter, looking up from one of Schuyler's letters, "is a cross a sign for love?" "Yes,"

Kate retorts spitefully, "and love often means a cross." The fair sex (God bless them) can be really extraordinary at times.

In our next glimpse of the lotus-eaters, in London, Schuyler has already begun paying the piper; his eyes are berimmed with kohl, his step is palsied, and his hair is covered with flour. Theda, contrariwise, is thriving like the green bay tree, still tearing up his correspondence and wrestling him into embraces that char the woodwork. Their idyl is abruptly cut short by a waspish cable from the Secretary of State, which reads, in a code easily decipherable to the audience, "ON ACCOUNT OF YOUR DISGRACEFUL CONDUCT, YOU ARE HEREBY DISMISSED." Remorse and *Heimweh*, those twin powerful antibiotics, temporarily dispel the kissing bug that has laid Schuyler low. He returns to the States determined to rid himself of his incubus, but she clings and forces him to install her in a Fifth Avenue mansion. Humiliations multiply as she insists on attending the opera with him in a blaze of aigrettes, and there is an affecting scene when their phaeton is overtaken by his wife's auto near the Public Library and his daughter entreats him, "Papa, dear, I want you." But the call of the wild is too potent, and despite pressure from in-laws and colleagues alike, Schuyler sinks deeper into debauchery. Kate, meanwhile, is keening away amid a houseful of relatives, all of them shaking hands as dementedly as ever and proffering unsound advice. There is such a hollering and a rending of garments and a tohubohu in the joint that you can't really blame Schuyler for staying away. When a man has worn himself down to the rubber struggling in a vampire's toils, he wants to come home to a place where he can read his paper in peace, not a loony bin.

Six months of revelry and an overzealous makeup man have left their stamp on the Fool when we again see him; the poor chap is shipping water fast. He reels around the mansion squirting seltzer at the help and boxing with double-exposure phantoms, and Theda, whose interest in her admirers wanes at the drop of a security, is already stalking a new meatball. Apprised of the situation, Kate goes to her husband bearing an olive branch, but their reunion is thwarted by his mistress, who unexpectedly checks in and kisses him back into submission. The action now grows staccato; Schuyler stages a monumental jamboree, at which his guests drink carboys of champagne and dance the bunny hug very fast, and then, overcome by delirium tremens, he violently expels them into the night. Kate, in the meantime, has decided to take his daughter to him as a last appeal. Preceded by her sister's beau (the Slob), the pair arrive at the mansion to find Schuyler in parlous shape. The child throws herself on him—a dubious service to anyone suffering from the horrors—and the adults beseech the wastrel to come home and, one infers, be committed to a nice, quiet milieu where his expenditures can be regulated. His dilemma is resolved by the reappearance of Theda; Schuyler grovels before her, eradicating any doubt as to his fealty, and the folks exit checkmated. The last few seconds of the picture, in a somber key unmatched outside the tragedies of D'Annunzio, depict the Fool, obsessed by a montage of his sins, squirming on his belly through an openwork balustrade and collapsing in a vestibule. "So some of him lived," comments a final sepulchral title, "but the soul of him died." And over what remains, there appears a grinning presentment of Miss Bara, impenitent and sleek in black velvet and pearls, strewing rose petals as we fade out.

FOR ALL ITS BATHOS and musty histrionics, *A Fool There Was*, I am convinced, still retains some mysterious moral sachet, if the experience I had after seeing it is at all indicative. As I was quietly recuperating in a West Side snug over a thimble of sherry and the poems of St. John Perse, a young woman who was manifestly no better than she should be slid into the banquette adjoining mine. So absorbed was I in the poet's meter that it was almost two minutes before I detected her wanton gaze straying toward me in unmistakable invitation. I removed my spectacles and carefully placed them in their shagreen case. "Mademoiselle," I said, "the flirtation you propose, while ostensibly harmless, could develop unless checked into a dangerous liaison. I am a full-blooded man, and one who does not do things by halves. Were I to set foot on the primrose path, scenes of carnival and license to shame Petronius might well ensue. No, my dear young lady," I said, draining my glass and rising, "succulent morsel though you are, I have no desire to end my days like John Schuyler, crawling through balustrades and being sprinkled with blooms." As luck would have it, her escort, whose existence I had somehow neglected to allow for, materialized behind me at this juncture and, pinioning me, questioned my motives. I gave him a brief résumé of *A Fool There Was* to amplify my position, but he acted as though I had invented the whole thing. Maybe I have. Still, who could have made up Theda Bara?

Swindle Sheet
with Blueblood Engrailed,
Arrant Fibs Rampant

CB

I PROMISE YOU I hadn't a clue, when I unfolded my *Times* one recent morning at the bootblack's, that it would contain the most electrifying news to come out of England in a generation —the biggest, indeed, since the relief of Lucknow. As invariably happens after one passes forty, the paper sagged open to the obituary page; I skimmed it quickly to make sure I wasn't listed, and then, having winnowed the theatrical, movie, and book gossip, began reading the paper as every enlightened coward does nowadays, back to front. There, prominently boxed in the second section, was the particular dispatch—terse and devoid of bravura, yet charged with a kind of ragged dignity. "BRITAIN'S INDIGENT LORDS ASK EXPENSE ACCOUNTS," it announced over a London dateline, and went on, "Some peers are too impoverished in the highly taxed present-day welfare state to travel to London and do their duty without pay, the House of Lords was told today. The Upper House, shorn by the last Labor Government of much of its power, was debating its own possible reform. One of its proposals was for giving expense money to those members who do trouble to come to Westminster. At present the Lords get no salaries and nothing but bare traveling expenses. On an average day no more than one peer in ten is present."

"Well, well!" I exclaimed involuntarily. "It's high time, if you ask me."

"What'd you say?" inquired the bootblack with a start, almost spilling the jonquil-colored dye with which he was defacing my shoes.

"This story about the British peers," I replied. "Poor chaps are practically on the dole—beggars-on-horseback sort of thing. Pretty ironical situation, what?"

He threw me a sidelong glance, plainly uncertain whether it was safe to commit himself. "You a peer?" he asked cautiously.

"No," I said, "but I do think England's in a hell of a state when your Gloucesters and your Somersets have to get down on their knees and scrounge expense money."

"Yeah, the whole world's falling apart," he said, scratching his ear reflectively with his dauber. "A couple of shmos like you and me, we can't even get up our rent, whereas them dukes and earls and all those other highbinders over there are rolling in dough."

"But they're not," I objected. "Judging from this, they've hardly enough carfare to get from their ancestral seats to London."

"That's what I said—it's all topsy-turvy," he returned. His inflection made it abundantly clear that he was humoring an imbecile. "Look, should I put some new laces in here? These are full of knots."

"I prefer them that way," I said icily, and retired behind the paper. The snub, though momentarily soothing to my ego, cost me dear; in retaliation, he gave me such a flamboyant shine that an old gorgon on the sidewalk mistook me for a minstrel and demanded to know where I was hiding my tambourine.

Fletcherizing the news item subsequently in a more tranquil setting, it occurred to me that while the projected expense accounts might seem a godsend at first glance, they could also be a potential source of embarrassment to the noble lords. No matter how august their lineage, they will eventually have to undergo the scrutiny of, and explain every last deduction to, a corps of income-tax ferrets rated among the keenest in the world. I have been speculating about just how, in these circumstances, one applies the thumbscrews to a man whose title dates back four or five centuries—how, in other words, the British tax inquisitor manages to grovel and browbeat at the same time. Obviously, the best way to find out is to secrete ourselves behind the arras at such an examination. Softly, then, and remember, everything you see or hear henceforth is in strictest confidence.

SCENE: *The office of Simon Auger, an inspector in the review division of the Board of Inland Revenue. A small, cheerless room equipped with the standard instruments of torture—a desk, two chairs, a filing cabinet. As a decorative touch rather than for its psychological effect, someone has hung on the wall a kiboko, or rhinoceros-hide whip. When the curtain rises, Auger, a dyspeptic of forty-odd, is finishing a frugal lunch of Holland Rusk, wheat germ, and parsnips, a copy of* Burke's Peerage *propped up before him. For the most part, his face is expressionless, but occasionally it betrays a wintry smile of the kind observable in barracudas. At length, he sighs deeply, stashes the book in the desk, and, withdrawing a bottle of Lucknow's Instant Relief, downs a spoonful. The phone rings.*

AUGER: Auger here . . . Who? . . . Ah, yes. Please ask His Lordship to come in, won't you? (*The door opens to admit Llewellyn Fitzpoultice, ninth Viscount Zeugma. He is in his mid-sixties, ramrod-straight, affects a white cavalry mustache and a buttonhole, and is well dressed to the point of dandyism. Having fortified himself with four brandy-and-sodas at lunch, his complexion—already bronzed by twenty-five years on the Northwest Frontier—glows like an old mahogany sideboard.*)

ZEUGMA (*jauntily*): Afternoon. Hope I'm not terribly late.

AUGER: Not at all. No more than three-quarters of an hour or so.

ZEUGMA: Frightfully sorry. This filthy traffic, you know. I defy anyone to find a cab in Greek Street.

AUGER: Your Lordship was lunching in Soho?

ZEUGMA: Yes, I found a rather decent little place there—Stiletto's. They do you quite well for five guineas—*coquilles St. Jacques*, snails, a tart, and a passable *rosé*. You must try it sometime.

AUGER: I could hardly afford to, at my salary.

ZEUGMA: Between ourselves, I can't either, but the Crown pays for it—ha ha ha. (*Blandly*) Necessary business expense in connection with my duties in the Upper House.

AUGER: Indeed. (*He jots down a note.*) By the way, I believe I had the pleasure of meeting a relative of yours about a fortnight ago—the Right Honourable Anthony de Profundis.

ZEUGMA: Wild young cub—Tony. What's the boy been up to?

AUGER: Little matter of evasion and fraud. He was sly, but we specialize in those sly ones—ha ha ha. (*Opening a dossier*) Well, let's get on with it, shall we? Your address remains the same, I take it—The Grange, Regurgingham-supra-Mare, Dotards, Broome Abbas, Warwickshire.

ZEUGMA: That's right. But why do you ask?

AUGER: Because your nephew changed his unexpectedly last week, if you follow me.

ZEUGMA: I—I say, it seems dreadfully warm in here. Could we open a window?

AUGER: I'm afraid not. Whoever designed this stage set forgot to include one. However, to resume. According to your return, you made thirty-one trips here from Warwickshire during the last Parliamentary session.

ZEUGMA (*muffled*): Whole avalanche of measures directly affecting my constituency. Crucial decisions. No time for shilly-shallying.

AUGER: I have no doubt. Still, in glancing over the minutes of the Upper House I notice Your Lordship didn't speak once in all that period.

ZEUGMA: Blasted committees chained me down. Paperwork from dawn to dark. Closeted with Winnie weeks on end. Barely able to snatch a sandwich.

AUGER: Yes, few of us realize how unselfishly England's public men give of their energy. Notwithstanding, you did find time to squeeze in sixty-three meals, excluding breakfasts, for a total of four hundred fifty-seven pounds thirteen shillings. These were all concerned with legislative matters?

ZEUGMA: Every blessed one. (*Spluttering*) Confound it, are you questioning my word?

AUGER: I wouldn't dream of it. I was merely giving you what we call a surface probe—to make certain there was no aura of peculation, as it were. Now suppose we cast an eye at your hotel appropriation. These five-room suites you habitually took at the Dorchester—weren't they a bit grandiose for an overnight stay?

ZEUGMA: By Gad, sir, if you expect me to crawl into some greasy boarding house in Kensington and fry my own kippers—

AUGER: Certainly not, certainly not. One can't conceivably imagine Lady Zeugma in such an atmosphere.

ZEUGMA (*unwarily*): She wasn't with me—er, that is, I was batching it most of the term—

AUGER (*smoothly*): I see. And the rest of the time you shared the accommodations with another legislator?

ZEUGMA: Well—uh—in a way. My staff secretary—or, rather, my secretarial adviser. Mrs. Thistle Fotheringay, of Stoke Poges.

AUGER: Ah, that explains these miscellaneous charges—one hundred eighteen quid for champagne, forty-two pounds ten for caviar, and so on. Naturally, neither you nor Mrs. Fotheringay ever partook of these delicacies paid for by the state?

ZEUGMA (*struggling to dislodge an emery board from his trachea*): N-no, of course not. I just kept 'em on hand for colleagues—for other viscounts, you understand. Haven't touched a drop of bubbly in years. It's death to my liver.

AUGER: Really. Then perhaps you'd care to examine this cutting from a recent issue of the *Tatler*. It shows you and your —ahem—secretarial adviser with upraised champagne glasses, dining at the Bagatelle.

ZEUGMA: Demnition . . . I say, old man, mind if I pass it along to Mrs. Fotheringay? Women like to preserve sentimental slop like this.

AUGER: I know. That's why I thought of sending it to Lady Zeugma.

ZEUGMA (*agitatedly*): Wait a bit, let's not—We mustn't go off half—By Jove, I've just had an absolutely wizard idea!

AUGER: Amazing how they pop out of nowhere, isn't it?

ZEUGMA: You revenue blokes have some kind of fraternal organization, don't you? I mean where you take the missus to Blackpool, toffee for the kiddies, all that drill?

AUGER: Quite. And if I may anticipate Your Lordship, you'd like to make a small donation to our outing fund.

ZEUGMA: Why, how did you guess?

AUGER: One becomes surprisingly clairvoyant in this line of work.

ZEUGMA: Fancy that. Well, suppose you put me down for about five hundred pounds. Needn't use my name, necessarily. Call it "Compliments of a Friend."

AUGER: Very magnanimous of you, I'm sure.

ZEUGMA: Nonsense—live and let live's my motto. Let sleeping dogs lie, I always say.

AUGER: Yes, and whilst you're raking up proverbs, don't forget there's no fool like an old fool. (*He replaces the dossier in the desk, extends a packaged handkerchief to his illustrious caller.*) Would you care for one of these? Your own seems to be wringing wet.

ZEUGMA (*undone*): Ah, yes, many tax—that is, you're most welcome. Pip-pip. Cheerio. (*He exits, tripping over his stick and ricocheting off the filing cabinet. Auger's eyes crinkle up at the corners and he hums two or three bars of a tuneless little melody. Then, reopening Burke's Peerage, he begins nibbling a carrot reflectively as the curtain falls.*)

Come On In,
the Liability's Fine

THE SUNLIGHT was so benign one recent forenoon in the country, and the air laden with such promise of spring, that, on the verge of entering my web to spin a few merchandisable threads, I decided to take a turn about the place and see what catastrophes I could unearth to impair my efficiency. It looked quite unpromising for a while; none of the barn doors had blown off during the night, the ruts in the lane—thitherto as deep as the Union trenches before Vicksburg—had mysteriously filled up by themselves, and the cistern containing our auxiliary supply of rain water had stopped rotting and exuded a fresh, invigorating tang of resin. I was forlornly kicking a terrace wall, in the hope of loosening the stones and embroiling myself in a long, exasperating hassle with masons, when an azure-blue sedan rolled up, backed swiftly around, and splintered the lower branches of a magnolia just coming into flower. A thickset, forceful man of the type who models Shurons in opticians' windows jumped out and cursorily examined the damage. Then, whisking a briefcase from the trunk, he strode toward me with hand extended.

"Howdy," he said, all wind and geniality like a barber's cat. "Chicanery's my name—Walt Chicanery. I'm with the Hindsight Insurance Company, over in Doylestown. Is the owner here?" I explained that though my clothes belied it, I held the fief, and he chuckled tolerantly to assuage my embarrassment. "You sure fooled me," he said. "I thought you were the handyman."

"I am," I replied evenly. "I do all the odd jobs, like pruning these trees after people drive over them."

"That's where you're missing a bet, neighbor," he said, stabbing me in the breastbone with his forefinger. "Don't prune 'em—replace 'em. I've got a policy whereby you're fully protected against loss to shrubs, hedges, sedges, vines, pines, creepers, rushes, and ramblers."

"So have I," I disclosed. "I've got any kind of insurance you can name—hailstorm, shipwreck, volcano, libel, frostbite, all of them. I'm even insured against meteors or a rain of red frogs. And now, if you'll excuse me—"

"One moment there," he said patronizingly. "You're pretty cocky, aren't you? Think every possible contingency's provided for, eh? Well, think again. What happens if your bowling ball slips and you break the bones in your companion's foot?"

I knew I should have whistled up my syce and had the fellow beaten off the place with lathees, but the sun felt so good on my back that I let myself be drawn. "The only kind I've ever dropped was a matzo ball," I said, "and I doubt whether it affected Jed Harris's gait. No, sir," I went on, "I don't get involved in those trick mishaps. I'm probably less accident-prone than any man alive. I just sit indoors and do my work, and that's where I'm going now." Entering the outbuilding where I worry, I immersed myself in a sheaf of papers. Simultaneously, Chicanery's hand slid into my field of vision, holding a printed page.

"You owe this to your family, friend," his voice purred into my shoulder. "Just look it over before you send me away."

"What is it?" I asked peevishly.

"A list of typical accidents covered by our new Allstate Comprehensive Personal Liability policy," he said, buttering each word like Svengali. "Go ahead, read it. Go ahead, I dare you." Robbed of my will, I read.

The list was formidable, an encyclopedia of disaster. "A passer-by breaks arm in fall on your icy walk," it intoned. "Your dog bites the deliveryman. Your wife injures a passer-by with her umbrella. Mailman slips on your front step—suffers a concussion. Your child knocks down an elderly person with his sled. Handyman tumbles from your stepladder. Friend suffers a crippling fall on your freshly waxed floor. While hunting, you accidentally shoot another hunter. Your baby-sitter breaks ankle tripping over baby's toy. Neighbor's child falls into trash fire. Your child accidentally hits playmate in eye with ball. Your child runs into bystander with bicycle. You accidentally burn stranger with cigarette. A guest trips over your rug. Your child accidentally sails toy airplane into playmate's face. Your golf drive injures another player. Your back-yard swing breaks, injuring a neighbor's child. A fellow bus passenger trips over your suitcase or package. Baseball bat slips from your son's hands—hurtles into spectator's face. Your trash fire spreads to a neighbor's home. Your child accidentally breaks plate-glass window. Your cat claws visitor's expensive fur coat."

I looked up at Chicanery, who, while I was absorbed, had flipped open my checkbook and was examining the balance with amused contempt, and handed back the prospectus.

"Listen, this is all very well for schlemiels," I said, "but I repeat —none of that stuff happens to yours truly. I've crisscrossed the ruddy globe, waded knee-deep in malarial swamps, slept cheek by jowl with hamadryads, shared my last catty of rice with head-hunters, and never even had a nosebleed. You're barking up the wrong tree, Tuan. Good day."

"Ta-ta," he said, without tensing a muscle. "Say, what's that whistling I hear down on your porch? A bird?" I admitted that I own a rather gifted myna acquired in Thailand, who speaks idiomatic Siamese, Chinese, and English, and who allows nobody but me to gentle him. "You don't say," he marveled. "What's he do when your guests reach into his cage?"

"Who—Tong Cha?" I asked carelessly. "Oh, he generally goes for their eyes. He thinks they're grapes."

"Be a shame to shell out fifty thousand damages for a grape," observed Chicanery with a yawn. "A party over here in Chalfont got hooked that way. His rooster bit off a little boy's nose. Time the courts finished with him, the poor devil was on relief."

"B-but Tong Cha wouldn't hurt anyone intentionally," I said, suddenly agitated. "I mean, basically he's sweet—he's just playful, full of beans—"

"Well, maybe he can explain that to the jury," said Chicanery. "Or maybe you'll be lucky enough to get a Siamese judge. Otherwise, you're going byebye with an iron ball soldered to your leg, as sure as you're born."

"Er—how much did you say that policy was?" I inquired, moistening my lips. "I might be able to swing it after all. I don't really need a bridge on these molars; I can chew on the other side."

"Sure you can," the agent agreed sympathetically. "Your cheeks are bound to cave in sooner or later, no matter what you do. Now, here's the deal." Within twenty minutes, and to the accompaniment of a spate of actuarial jargon I only half

understood, I was formally indemnified against a host of action-
able casualties that might befall me or my dependents, whether
human or members of the brute creation.

As Chicanery finished ticking off the complex provisions, he
caught himself abruptly. "Danged if I haven't forgot the drown-
ing clause," he exclaimed. "That's what comes of somebody
jabbering in your ear."

"There's no water on this place," I objected. "Just the little
creek you drove through in the lane. You couldn't drown a chip-
munk in that."

"Hunh, that's what Dr. Bundy over at Keller's Church
thought," rejoined Chicanery. "His wife's brother came home
one night drunk as a boiled owl, fell in the brook, and goodbye
Charlie. Widow collected seventy-four grand and poor Bundy
blew his brains out. I don't want you coming around with a beef
if it happens to you."

"O.K., O.K.," I said impatiently. "Is the policy in effect from
now on?"

"Yup, soon as your check clears," he said. "Personally, I always recommend paying cash so you get immediate protection." I at once yielded up what currency I had in my clothes,
then repaired to the house and levied on the kitchen funds, and
finally amassed the premium, a good share of it in pennies.
Chicanery stowed it away in his poke and, teetering back in
my mid-Victorian swivel chair, beamed paternally at me.

"Someday you'll bless me for this," he declared. "A stitch
in time—" There was a fearful crack of wood and metal, the
chair crumbled into matchwood, and Chicanery catapulted
backward, describing the figure known among movie stunt
men as the Hundred and Eight. In landing, he unfortunately
dislodged a pile of atlases and gazetteers, which rained down
on him like building blocks and almost hid him from view. I
sprang up and flung aside the sailing directions for Macassar
Strait and the copy of *Menaboni's Birds* resting on his head.

His face had gone the color of an old Irish towel and he was breathing heavily through his mouth.

"Are you all right?" I demanded, seizing his shoulders and shaking him vigorously. Two years as a biology major, plus wide reading of illustrated hygiene magazines along Sixth Avenue, have taught me that in possible concussions the patient should be stimulated to keep the circulation brisk.

Chicanery opened his eyes and goggled about stupidly. "Where am I?" he murmured.

"Right here in the Pennsylvania Dutch country, about nine miles from Riegelsville," I assured him, endeavoring to keep my voice buoyant. "Is anything hurting you? Can you twist your neck?" With a grunt, he shook me off and clambered to his feet. A normal healthy flush was momentarily replacing his pallor. He looked fit as a fighting cock, and I said so.

"Leave that up to my doctor," he snapped, dusting off his pants. "It could be internal injuries, like as not. Whatever it is, we can settle it between us. You won't have to go to court."

I had some difficulty in enunciating clearly, but I made my point at last. "You just sold me a policy that covered this type of accident!" I bellowed. "I thought you were sincere! *I* was sincere! Now you tell me—"

"Look, Mister," said Chicanery, his eyeballs shrinking to two bits of flint. "No use trying to bluster your way out of it. If you wanted protection against falls sustained from furniture, you should have specified. That chair is a death-trap, and you could be jailed for using it. You'll hear from my lawyer." He sailed out, slamming the door with such force that a loose slate pitched off the roof and struck him between the shoulder blades. Through the window, I saw him sink to his knees in a position of deep meditation, like a Buddhist monk. Then he arose heavily and, making a notation on a pad, tottered to his car. Five seconds later, it disappeared over the brow of the hill, trailing a flowering magnolia from its bumper. I haven't heard a rumble out of him since, but one of these days my heirs and assigns will undoubtedly receive a bulky envelope with a Doylestown postmark. I must leave word behind to forward it on to Singapore.

This Little Piggy Went to Market

I WAS A FIRST-BORN (there were forty of us in that first year of my mother's maturity), she was eight years old at the time if I remember rightly. Swinging high and joyously in my lofty cradle —feeling myself grow and grow; basking in the sunlight, loving my green satin coat, I grew the fastest and was handsomer and bigger than all the rest.

Like all families we have our troubles, a bit of hardship during the hot dry season (thirsty and all that), and wretched coconut beetles who do their best to bore into our supports. When the typhoons come, wind and rain tear through our house, the palm leaves whip straight out! Plunk! Thud! Children drop out of their cradles.

When I was old enough to lean safely over the edge of my cradle, I had lots of fun watching the world below. The clumsy man animals sorting the fallen; stacking them in piles to await the coming of the carabao and his creaking cart. They'd grab a coconut and crash it down on a spike they had wedged in the ground. A couple of twists, presto! A coat torn off and a victim thrown aside. . . . Afterwards, a whack of the bolo and the poor things were split wide open and left to dry! One gets hardened to such things, and too, it was someone else's life, which makes the difference.

One day as I was watching the spectacle below I felt my stem give—an instant later, I was hurtling through space! Those awful seconds! Me there on the ground . . . exhausted, fear in my heart! What would be my fate? Lose my shiny green coat? A swift bolo baring my inner self to the sun?

I smile now at that poor innocent! My fate was never in doubt. My very size and perfection was a guarantee. I was placed in a seed bed for propagation, *of course!* Side by side with the elect of our species I was left to drowse and dream, and wait. . . .

Nice coconuts go into syrup and candy kettles, into beauty creams, and fragrant soaps, and of course, into vegetable shortening.—*From "Autobiography of a Coconut," a leaflet advertising Mandalay Coconut Syrup.*

HONESTLY, it's enough to make you blow the cover off your jar, the way some coconuts run off at the mouth. You'd think nobody else had ever done anything significant or exciting, and coming from your own sister, it's twice as provoking. She always was stuck on herself, even when the clump of us used to sway out there in the Philippines, and now, since she managed to break into print, she's intolerable. Well, I've got news for her: I've had ten times the career she's had. I've traveled, I've rubbed elbows with cosmopolitan, glamorous people—or been rubbed on their elbows, which amounts to the same thing —and I'll bet I've had more weird, hair-raising experiences, ounce for ounce, than any beauty cream with a coconut-oil base *she* could name. But you be the judge; I'll just put it down as I recall it, and if it brings a blush to the unsophisticated cheek, so much the better. After all, that's why I was compounded in the first place, *n'est-ce pas?*

My earliest recollections, after being sundered, squeezed, and boiled, are naturally vague; I was swirling around turbidly deep in the hold of this freighter, part of a glutinous white purée consigned to a wholesale-cosmetics firm in New York. Then a confused interval—grim-faced customs inspectors rummaging through me for opium, the rough persiflage of roustabouts and truckmen, and, finally, a scrubby loft in the West Thirties full of noise and commotion. When I eventually got my bearings, the establishment proved to be a fly-by-night laboratory styling itself La Pulchrituda Lotions, operated by two grifters named Victor Spatula and Morty Krisp. They were both sallow, ulcerous dwarfs, treacherous as quicksand, ever on the *qui vive* to fleece the public and each other. Spatula, whose previous scientific experience had been confined to adulterating bourbon, was officially head chemist of the concern; Krisp, the one-man sales force, scurried about town hawking their products to hairdressers and department stores. I well remember the afternoon they originated me—in my present form, that is. Amid half a dozen other ingredients chosen at random, like capsicum, sage, oil of cinnamon, and buckwheat flour, I had been revolved a few hasty seconds in a centrifuge and decanted into a number of small opaque jars. Just as I was settling, I overheard the partners conferring.

"What'll we call this gunk?" asked Spatula. "We already used every name there is—Stimulose, Velveena Nose Unguent, Rejuvenola . . ."

"Wait, I thought of one yesterday," said Krisp, pondering. "How about Monadnoid Cream? It's a combo of hormone and adenoid."

"Say, that sounds beneficial," the other assented. "It lacks feminine appeal, though. How about Monadnoid Youthifonium Cream?"

"The greatest!" exulted Krisp. "I'll go ask the printer to knock out the labels on spec. Here, give me a couple of jars for his wife."

The contrast between their squalid hive and my next home was refreshing. Less than a week later, I was the apex of a window display in a chic little salon on East Fifty-fourth Street, lording it over a whole phalanx of gilt nail polish and costly wrinkle removers. It was enthralling to study the women who paused to stare in at us—pert secretaries and models with hatboxes, basilisk-eyed dowagers, housewives bearing rib roasts, *poules de luxe*. Invariably, their nostrils dilated when they saw my legend, and they yearned toward me like iron filings in a magnetic field, but they were either too busy or too timid to gratify their longing, because I remained where I was. The dogs resident in the neighborhood behaved even more curiously. Impossible to drag them past; there was always a poodle, a boxer, or a Bedlington gazing through the plate glass in stupefaction, sniffing and whimpering feverishly. I presume that Spatula, in his creative frenzy, must have unwittingly included some element in my formula, like beef extract, that aroused their desire. At any rate, one midmorning I was plucked from the window by the proprietress, a highly synthetic Parisienne, and exhibited with a flourish to a young lady. She was a vivid, shapely brunette in expensive sports clothes, with sloe eyes and the kind of mouth traditionally referred to as a scarlet wound.

"You really recommend this?" she asked hesitantly. "You see, I have a special problem with my skin. It's as tender as a baby's."

"But *mais certainement!*" the shopkeeper effervesced. "Zis is *absolument* miraculous—astringent but not harsh, oily but not greasy. Eet supplies the very essential Mademoiselle needs." She lowered her voice portentously. "Eet comes from an old Aztec recipe."

The tiny flat in the Upper Seventies that Jasmine Lispenard took me home to was, I shortly deduced, typical of those occupied by most career girls, though I never quite ascertained what Jasmine's career was. She had evidently been married at one time, to judge by her frequent appeals to her lawyers, Howells & Imprecation, to collect back alimony. Once or twice,

I heard devout resolutions about a course in Greek drama at Hunter, a television appearance, and some abstract jewelry Jasmine meant to design, but they dissipated along with her hangovers. From eleven, when she awoke, she clung like a limpet to the phone, relaying gossip, arranging dates with beaux and playing them off against each other, and analyzing their potentialities to her girl friends. The apartment was usually in disorder, except on the day the maid came in, when it became a shambles. The latter, a Hungarian lady afflicted with *folie de grandeur*, fiercely disdained the chores expected of her and did nothing but dust the neo-Calder mobile, scream vilification at the cat, and read her employer's mail. As a result, the place was ankle-deep in old theater programs and tangerine peels, discarded stockings, and crumpled Kleenex. Fresh from an elegant shop window off Park Avenue, it required time to accustom myself to this informal atmosphere. Nonetheless, I soon adapted to the clutter on Jasmine's vanity—the pots of mascara, the eyebrow pencils, and the manifold skin tonics and bracers—and, indeed, found it a quite cheery *ambiance*.

My chatelaine's single attempt to use me was, I fear, rather disastrous. One evening, her amatory scheming misfired; three of her cavaliers canceled out, and, willy-nilly, she was forced into the kip at nine o'clock. Placing a volume of Turgenev on the night table and me on top of it, she got into bed and opened the *Journal-American*. As she thoughtfully digested Cholly Knickerbocker, chewing a salami sandwich the while, she massaged me on her forehead and cheeks. Suddenly, she emitted a choked cry, sprang out of bed, and caught up a hand mirror. A chain of horrifying red welts had risen on her face, giving her the uncanny aspect of one of those old-time testimonials for Poslam Ointment. I vanished forthwith into the wastebasket, where I sojourned for three days until the maid, piecing together a letter of Jasmine's, discovered me. My label obviously intrigued her, and she applied me in quantity to her jowls, studying the effect critically in the mirror. Then, yielding to her ungovernable inclination to identify herself with the *haut monde*, she procured an evening cape from the closet, wrapped it about her, and paraded languidly before the vanity.

"How do you do, Mrs. Astorbilt?" she drawled in a haughty, aristocratic voice. "So divine to see you again since we had tea together in your cabaña at Newport. Tell me, how is dear Reggie? Is he still coining money hand over fist down there in Wall Street?"

When she had departed, leaving me on the vanity with my cover askew, the cat reappeared and prowled around, stalking me with intense curiosity. He managed to insinuate his paw and extract a dab, but the taste plainly revolted him, for he arched his back, spat, and withdrew under the bed.

Life in the apartment pursued its uneven tenor for a while thereafter. Absorbed in a new and unusually promising conquest, Jasmine forgot my existence, and I made myself as inconspicuous as possible. The latest admirer, it appeared from reports to her intimates, was a big advertising executive—no less than the copy chief of Phlebotomy, Stinch & Mercer, she told them carelessly. His name was Raoul Paltry, and according to Jasmine he was criminally good-looking, even if his hair had begun to thin out and he *was* a trifle heavy in the seat. Raoul's manners were exquisite; he wore the most beautiful suits—dispatched from Savile Row, he had confided to her, in dozen lots semiannually—and his largess in places like the Chambord and Le Pavillon was legendary. As she reconstructed it, his wife, a withered crone, had not kept pace with his rise to success, but Jasmine understood him fully. To her, he was just a small boy who had lost his way.

From the outset, it was a stormy romance, if the skirmishes over the phone, the duplicity, and the recriminations were at all indicative. To fan Raoul's ardor, Jasmine invented a rival named Don Carlos Morales y Muñoz Carvalho, heir to Brazil's greatest coffee fortune and a Neronian spendthrift. She tortured Raoul by the hour with inventories of Don Carlos's toys—his Rolls-Royces and Ferraris, his yachts, planes, and shooting boxes—and his mulish insistence on plying her with gifts. No morning dawned, she asserted, without some new bauble from Winston's or Olga Tritt's, which, to be sure, she instantly returned out of principle, but the strain was driving her to the edge of neurasthenia. I went liquid as she retailed scenes of Latin jealousy, bloodcurdling threats Carlos had made to disembowel Raoul on sight. The latter, caught between his wife, his analyst, and Jasmine, must have led a dog's life; one could visualize the poor devil striving to compose elegiacs to shoe polish or laxatives while disentangling his emotional problems. With the affair gaining momentum daily, I grew increasingly concerned for the man and most eager to see him, for as yet he had never set foot on the premises. What pretexts Jasmine used to hold him at bay I cannot imagine, but the hour of reckoning arrived at last. Late one night, I heard her unlock the outer door and engage in a protracted debate too muffled to comprehend.

"Oh, all *right*, Raoul," she said impatiently, after a bit. "But remember, just one drink and off to your beddie-byes. Promise?"

The promise was forthcoming, in an unsteady basso; there then ensued a series of predictable sounds—the slam of the icebox door, the tinkle of ice cubes, a glass crash. From my situation on the vanity, I could follow the succeeding dialogue only imperfectly, and the record-player did not help matters, but I gathered Raoul sought the conventional return on his investment and Jasmine was proving obdurate.

"What do you mean, I'll think less of you?" His voice, hitherto cajoling, contained a note of exasperation. "I'll think *more* of you! After all, you're a man—that is, I'm a man and you're a woman, and when two people—"

"Look out, for God's sake. You're dislocating my arm!" she protested. "Now, go on, dear, fly away home. You have to finish that exciting advertisement you were telling me about."

"Aw, sugar, this is no time to bring up linoleum," Raoul whined. "Listen, why don't you slip into something like a negligee?"

"Yes, and you slip into something like the Pelham local," she retorted. "Let me *go*, I said!"

In the next breath, the two of them were framed in the doorway, Jasmine struggling manfully to escape her suitor's clasp. She kicked out at his ankle and, as he jumped back, broke away. Then, seizing the weapon closest to hand, she whisked me off the vanity and shied me at Raoul's head. I landed square on his right temple. With a peculiar sobbing intake of breath, he collapsed over a Hitchcock chair and sprawled on the floor, out for the count. Immediately, Jasmine's whole mood changed. She ran to him, uttering little broken moans of contrition, loosened his collar, bathed his forehead with a washcloth, hysterically begged his forgiveness. Within the minute, Raoul had revived and they were babbling assurances of mutual esteem couched in the most repugnant baby talk.

As for me, I've been on pretty much of a retired basis since then. Jasmine's circumstances improved strikingly soon afterward, and she moved to a far roomier apartment on Central Park South. Along with a spavined Venetian blind and innumerable soda bottles, I was transferred to the janitor's quarters in the basement, where his wife has earmarked me for future experiment. Ah, welladay, life's a whirligig. I may be ousted from this jar to make room for a handful of bobby pins or I may wind up greasing a window cord, but at least I haven't stagnated. That's more than I can say for a certain gasbag of a coconut out in the Philippines. No need to mention names. Maybe, if she's so goddam adept at writing, she can also read.

I'm Sorry I Made Me Cry

Cⱻ

THE CONSULTING ROOM I sat in that dun December afternoon in 1920 was a perfect setting for a senior Rhode Island eye specialist, and Dr. Adrian Budlong was perfectly cast in the role of the specialist. A septuagenarian with a sunken, emaciated face, and as angular as a praying mantis, Dr. Budlong bore a chilling resemblance to the mummified Rameses II, and it would not have surprised me to learn that he kept his entrails in an alabaster canopic jar under his desk. The room itself was rather like a crypt, dark and redolent of musty bindings and iodoform; behind the Doctor's head, in the shadows, a bust of Galen just large enough for a raven to perch on scowled down at me balefully. For forty-five minutes, Dr. Budlong, in an effort to discover why my eyelids were swollen like Smyrna figs, had submitted me to every test known to ophthalmology.

He had checked my vision with all manner of graduated charts and images, made me swivel my eyeballs until they bellied from their sockets, peered endlessly into my irises with sinister flashlights. The examination, clearly, had been fruitless, for he was now bombarding me with questions that struck me as irrelevant, if not fatuous. Had I eaten any toadstools recently, been stung by any wasps or hornets? Had I wittingly stepped on a rattlesnake or serpent of any description?

"I—I swim under water a lot at the Y.M.C.A.," I faltered. "Maybe the disinfectant—"

"Chlorine never hurt anybody," he snapped. "Clears the brain." With a palsied clawlike hand, he plucked the optical mirror from his death's-head and dropped it on the blotter. "Humph—no reason a boy of your age should suddenly start looking like a bullfrog. Have you been under any mental strain lately? What kind of stuff d'ye read?"

"Er—mostly history," I said evasively. "Balzac's *Droll Stories*, the *Decameron*, Brantôme's *Lives of Fair and Gallant Ladies*—"

"Nothing there that would affect the lids especially," he said, with what I considered unnecessary coarseness. "Now let's stop paltering around, young man. What have you been crying about?" Somewhere deep in my consciousness, a louver flew open and I saw the façade of the Providence Opera House, the temple where every moviegoer in town had been snuffling uncontrollably over D. W. Griffith's great tear-jerker *Way Down East*. Choking back a sob, I confessed shamefacedly that I had seen the picture three times. Dr. Budlong regarded me for a full twenty minutes in silence, patently undecided whether to have me certified or bastinadoed. Then, making no effort to conceal his spleen, he prescribed cold poultices and a moratorium on cinematic pathos, and flung me out. By an evil circumstance, the trolley car that bore me homeward passed the Opera House. Hours later, streaked with tears, and blubbering from my fourth exposure to the masterpiece, I informed my folks that Budlong had pronounced me a victim of winter hay fever.

The diagnosis aroused no visible furor. By then the family was impervious to shock.

NOT LONG AGO, examining the network of laughter lines around my eyes in the mirror, it occurred to me that I was in peril of becoming a slippered popinjay. Life since forty had been so rollicking and mirthful that I had allowed my sentimental, nobler instincts to retrogress; what I needed, and pronto, was a profound emotional *nettoyage*. Accordingly, I downed twenty pages of Thomas Merton, the spiritual equivalent of sulphur and molasses, listened to Jan Peerce's superbly emetic record-ing of "What Is a Boy?" and topped it off with a matinée of *Way Down East* at the Museum of Modern Art. I can get around the house passably by holding on to the furniture, but I still feel a mite queasy.

The leitmotiv of *Way Down East*, like that of so many early film melodramas, was innocence betrayed, virtue—doggedly sullied through ten reels—rising triumphant and kneeing its traducer in the groin. The sweet resignation with which Lillian Gish, the heroine, underwent every vicissitude of fortune from bastardy to frostbite, and the lacquered, mandarin composure of Richard Barthelmess in the face of ostracism and blizzard, have rarely been surpassed on celluloid. It was, however, Lowell Sherman, that peerless actor, who, in his delineation of the villain, copped the honors. Exquisitely groomed, a trifle flaccid, the epitome of the jaded roué, he moved catlike through the action, stalking his prey, his face a mask of smiling insin-cerity that occasionally let slip a barbered sneer. When he tapped a cigarette deliberately on his silver case and cast a cool, speculative glance into a woman's bodice, you knew she would never survive the rabbit test. Sidney Blackmer, Henry Daniell, Robert Morley—there have been many able varmints since, but none quite as silky or loathsome as Lowell Sherman. They had to spray him with fungicide between takes to keep the mushrooms from forming on him.

Way Down East, billed in its opening title as "a simple story for plain people" (the adjectives would seem to be interchangeable), starts off with a windy hundred-and-twenty-two-word essay containing far less juice than pulp and seeds. Its general content is that while polygamy is on the wane, monogamy is not yet worldwide—an assertion calculated to lacerate nobody's feelings, whether Bedouin or Baptist. The locale of the drama, continues the preamble, is "in the story world of make-believe; characters nowhere, yet everywhere." Having slaked the passion for universality that constantly assailed him, Griffith yielded the stage to his puppets. Anna Moore (Miss Gish) and her widowed mother, destitute in a New England village, decide to put the sleeve on the Tremonts, their rich Boston relatives. Clad in gingham and a black wide-awake straw, Anna sets off for their mansion, bumbling into a stylish musicale they are giving and discomfiting her snobbish female cousins. In order to make character with a rich, eccentric aunt, however, the Tremonts swallow their resentment and take Anna in. Simultaneously, the girl has a fleeting encounter with her seducer-to-be, dashing Lennox Sanderson (Lowell Sherman), who smirks into her cleavage and earmarks her for future spoliation. We now whisk to the countervailing influence in Anna's life, David Bartlett (Richard Barthelmess), as he scratches a pigeon's neck on his father's farm, adjacent to Sanderson's country estate. "Though of plain stock," the subtitle explains, "he has been tutored by poets and vision wide as the world." He has also had access, it might be noted, to a remarkable pomade, which keeps his hair snugly plastered to his scalp no matter how turbulent the action becomes. The secret of Barthelmess's hair has never ceased to fascinate me. In every picture I recall him in, from *Broken Blossoms* and *Tol'able David* to *The Idol Dancer* and *The Love Flower*, nothing ever disturbed that sleek coiffure. Cockney bruisers beat the daylights out of Barthelmess, bullying mates kicked him down hatchways and flailed him with marlinspikes, and Papuans

149

boiled him in kettles, but he always looked as though he had just emerged from the Dawn Patrol Barbershop. Of course, there is no external evidence that his hair was real; it may merely have been Duco, sprayed on him between takes, like Sherman's fungicide, but how they ever prevented it from cracking is beyond me.

Anna's downfall, the next item on the agenda, is one of the most precipitous and brutal since the sack of Constantinople by the Turks. Sanderson spies her at a society rout, almost unbearably ethereal in soft focus and a cloud of tulle, and, closing in, murmurs thickly, "In your beauty lives again Elaine, the Lily Maid, love-dreaming at Astolat." Enchanted by this verbal zircon, Anna dimples from head to toe and implores, "Tell me more." He obliges, with such notable effect that she ultimately agrees to a secret marriage ceremony, unaware that the parson is bogus and the witnesses fixed. From then on, the poor creature is fed through the dramatic wringer with relentless ferocity. After her return home, she finds she is gravid, appeals to Sanderson—who, meanwhile, has gone on to other amorous diversions—and discovers that she has been euchred. Sanderson callously deserts her, on the pretext that he will be disinherited if their liaison comes to light, and Anna's mother, with typical maternal spitefulness, dies off just when she is most needed. The baby languishes from birth; when it succumbs, giving Anna endless golden opportunities for histrionics, she is expelled from her lodgings by a righteous landlady, and the first portion of her Gethsemane concludes. The least sophisticated movie fan senses, though, that his tear ducts are being permitted only the briefest respite. Better than any director before or since, Griffith understood the use of the bean ball, and he now prepares to pitch it square at his leading lady and reduce everyone to jelly.

Drawn by the peculiar magnetism that polarizes movie characters, Anna wanders to the Bartlett farm, meets David, and so generally excites pity that Squire Bartlett, his gruff, bigoted father, gives her a minor post agitating a churn. The farm hums with all sorts of romantic activity. There is, for instance, a visiting niece named Kate who is alternately being courted by Hi Holler, the hired man, and the Professor, an absent-minded pedagogue with a butterfly net. Gusty bucolic comedy ensues when the former, daubing his shoes and hair with axle grease to enhance his charm, is struck on the head by a new-laid egg and backs into a pitchfork. Also on hand to provoke chuckles is a rustic twosome made up of Martha Perkins, the village gossip, and her perennial admirer, a hayseed in a linen duster who quaffs Long Life Bitters. The story meanders sluggishly along for a spell, washing up tender symbols like cooing buds and bursting doves to blueprint David's bias for Anna, and then Lennox Sanderson pops in again, this time mousing around after Kate. He berates Anna for remaining in his bailiwick and, in truly heartless fashion, orders her to clear off. As she is about to, though, David shyly confesses his *béguin* for her (and nobody could confess a *béguin* more shyly than Barthelmess, without moving so much as a muscle in his face). At length, sorely troubled, she decides to stay—a difficult decision and similar to one that I myself, by a coincidence, was having to make. Confidentially, it was touch and go.

Except for love's gradual ripening, the next thousand feet of the film are as devoid of incident as a Fitzpatrick travel talk on Costa Rica, Land of the Coffee Bean. There is a plethora of fields choked with daisies, misty-eyed colloquies, and orotund subtitles like "One heart for one heart, one soul for one soul, one love, even through eternity. At last the great overwhelming love, only to be halted by the stark ghost of her past." With the onset of winter, the plot registers a sudden galvanic twitch. Just as Anna is stalemated between David's proposal, which she cannot bring herself to accept, and Sanderson's renewed persecutions, her onetime landlady happens into the village, recognizes her, and recounts her shame to the sewing circle. Martha Perkins, of course, instantly hurries to the Squire to apprise him that he is harboring a Jezebel, and the fat is in the fire. Anna is excoriated in front of the entire household and driven forth despite David's protestations, but not before she castigates Sanderson as her betrayer. A blizzard, which has been picking its teeth in the wings, now comes in on cue, and enfolding the outcast, whirls her toward the icebound river. David, who meanwhile has been locked in mortal combat with Sanderson (without having his hair mussed, naturally), flattens his adversary and runs to intercept Anna; the ice goes out, she is swept to the brink of the falls, and her lover, exhibiting the nimblest footwork since Packy McFarland, saves her from annihilation. The rest of the spool portrays Sanderson, surprisingly natty after his drubbing, offering his dupe legitimate wedlock and sighing with relief when she disdains him, and a multiple marriage in which Anna and David, Kate and the Professor, and Martha and her apple-knocker are united. So ends the morality, with no hard feelings except in the gluteus, and with that unique sense of degradation that attends a trip to the movies during daylight.

As IT HAPPENS, the only known antidote for the foregoing is a double banana split with oodles of fudge sauce, and immediately on quitting *Way Down East* I sought one out at a neighboring drugstore. As I was burrowing into it like a snowplow, I became conscious of the soda jerker's intent scrutiny. "Say, din I use to see you around the old Opera House in Providence?" he inquired narrowly. "I took tickets there when I was a kid." Judging from the man's decrepitude, I would have had to dandle Bronson Alcott on my knee to be his contemporary, but I waived the point and held still for a spate of theatrical reminiscence. At last, as a sort of tourniquet, I mentioned *Way Down East* and suggested he might enjoy seeing it again. He drew himself up, offended. "Listen, wise guy," he retorted. "I may handle slop for a living, but I don't have to look at it." I slunk out with flaming cheeks, made even pinker by the cashier's recalling me to settle the check. Altogether, it was a shattering afternoon. The next time my nobler nature gets the upper hand, I aim for the nearest Turkish bath.

Danger—Molting Plumage

MEN, here's the opportunity of a lifetime. How would you like to acquire a garment for only two dollars and ninety-eight cents that, if you tried to duplicate it at James Bell, Bernard Weatherill, or any other leading Fifth Avenue tailor, would stand you in the neighborhood of two hundred and twenty-five dollars? I'm speaking of a genuine Chinese shantung suit, equally ideal for resort or town wear, custom-tailored throughout from the finest imported material, and guaranteed wrinkleproof, with absolutely dreamy trousers—hand-sewn pockets, double cuffs, and a huge, roomy seat. Anyone lucky enough to have a waist measurement of twenty-seven inches and a pair of short, fat thighs like a West African mandrill's had better hurry right down to my apartment, because I intend to close out the suit, especially the pants, even if I have to burn them. Every time I

154

look at them, the room swims around and I feel as though I were going to have a syncope.

It was about three years ago, in Hong Kong, that I first became involved with the idea of a shantung suit. I'd remarked several taipans wearing them around Ice House Street and the Peninsula Hotel, over on the Kowloon side—fastidious types, don't you know, umbrellas at the furl and that sort of thing, nothing showy but everything in quiet good taste. I mean the kind of chap you might see along Jermyn Street or Piccadilly selecting a cravat at Hilditch & Key's or a serviceable Malacca at Swaine Adeney Brigg & Sons. I was around H. K. at a loose end just then, waiting for a Dutch tramp I'd booked east to Macassar to complete her manifest, and I thought, damn it, old boy, here's your chance. Why not pick up a few yards of decent shantung in Queen's Road Central and have some local tailor run you up a suit? Cleverest beggars on earth, these Cantonese, copy anything overnight and you can pay them off under an old ginseng root. Well, I flagged a trishaw and told the boy to take me to Wing Yan's silk shop down near Upper Lascar Row. Wing's a pretty sharp trader, the old reprobate; *he* knew what I was after, in that clairvoyant way Orientals do —don't ask me how—and pretended to be busy in the rear nailing a whitefish sandwich to the floor. Rather than lose face doing business with his clerks, I waited about till the store closed, returned to my hotel, and came back the next morning. That did it, all right; I could tell straight off from his bland heathen smile that I had him on the defensive.

"No first-chop shantung along here," he said evasively. "Plice plohibitive." I blew a thin plume of smoke over his head and casually mentioned the name of a C.I.D. inspector over in the New Territories who might like to know that Wing was nailing whitefish sandwiches in the rear of his shop. He immediately lost his fried-noodle accent and produced a bolt of superb, close-textured stuff almost as heavy as brocade. The legend in the selvage, "Winograd Bros. Mills, Paterson, N.J.," disturbed me somewhat, but Wing swore it had been loomed on the Shantung peninsula and that some opium-befuddled coolie had stenciled it erroneously. We then fell to bargaining in the traditional fashion, bandying veiled gibes at each other's legitimacy and sluicing down hell's own quantity of Lapsang souchong, and I finally got the cloth for a cool two dollars less than it would have fetched at Gunn & Latchford's at home. It was ticklish work, of course, and your average tourist could never have brought it off. But pshaw, when you've kicked about the Treaty Ports as long as I have, dealing with the Chinese temperament gets to be second nature to a man. I can't explain it. It's kind of a knack you develop.

Well, a Stateside Johnny who'd just come transpacific would have popped into the first tailor along Chater Road and gone out with a botch. Not I, though; I know chalk from cheese, if I do say so myself, and I meant to have the job done right. There's a little hole in the wall off Connaught Road, squeezed in between a ship's chandler and a rattan export firm (which exports a good deal more than rattan, I'll be bound). Chap in the Gloucester Hotel bar who'd got a bit tiddly on gimlets put me on to it. Says he, "Chen's the name. Best cutter in H. K. Simply wizard. Just mention Froggy Lamprecht."

"Make *your* suit?" I asked, as though I hadn't noticed it before. Gad, what a fit. Paper on the wall.

"*And* Lord Louis Mountbatten's," he said. "Real artist, that blighter. Poet of the scissors." Then, fearing he'd said too much, he dummied up and fell down. I looked Chen's place over from the outside; rather grubby, couple of dusty naval uniforms in the window, but sound. Thin, scholarly bird stitching a coat inside pricked up his ears when I mentioned Lamprecht.

"Him still on flo' in Gloucester Hotel?" he asked. That's how fast news travels in Hong Kong.

I swallowed hard and did some quick figuring. If he was

playing it inscrutable, so could I. I wasn't giving anything away for free. "No savvy plesent status along Floggy," I rejoined impassively. "Him allee samee inexplicable quantity." I brought out the material, together with a jacket to use as a model, and stipulated I must have the initial fitting within forty-eight hours.

"Can do," said Chen. "You bling along ginseng root to pay off under. Everytling shipshape, no bobbery. Number-one job."

And it would have been, too, if the skipper of the *Balikpapan* hadn't sent around a chit to my digs ordering my gear aboard chop-chop, as his vessel was sailing on the tide. I nipped back to Chen's posthaste and luckily caught him just as he was laying out the pattern. Of course, he raised the most fearful din, insisted I reimburse him for his trouble and what all. But I know these gentry; once they sense you've the whip hand, they back down fast enough. I merely peeled off a couple of those small-denomination express checks—tens or twenties, I forget which—and Chen at once became all smiles. I couldn't help chuckling, as the *Balikpapan* moved downstream, at the way I'd put it over on him. Ordinary bloke in the same spot might easily have wound up with a knife in his ribs, whereas I had, potentially, one of the finest shantung suits that ever came out of the Far East. Luck? Cunning? No-o-o—the difference between the tyro and the experienced traveler, is all.

Well, come one thing and another, it was three years before I got around to the suit again. One day last summer, pricing some suspenders braided out of human hair at a clothier's in Beverly Hills, I noticed a tropical coat whose material was a dead ringer for mine. The manager of the place, Roger Fly, was an old friend who used to work for the students'-and-misfit clothing firm on Madison Avenue I patronize. When he heard about my shantung, he turned pale with excitement.

"See here," he said, lowering his voice. "I'll get canned if this leaks out, but do you want that suit made for fifty dollars?"

"Rot," I said. "Why, the cheapest custom tailor charges a hundred and sixty—"

"Yes, yes," he said scornfully. "Brigands, all of them. I've got a little man down in L. A. who's a genius—makes clothes for Cary Grant, Charles Coburn, all the best-dressed men in pictures. How he does it for fifty bucks, I don't know, but he even supplies the thread. Now, listen," he went on hurriedly, "you ever heard of Vladimir Horowitz?"

"The pianist?" I asked. "Is he making clothes now?"

"No, this is his uncle or his cousin or something," said Roger. "Calls himself Lance Argyle. The shop's on Figueroa, just off Wilshire. Don't use my name. Just mention Froggy Lamprecht."

"Hey, wait a minute!" I protested. "I mentioned him to a Chinese in Hong Kong and almost got a knife—" But it was too late; Roger, obviously fearing he'd said too much, had vanished into the mackintoshes. That afternoon, chancing to be at Bernstein's Fish Grotto in the vicinity, I dropped by Argyle's. A bald, misanthropic gentleman in shirtsleeves, ironing a vest, removed some pins from his mouth and identified himself as the genius. Halfway through my explanation, he cut in with a superior smile.

"Sonny, you don't have to tell Lance Argyle his business," he said. "Thirty-two years I'm making clothes for the stars. You like Adolphe Menjou's suits? You like Fred Astaire's? I'll give you an outfit which you wouldn't be ashamed to wear it to the White House even. Stand still while I take your measure." During the process, I took pains to impress on him the value of the cloth involved, its rarity, my exacting taste. "Yeah, yeah," he muttered. "A real conservative drape, leave it to me. Send the goods and I'll copy you the exact same thing."

By means of a series of frantic telegrams and phone calls to New York and the outlay of a small fortune in air-mail postage, I managed to get the shantung flown across the continent to

Mr. Argyle in a hurry, as well as to engender universal suspicion about my sanity, and, a fortnight later, reported back to
him for a fitting. The coat—or, rather, the vestige its creator
helped me into—looked promising, though it possessed only
one lapel and a sleeve, both of which he proceeded to rip apart
viciously, murmuring some incomprehensible rune to himself.

"Is—is anything wrong?" I asked, scenting disaster. Argyle,
plainly a man prone to taking umbrage, instantly took an over-
dose. Had I forgotten that for thirty-two years . . . Menjou . . .
Astaire . . . Coburn? If there was one thing he found insupportable, he went on violently, it was smart-alecks. The world was
full of boneheads posing as experts, buttinskies trying to teach
a craftsman his job. Nervously parrying the shears he bran-
dished, I apologized for my *gaffe*, and soothed his vanity with
the most fulsome compliments. The jacket was masterly, I proclaimed, and I was confident the same was true of the trousers,
which, I continued with an ingratiating smile, I would now be
delighted to try on.

"The trousers?" Argyle demanded, in the tone Winthrop
Aldrich might employ toward a depositor questioning his solvency. "Lance Argyle don't try on no trousers. You think after
thirty-two years I can't cut a lousy pair of pants?"

"Gollies, of course you can!" I agreed slavishly. "But in case
I have to leave suddenly— I mean couldn't we just slip on the
pants together—that is, *I* slip on the pants together—"

Argyle wheeled about in a fury, snatched up his handiwork,
and began wrapping it in an old newspaper. "Take it!" he
shouted. "You finish it! I kill myself, I ruin my eyes for a *nud-
nick*, and this is the thanks I get. I was better off in Odessa,
living six in a room!" The rhetorical gamut he ran, while not
quite as florid as Rudolph Schildkraut's in *The God of Vengeance*, eclipsed it in vigor, but eventually hoarseness pre-
vailed, and I cozened him into forgiveness. Pocketing the sawbuck I had forced on him as heart balm, Argyle commanded

159

me to banish all my worries and return a week thence for the final fitting. "Mind you, it ain't necessary," he added, "but a customer like you and Menjou, that they're practically a walking advertisement for me, I got to make every buttonhole perfect, every seam. Otherwise, I couldn't sleep at night."

Evidently the burden of insomnia was less than crushing, for when I saw Argyle again, he seemed unable to recollect me, and considerably damaged my morale by asserting that he had never made a shantung suit in his life. After an intensive search, however, he reappeared with the coat over his arm. "It was laying on the floor behind the radiator," he said sheepishly. "Must have slipped off the hanger." Whatever had happened, it was an appalling sight, a patchwork of unrelated fragments loosely basted together and striped with gray fuzz.

"Look," I said desperately, seizing the mosaic and draping it over me, "I'm flying back to New York tonight. Finish this up and send it on to me. And remember, for God's sake, enough room in the pants."

"Mister, one thing I'll guarantee you," promised Argyle, placing his hand on his heart. "Room you'll get in the pants or my name ain't Lance Argyle." The fact that it wasn't seemed too obvious to dispute, and in any case I had no time for polemics.

Six weeks later, just as the entire affair was receding into limbo, a postman awoke me one morning with a C.O.D. parcel from Los Angeles. The seventy-eight dollars he demanded was preposterous, but in view of the investment I had already made, I let myself be cajoled into paying it. Right after breakfast, I locked the bedroom door, unwrapped the trousers, and began drawing them on. Fortunately, my wife, who was sewing in the breakfast nook at the time, heard the crash and got the superintendent to force the door—a mighty providential thing all around, for, as the doctor said afterward, it could easily have been slow strangulation and nobody the wiser. That is, nobody but Froggy Lamprecht, who I still think may have engineered the whole thing from the start. Whoever did, I know where there's a really sensational bargain to be had in men's apparel. Owner, a onetime fop, has just switched over to seersucker.

Sorry—No Phone or Mail Orders

⊂≡

WHEN A PERFUME called Chaqueneau-K was launched a couple
of seasons ago with a campaign designed to prevent women
from buying it, there was a lot of headshaking around the Advertising Club of New York, and more than one scarlet-faced
old member gloomily prophesied, over his gin-and-French, the
death of retailing. "Damn it all, sir, it won't go down," the
Tories sputtered. "Bullyrag the consumer, deride him if you
will, but you can't dispense with the beggar altogether. Someone's got to move the bloody stuff off the shelves." The fore-
bodings were, as it turned out, groundless; ladies bent on
achieving the unattainable cozened their menfolk into procuring it for them, and today any *femme soignée* would consider herself *vieux jeu* without a flacon of Chaqueneau-K in her
parfumoir. (Well, almost any *femme soignée*.) Quite recently,

the technique has been gaining ground among other storekeepers, notably Macy's and a men's-apparel firm in Baltimore named Lebow Brothers. The former's announcement of a fur sale, while not out-and-out preventive advertising, narrowed down the market to a mere handful of the élite: "Just 10 very precious natural ranch mink cape stoles go on sale tomorrow—$377. Hard to believe a lustrous, deeply piled natural ranch mink cape stole could cost so little? It's true true true at Macy's tomorrow! Just 10 very lucky women will get ten very precious mink buys," etc., etc. Lebow Brothers, apostrophizing a men's cashmere jacket in the pages of *Vogue*, was even more dickty: "Cashmiracle . . . so rare each coat is registered. Woven by the famous Worumbo Mill. This miracle in cashmere makes a truly proud possession. The finest underdown of 20 goats makes one jacket. In Oyster White, Moonlight Blue, Mulberry, Bamboo." The text opens a whole host of nerve-tingling possibilities, such as the hijacking by goniffs of an armored car laden with Cashmiracles, or the crisis at Worumbo when, in the course of looming a jacket for some noted coxcomb like Danton Walker, one of his twenty sacrificial goats is found to possess no underdown. The temptation to substitute the hair of a Bedlington terrier or a yak might understandably arise, though I imagine Worumbo's blenders are incorruptible—and heavily bonded, to boot. In which case, of course, the suspense would stem from some rival columnist, say Ed Sullivan or Barry Gray, attempting to suborn a blender into using the ersatz to discredit Walker. In short, the dramatic complications could be hilarious, especially if you added a Shakespearean holocaust and killed off all the protagonists in the end.

The upshot of this constricted merchandising, foreseeably, is that the average shopper may soon be frozen out of the picture, and, unless he has a controlling interest in the United States Gypsum Corporation, a listing in Debrett, and a membership in the Jockey Club of France, will be unable to purchase the ordinary necessities of life. The easiest way to appreciate his plight, perhaps, is to follow an exemplar named Leo Champollion, whose garter has snapped while crossing against a light, into a haberdashery in the East Fifties. The establishment, deeply carpeted and indirectly lit, has no vulgar fixtures like showcases or spittoons to identify it as an outfitter's; given another urn or two, it could be a mortuary or a gastroenterologist's waiting room. As Champollion enters in a crouching position, tugging at his socks, Elphinstone, a lard-faced salesman, finishes pinning a camellia in his lapel and approaches languidly.

ELPHINSTONE (*from across a gulf*): You wished—?

CHAMPOLLION: I busted a garter just now—the elastic's all shot.

ELPHINSTONE: Soddy, we don't vulcanize old rubber. There's a garage over on Second Avenue that may conceivably aid you.

CHAMPOLLION: Aw heck, she's not worth fixing. I'll take a new pair.

ELPHINSTONE (*suavely*): Indeed? May I have your name, please?

CHAMPOLLION: Why—er—Champollion. But what difference does it make? I just want an inexpensive—

ELPHINSTONE: Champollion, eh? Any relative of the distinguished Egyptologist?

CHAMPOLLION: No-o-o, not as I know it. I'm with the Cattaraugus Yeast Company, in the enzyme division.

ELPHINSTONE: I see. And who recommended you to us?

CHAMPOLLION: Nobody. I happened to look up and see your sign "Cravatoor."

ELPHINSTONE: You mean you haven't been previously introduced or filed application to enroll as a customer?

CHAMPOLLION: I—I didn't know you had to.

ELPHINSTONE: My dear fellow, the clientele of this shop comprises some of the biggest gazebos in the country. If we were to bother with every whippersnapper who blunders in off the street, how long do you think we'd stay in business?

CHAMPOLLION (*piteously*): But I can't walk around this way, like a college boy! How can I call on the prospects with my sock hanging down?

ELPHINSTONE: That's your headache. Mine is to safeguard the stock so that pikers won't sneak in and buy it out from under our nose. Good day.

CHAMPOLLION: Look, I'll pay double the usual price! (*His voice becomes incoherent.*) I'm a family man, with two little chiggers—I mean two little nippers—

ELPHINSTONE (*relenting*): Well, I'll make an exception this time, but if it ever leaks out, it'll cost me my job.

CHAMPOLLION: I won't tell anybody—honest I won't. I'll say I stole them.

ELPHINSTONE: All right, then, sit down and I'll take your measurements. (*Pulls on surgical gloves.*) Now, hoist up your trousers; I don't want to get these septic. . . . Hmm, that's a pretty scrawny-looking calf you've got there.

CHAMPOLLION: It's wiry, though. I used to beat everybody at stickball.

ELPHINSTONE: Well, you could have done with a bit of polo. Let's see, we might anchor a catch here—

CHAMPOLLION (*diffidently*): Look, wouldn't a regular-sized garter fit me? You know, just ordinary ones—maroon or navy blue. There don't have to be those naked girls on the webbing.

ELPHINSTONE: It isn't a question of size, and anyway, when the times comes *we'll* decide what pattern is best on you. What I'm concerned with now is the contour of your leg so I can fill out my sculptor's report.

CHAMPOLLION: Hanh? What's that for?

ELPHINSTONE: To aid him in modeling the garter, man. (*Impatiently*) Don't you understand? Each pair is sculptured to the wearer's individual requirements by an artist specially commissioned for the task. In your case, it could be one of the academicians, like Paul Manship or Wheeler Williams, if your knees aren't too knobby.

CHAMPOLLION: Wh-what if they are?

ELPHINSTONE: Ah, then we'd have to call in an abstractionist —Henry Moore or Calder. Naturally, their fees are higher and you'd have to sustain the cable charges should we send your specifications abroad.

CHAMPOLLION (*uneasily*): I wasn't figuring on too much expense, to tell you the truth.

ELPHINSTONE: Possibly not, but you don't realize the trouble involved. First, we have to make a plaster-of-Paris form of your shinbone, then a mockup in laminated wood, which is baked under pressure, sanitized, and aged. This guides the sculptor so he can rough out his cast.

CHAMPOLLION: But I can't wear stone garters! I have to be on my feet all day.

ELPHINSTONE: We wouldn't allow you to. They're simply the matrix from which we execute your personalized accessory in a variety of materials. Here's a swatch to give you an idea. This one, as you see, simulates pickled pine.

CHAMPOLLION: What's that one—plastic?

ELPHINSTONE: No, it only simulates plastic; it's infinitely more costly. Here's one in a fabric so nearly resembling human flesh that customers frequently can't find their garters once they're on.

CHAMPOLLION: Is that good?

ELPHINSTONE (*stiffly*): We're not here to answer metaphysical questions, Mr. Champollion. We're here to not sell merchandise.

CHAMPOLLION: I was only asking. I didn't mean to sound fresh. (*Peering at another sample*) Say, isn't this what I've got on?

ELPHINSTONE: Hardly. That's what we call *trompe-l'œil*. It may look like worn-out elastic, but it's not elastic at all. It's grypton, the sleaziest plastic known.

CHAMPOLLION: Jeekers, you can't keep up with science nowadays, can you?

ELPHINSTONE (*with Olympian amusement*): No. I suppose it must be rather confusing for a layman. Well, let's start with the mold—

CHAMPOLLION: Uh—I was wondering—couldn't you advance me a pair of garters just for the time being, till I get back to Yonkers?

ELPHINSTONE: Quite impossible. Our vaults close at three.

CHAMPOLLION (*supplicatory*): Or even a piece of twine, so's I could finish my calls. I'd send it back by messenger.

ELPHINSTONE: No, but in view of the circumstances, I'll stretch a point and expedite the psychological quiz. (*Flicks the switch of a Dictograph concealed in an urn.*) Elphinstone to Glintenkamp. Will you be good enough to come in here, Doctor? (*Before Champollion's motor apparatus can function, a dynamic young man enters from rear. He wears a speculum and a physician's smock improvised from an old flour sack, on the back of which is visible, in faded blue letters, the legend "Ceresota—Best by Test."*)

GLINTENKAMP: Eligibility prognosis?

ELPHINSTONE: If you please. Solvency dubious, physique zero minus four.

CHAMPOLLION (*eyes rolling affrightedly*): I can't stay any longer. My boss'll have a connip—

GLINTENKAMP: Now, now, nobody's going to hurt you. Just look at these cards and tell us what the various shapes suggest to you. Come on.

CHAMPOLLION: S-someone spilled gravy on it. Juice of some kind.

GLINTENKAMP: No, no, they're blots of ink. Try to concentrate, now—don't they remind you of anything?

CHAMPOLLION: Well, the top part there . . . um . . . that could be a face, a man's profile.

GLINTENKAMP: Anyone you know?

CHAMPOLLION: Uh-uh. Wait a minute, though. It's a little like Mr. Bastinado.

167

GLINTENKAMP: Your boss?

CHAMPOLLION: No, a credit manager up our way. He works for the Procrustes Finance people.

GLINTENKAMP (*significantly*): I see. Go ahead, keep trying.

CHAMPOLLION: This one on the side looks like—well, like pencils in a cup.

GLINTENKAMP: That'll do. (*To Elphinstone*) Impoverishment fixation. Strictly a vag. Boost him.

CHAMPOLLION (*anxiously*): Did I pass? Am I going to get the garters?

ELPHINSTONE: Just close your flap and pretend to be a special-delivery letter. You're practically in Yonkers. (*As one man, he and Glintenkamp sweep up Champollion, propel him to the door, and toss him into oblivion.*)

GLINTENKAMP (*consulting his watch*): Well, five o'clock. The end of a perfect day.

ELPHINSTONE: Yep, all the goods intact and not a cent in the register. I tell you, Doc, this business is going places. Another year like this and we'll be moving over onto the Avenue. (*Radiant, the two of them exit to prepare a banner advertisement for* Vogue *celebrating their collapse.*)

CURTAIN

Don't Tell Me,
Pretty Gypsy

WHEN ONE exercises his inalienable right to line a bureau drawer with newspaper on a humid day and deposit in it a couple of freshly ironed shirts, it's a cinch the resultant decalcomania on his bosom will eventually elicit comment from some busybody or other. I was at my optician's the other morning, myopically waiting for him to finish soldering the bridge of my glasses, when he broke off his labors and leaned closer.

"Well," he said with the relish people invariably evince in reporting a theatrical debacle, "I see where the New York *Post* didn't exactly rave over that show down on Second Avenue, *Girl of My Dream*."

"Where'd you see that?" I asked.

"On your shirt," he replied pleasantly. "Like me to read it to you?" He lifted aside my cravat for a better view and removed from his tongue a particle of solder that impeded his diction. " 'Nobody, I suspect, has gotten, or is going to get, very excited about the plot of the Yiddish musical, *Girl of My Dream*, closing the season for Edmund Zayenda and Irving Jacobson at the Second Avenue Theater this weekend,' " he read. " 'The story of the air pilot lost at sea, who turns up as a member of a gypsy band with amnesia, is pretty old hat.' The next part is kind of wrinkled from your tie clasp, but he says down here, '*Girl of My Dream* is not going to start any innovations in the Yiddish theater.' "

"Well, it's only one man's opinion," I returned shortly, tucking the review back into my waistband. "The idea sounds breezy enough to me."

"Me, too," he concurred. "Say, how come you stenciled that on your shirt front? You a friend of the critic?"

"No, he pays me to do it," I said. "I'm a sandwich man for the drama critics. Yesterday I had on a plug for Brooks Atkinson." The novelty of this so overwhelmed him that I finally had to abandon the glasses and feel my way home. As I was reversing the shirt, though, I began to ponder the summary of the plot, and it struck me again as being most cavalier. I felt that the idea of a shipwrecked airman becoming a member of a gypsy band with amnesia, far from being démodé, could make a corking musical if handled right. (That is, if only the pilot had amnesia; if the whole band had it, as the *Post* implied, the device might be a shade cumbersome.) After all, what was so world-shaking about the premise of a romance between a Navy nurse and a French colonial resident, or an English governess and a Siamese potentate? Yet each of these was the basis of a smash: *Hit the Deck* and *Chu Chin Chow*. In other words, the librettist desirous of fashioning a silk purse can use any sow's ear that presents itself, and, buoyed up by this maxim, I have been formulating a tight, workable outline that grows naturally out of the original situation. Inasmuch as the Second Avenue production, written by Joseph Rumshinsky and William Siegel, snapped shut without my seeing it, any resemblance between our two efforts is, of course, illusory; in fact, I have deliberately eschewed all standard motifs like tambourines, horse thievery, and hidden birthmarks to avoid possible conflict. Nothing could be fairer than that.

Our opening scene must, to my way of thinking, have a nautical tang, with a locale off the Balkan coast wherever gypsies tend to forgather—Dalmatia, let us say. On the horizon, the famous blue cliffs of Dalmatia rise sheer, and at center stage, half dead from exposure to the cruel Dalmatian sun, lies Speed Wintringham on an inflated rubber raft. From his rather incoherent soliloquy—a futuristic background of woodwinds and strings suggests that the exposition may really be going on in his head—we gather that he remembers bailing out of his plane but naught else. In short, a good-looking, brawny young American flier, temporarily discombobulated but not medically certifiable. Just as his hopes of rescue are dwindling, a felucca manned by gypsies appears. Their presence in these waters—or, indeed, in any waters—may take a bit of justification, as gypsies are not notably a seafaring folk; however, we weave in some skillful allusion or other to their inherent restlessness, their hatred of fetters, and package it in a ringing chorale wherein they joyously pound their canisters on the gunwales, and the audience won't have time to speculate. You never let grass grow under your feet on such occasions. In a musical I once helped confect that perished in Philadelphia, the actors paused to explain how some Thracian hoplites had strayed into Dolores Gray's bedroom. When they looked up, they had an unobstructed view of the interior of the Erlanger Theatre clear back to Chadds Ford. Even the candy concessionaires had vanished.

Anyhow, hanging over the ship's rail, and a veritable orchid among thistles, is a lovely ash-blond vision named Darleen, whose blouse continually slips off her shoulders—a good comedy touch and highly authentic costumewise in a nomad lass. Darleen is, supposedly, the daughter of the gypsy chieftain, Stanislas, but in the confusion of hauling Speed aboard, chafing his wrists, and reviving him with fiery Dalmatian brandy we plant that there is something fishy about the girl's actual origin. I mean just a glancing reference, like spurts of revulsion at her companions' mentality and table manners, little signs of fastidiousness that will pay off plotwise later on. One hinge at Speed and, needless to say, Darleen falls. She sings "My Heart Floats Up," a ballad that subtly combines love's yearning with the sea, our common mother. While not wedded to the lyric that follows, I believe it will serve as a beacon:

> Out where the whelks and starfish crawl,
> Amid the sea wrack and the combers,
> I found a pearl in my deep-sea haul
> That spells one of Cupid's diplomas.
> My heart floats up when I discern
> A castaway so taciturn.
> I'll nurse and tend you, mend you, bend you,
> Rend you, send you from my orbit nevermore.

Speed, as yet, is too bushed to return Darleen's love, and hovers between life and death (it might be preferable, for the sake of more squeamish patrons, to have him hover offstage), but meanwhile Zilboor, a darkly handsome young gypsy who has long craved the girl, starts resenting the newcomer and musically plots his destruction. This is an ideal opportunity for an imaginative dream sequence in which Zilboor envisions himself bowstringing Speed and being hounded by the devils of remorse. Actually, the rivalry theme is an ingenious subterfuge on our part, because once it is built up, we never refer to it again. The next scene introduces a distinct change of pace. The setting is present-day New York—an exclusive discount house on West Forty-seventh Street, one of those establishments that sell toasters, radios, waffle irons, and similar appliances, where Gotham's socially elect converge to exchange gossip and seek bargains. Speed's mother, a *grande dame* descended from early Dutch patroons, has come here to buy an egg timer, and encounters a bridge friend she has not seen for years. Their conversation reveals that Speed, only heir to a great real-estate fortune and betrothed to Bibi Witherspoon, a leading débutante, tired of his playboy existence a few months before and took a job with an obscure Greek airline. Mrs. Wintringham voices fears for his safety, knowing that he flies one of the world's most treacherous routes, the Dalmatian run. She wishes he would return home, wed Bibi, and head up his father's manifold realty ventures. What she doesn't suspect is that Speed is in Manhattan at this very moment. The gypsies, chafing under tyranny, have migrated thither and are encamped in a store on Eighth Avenue. While Darleen tells fortunes and tenderly ministers to Speed, still convalescent on a pallet in the back room, Stanislas and the others strive to gain a foothold in the New World by marking cards, playing the handkerchief switch, and glomming laundry off the lines. A good contrast here between a primitive, unspoiled people and the staccato dynamism of the metropolis engulfing them. It can be musically underlined or not, as the case may be.

The plot now goes into high gear. Bud Zapotecky, a fledgling theatrical agent, has been combing the town for a blond gypsy singer to star in a forthcoming ice show. Frustrated at every turn, he is wending his melancholy way homeward down Eighth Avenue—we have established that he lives on Varick Street—when he hears Darleen's glorious soprano issuing from the store. Her glowing beauty surpasses his anticipations; this is the girl for the role. What is more, he falls desperately, hopelessly in love with her, and declares it in a number I provisionally call "You're the Answer to My Unremitting Quest." The words are flexible enough to be rearranged in almost any way required:

> Cortez sought everywhere for gold,
> And Peary the Pole in unimaginable cold,

> Ehrlich the pallid spirochete unfroze,
> And I found you under my very nose.
> Through deepest gloom, like Speke and
>   Mungo Park,
> I've followed your chimera in the dark.
> No trophy could compare with you, I
>   want to share my lair with you,
> Dispel my every care with you and then
>   let down my hair with you,
> My lovely meadow lark.

Darleen, seizing on a mummer's career as a means of procuring Speed the delicacies he needs to get well (his character, incidentally, seems to be developing into the most valetudinarian in the history of show business), gives up her palmistry and begins rehearsals. As a result, the gypsies fall into arrears on their rent, and the landlord—i.e., Speed's own father—hastens down to evict them. The sight of Mr. Wintringham instantly restores his son's memory, but the joyful reunion curdles when the elder learns that the boy worships Darleen. Threatening to disinherit him if he does not accede, he hales Speed off to marry Bibi Witherspoon, and Act I ends with Darleen, brokenhearted, sobbing in her agent's arms. Thus far, it must be admitted, Speed's part in the story has consisted mainly of hollow groans, and it may not be easy to find an actor of the first magnitude to play him. We might have to draw on someone of the second, or even cut the part altogether, if this can be done without weakening the structure.

Time has wrought substantial changes by the opening of Act II. Overnight, Darleen's ethereal loveliness has captivated blasé playgoers, and she is ensconced as the reigning star of Broadway—a bitter triumph, for the personable young birdman remains ever verdant in her thoughts. A poignant scene this, in her dressing room, as she stares into a mirror and sings "I Have a Plenitude of Everything but You," a panorama of lovers' tribulations through the ages. Deftly woven into the lyric are famous attachments paralleling hers, such as those of Jubilee Jim Fisk and Josie Mansfield, Blazes Boylan and Molly Bloom, Swann and Odette, etc. As for Bud Zapotecky, now the ranking agent of theaterdom and still her ardent slave, Darleen cannot bring herself to accept him, fearing he loves her merely for her commissions. She intimates this to him musically that evening in "Is It the Girl or the Client You Love?" when they dine vis-à-vis at an ace nitery. The mood of the song is lightly mocking, but underneath runs a vein of seriousness:

> Ten per cent of me is yours,
> By legal ties we're bound,
> Yet though the repetition of it bores,
> An ounce is but a fraction of a pound.
> I'll pay my debt of gratitude,
> I'll speak of you with all esteem,
> To you I owe my clothes and food,
> But love? You must not dream this dream.

Hence, by cleverly blending our story elements we have now brought about an impasse that will require ingenuity aplenty to resolve. Zapotecky provides the key. Realizing he stands between Darleen's happiness, he goes to Bibi Witherspoon, who he has reason to believe nurses ambitions of becoming a nightclub songstress, and proposes to her. Avid for success, she breaks her engagement to Speed, and, without quite knowing how it happened—though *we* know—the lovers are reunited. Then, thunderclapwise, comes the revelation of Darleen's birthright that smooths the path to marriage. Stanislas, stabbed in a gypsy fray offscene, confesses she is not his child but the daughter of a Milwaukee flour titan, abducted from the latter's yacht in the Adriatic. The Wintringhams extend their heartfelt blessing to the nuptials, and the curtain falls on a glittering wedding reception at which gypsies rub elbows with the *haut monde*.

Of course, a bare outline can't possibly convey the effervescence and sparkle the show would have opening night; there are myriad opportunities for boffs—for instance, in a scene where some Thracian hoplites get into Darleen's bedroom by mistake. What it needs now is sponsorship—a group of investors willing to gamble forty or fifty thousand to subsidize one while he works out the intricacies. If I were to accept the task —mind you, I'm not saying I would, unless I had the money in five-dollar bills, say—I'd fly over to the Dalmatian coast, spend a month or two trying to get the feel of the thing, and then keep right on going. I don't think the script ought to be readied for next season anyway. Better to skip a year or two, until the critical fraternity begins hungering for a good gypsy musical. You'll get intimations of it when the time is ripe. Just keep an eye on the drama columns—or, better still, my shirt.

CLOUDLAND REVISITED:

By the Waters of Razz-Ma-Tazz

TOWARD THE END OF 1920, or just about the time the fencing foils on my bedroom wall were yielding to sepia portraits of Blanche Sweet and Carol Dempster, I became briefly enamored of a Rhode Island schoolmate named, if memory serves, Celia Cahoon. Together with a dozen other unemployables that semester, Miss Cahoon and I were retracing Xenophon's footsteps to the sea, and as we toiled our daily twenty parasangs over the stony Mesopotamian plain, leaving a wake of dead and dying gerunds, I felt myself involuntarily succumbing to her spell. Though hardly the comeliest girl in the class, Celia possessed a figure so voluptuous that it addled every male within a radius of fifty feet. Whenever she was called on to recite, chairs began to scrape, pencils rolled off the desks, people upset ink on their pants, and the quickened exhalations formed a steam that fogged the windows. In her senior year at Classical High, Celia undoubtedly came in for more accidental jostling in corridor and lunchroom than anyone prior to Sophia Loren.

It was, therefore, with as much exultation as though I had been singled out of the ranks by Catherine of Russia that I mounted the stoop of the Cahoon residence one December evening, painstakingly groomed for the soirée Celia had bidden me to. In both dress and deportment, I was patterning myself after Wallace Reid, the brightest star in my movie galaxy; I wore a yellow butterfly bow and a wasp-waisted tweed suit with globular leather buttons, my hair (modishly parted in the middle) exuded a paralyzing scent of bay rum, and my swagger was debonair to the point where I was having trouble retaining my balance. Whom Celia was impersonating at the moment I have no idea, but I remember bee-stung lips pouting out of a heavy mask of rice powder, and a hairdress of those unlovely puffs we used to call "cootie garages," accentuated by a wicked spit curl. The lights in the parlor were low, and another couple, also from our class, was executing a vertiginous tango to "La Veeda." While Celia hastened to fetch me a glass of some ghastly punch made of muscatel and sliced oranges, I adopted a *dégagé* pose on the arm of a Morris chair and, stifling a well-bred yawn, covertly studied my surroundings. The family's taste in art was plainly cultivated; in addition to the standard chromo of Landseer's "Dignity and Impudence," there was a side elevation of a pearly nude with red hair by Henner and half a dozen etchings by Anders Zorn. Their library also hinted at a wide intellectual horizon, ranging from fluff by Peter B. Kyne and James Oliver Curwood to substantial works by John Spargo and Brand Whitlock.

"Now, don't be an old bookworm," said Celia effervescently, seizing my wrist. "Come on, slowpoke, let's shake a tibia!" To be in close proximity to the figure I had so long admired was an exhilarating experience, and when my hostess coyly disclosed that her folks would not be home until midmorning, I figured I had hit the mother lode. As the punch took effect, the pace grew markedly giddier; there was a rare amount of tickling and squealing, and the ladies had frequent recourse to the lipstick that dangled from the chain of the floor lamp—a fribble that I pretended to sneer at but that actually impressed me as the acme of sophistication. But whatever the romp I contemplated in the Elysian fields, the gods had ordained otherwise. Made overconfident by wine, I decided to re-enact an adagio Wallace Reid had performed in his latest vehicle, *The Dancin' Fool.* I clasped Celia in a cheek-to-cheek embrace and, to the cadences of Coon-Sanders and their Blackhawk orchestra, began a series of improvised pirouettes in the style known as the balconade. Just as we were completing a dizzying backward dip, my partner's heel caught in the green plush portieres suspended from an archway, and we fell heavily, demolishing a rubber plant and the lower panel of a Globe-Wernicke bookcase. At that instant, the door opened and two old crabs by the name of Cahoon entered. They had unexpectedly altered their plans, and, it shortly transpired, my own.

NORMALLY, nothing could have persuaded me to revive such painful memories, but they crowded in pell-mell to a screening I was granted recently, by the Museum of Modern Art, of this very Wallace Reid classic. Like *The Roaring Road* and *Excuse My Dust,* his automotive sagas of the same epoch, *The Dancin' Fool* was a breezy success story, altogether synthetic and as devoid of motivation as Happy Hooligan. Its leading man, for all his dazzle, was probably the least gifted actor of the century —a sizable achievement in a medium that begot Nelson Eddy, Henry Wilcoxon, and Mario Lanza. At the risk of alienating readers wholesale, I submit a précis of the plot, but it must be understood that I act merely as an intermediary, or vector.

179

The management will not be responsible for any lost illusions, heartbreak, or ennui poisoning.

The Jones Jug Company, the setting of Wally's initial exploits, is an old-fashioned pottery concern headed by his Uncle Enoch (Raymond Hatton), a stereotyped curmudgeon who bitterly resents progress. Into this milieu bounces Reid, cast as a fresh young hayseed named Sylvester Tibble (or Ves Tibble, naturally), seeking a business career. Given the post of office boy, he at once pantomimes cyclonic energy, raising clouds of dust with his broom, ruffling the bookkeeper's wig, scoffing at the filing system, and generally roiling his elders. After dusk, his uncontrollable zest for dancing leads him into a basement cabaret whose songstress, Junie Budd (Bebe Daniels), seeks his protection from a masher. Wally flattens the offender, and Junie, captivated by his dimples, invites him to her mother's boarding house and offers to coach him in ballroom technique. "You've got regular rattleboxes in your feet," she declares, obviously unaware of a pair that were making every cake-eater in Rhode Island drool with envy. In no time at all—one lap dissolve, in fact—the couple have blossomed out as a dance team in the cabaret, doing a Dutch specialty at their *première* that establishes new frontiers in bathos. Among the patrons, it just so happens, is a wealthy pottery tycoon named Harkins (Tully Marshall), who is established as avid to gain control of the Jones Jug Company's clay pit, a circumstance without burning relevance to the floor show but that provides a yeast for future villainy. Wally and Junie now reappear in an apache number so sensational, presumably, that a rival café owner signs them up at two hundred a week, whereupon they run home to apprise Junie's mother of their success and Wally proposes to her. To Junie, that is, not her mother, although actually it wouldn't have made much difference. By this point in the proceedings, it was crystal-clear to me that the engineer was drunk in the cab, the locomotive out of control, and the switches wide-open.

At the Jones Jug Company, where our hero continues as office boy while dancing professionally at night—a movie premise as plausible as most of them—the firm's drummer, a blowhard and wineskin, returns from a sales trip and angrily resigns when Wally questions his expense account. Thereupon, in a comic routine that has begun to lose some of its sizzle with repetition, Uncle Enoch upbraids his nephew for exceeding authority, fires him summarily, and hires him back at once. Disclosed next are Junie and Wally at their cabaret that evening, clad in leopard skins and presenting a divertissement billed as "Antediluvian Antics," which it would be flattery to describe as the nadir of choreography in our time. Nonetheless, Harkins (who apparently uses the crib as his headquarters) applauds it vociferously from ringside and invites Wally to his table. There the latter overhears him confide to a subordinate, "The way to get old Jones's business is to buy up his pottery, and I believe he'd sell out for a dollar." Sensing the machinations that threaten his uncle, Wally racks his brain for some novelty that might stimulate sales, and evolves a repulsive line of containers with human faces he calls B-Jones B-Jugs. Uncle Enoch, betraying the one flicker of taste visible anywhere in the picture, quite properly refuses to countenance them, but, to rid himself of Wally's paranoid schemes, permits him to take over as traveling salesman. When Junie discovers her partner has doffed his leotards for commerce, she breaks their engagement in the best musical-comedy tradition, and Wally, approximately as grief-stricken as if a caraway seed had lodged in his teeth, exits nonchalantly to pursue his destiny. The temptation to emulate him pierced me like a knife. I half rose from my chair; then, detecting the projectionist's baleful eye fixed on me through the peephole of his booth, I twisted my features into a sickly placatory grin and sank back, resigned to perishing like a rat in a trap.

In the ensuing reel, Harkins, repeatedly bilked in his attempts to flimflam Uncle Enoch out of his pit, cunningly de-

cides to show the old gentleman the fleshpots, and inveigles him
to dinner at the cabaret. Junie has meanwhile found herself
another dancing partner, though still torchy for the Ragtime
Kid. The evening the new team is unveiled, Wally bursts in
unexpectedly—unexpected by the washroom boy, it would
seem, for nobody else exhibits surprise—and, shouldering aside
the interloper, struts a duet with Junie to universal acclaim.
Uncle Enoch fumbles on his glasses, recognizes his scapegrace
nephew, and once again thunders, "You're fired!" By some
process of reasoning I was too dense to comprehend, the revelation that he had been nurturing a gigolo determines Uncle
Enoch to sell out to Harkins. The two retire to a banquet room
to sign the necessary papers; there is the usual zabaione of
misgivings, phony legalities, and the fountain pen that runs
dry, and inevitably Wally comes bounding in with the cornucopia of orders he has garnered for B-Jones B-Jugs. Uncle
Enoch, exuberant, makes him a full partner on the spot, and
his competitor, after a token display of pique, proves that he
has a heart of gold under his knavish exterior. "We're beaten.
It serves us right," he says sheepishly. "All along we've been
calling him a dancin' fool and really he's a commercial whiz."
The butchery terminates with Wally imprinting a peck on his
sweetheart's cheek and declaring, with a brisk insincerity
guaranteed to reassure his female fans, "B'gosh, you're going
to be my little B'Junie, and b'join the B'Jug family."

You might suppose that a victim of such cinematic mayhem
would excite some measure of pity, and that when I reeled out
into Fifty-third Street and collided with a pair of elderly drag-
ons laden with Christmas shopping, I would have been ac-
corded a helping hand. On the contrary, both ladies recoiled
and gaped at me as though I were aswarm with caterpillars.
"Well!" snapped one of them, pursing her lips. "Pickled in the
middle of the afternoon, and in a museum, too. I always won-
dered what went on in there."

I removed my Borsalino and gave her as courteous a bow as I could muster. "If I told you what went on in there, Medusa," I said, "those dentures would drop out of your head. Did you ever hear of a dancing salesman named Ves Tibble—I mean an office boy called Wallace Reid?" Before I could adumbrate the plot, the two of them turned tail and streaked for Fifth Avenue. I worked over toward Sixth, found myself a cool, dark clinic with a sympathetic interne, and eventually managed to justify their diagnosis. What the hell, you might as well be hung for a sheep as for a lamb.

Next Week at the Prado:
Frankie Goya
Plus Monster Cast

☞

IT MUST HAVE BEEN about a quarter to four when I entere
Rumpelmayer's the other afternoon, and except for a pair c
spurious Hungarians crouched over their *Guglhupfe*, hissin
objurgations at Sir Alexander Korda, the place was empty c
customers. A headwaitress, all whalebone and basic blac
undulated in my direction, executed a crisp sergeant major
flourish toward a table reserved for pariahs, and dismissed m
with a venomous glare as I chose another, at dead center. M
request for cinnamon toast and tea engendered such disma
that I ordered a *Dobos Torte* I needed like a hole in the du
denum, but I figured that perhaps my friend Federbush mig

eat it when he arrived. He had always been an incurable pastry addict; I recalled how years before, while we were collaborating on *Mother Carey's Chiclets*, an abortive musical comedy based on a book by Kate Douglas Wiggin, he used to consume éclairs, napoleons, *petits fours*, and strudel by the trayful, and the fact he had proposed Rumpelmayer's for our reunion intimated that he was still on the starch.

Even so, I was unprepared for the moonfaced dumpling who presently spun out of the revolving door enveloped in a billowing balmacaan, a green velours dicer cocked on his head, and bore down on me with outspread arms. The duckbill nose and shoe-button eyes were still Federbush's, but fifteen years of lotus-eating in Hollywood had not made him any more ascetic. To put it conservatively, he had ballooned.

"Lover!" he sang out, enfolding me. "You look younger than springtime—exactly like the day we died in Wilmington! How the hell do you do it?"

"Well—er—you see, my face never changes," I replied evasively, "but there's this portrait of me that ages instead."

"And eventually we build to a dénouement where you stab the picture and are found dead beside it, a loathsome old man," he finished, tossing his coat at the waitress. "It's threadbare, kid. Oscar Wilde lifted it from Goethe, who copped it from Marlowe, who probably got it from the *Upanishads*. Anyway, you certainly don't look your age. If it wasn't for the bald spot, you could pass for a man of fifty-one."

"Gee, thanks," I said, with the sort of boyish twinkle Lon Chaney used to excel at. "You haven't changed either. Listen, what'll you have? I got you some pastry—you always liked it in the old days."

"Ancient history, my boy," he said tragically. "Shades of young men among the *mille-feuilles*. It's strictly fronds and hot water now—no more carbohydrates for me. One French cruller and I'm liable to drop in my tracks." He waved aside the menu the waitress was presenting and ordered two soda crackers and a cup of Ovaltine. Then, his lower lip atremble with nostalgia, he fell to musing over the past. Did I remember Dave's Blue Room, a delicatessen at the corner of Sixth Avenue and Washington Place along about 1926? "Boy, what groceries," he sighed. "That Dave was the Michelangelo of the sandwich world. I'll never forget the one he called the Dr. Flandina Reducing Special—goose liver, raisins, Swiss cheese, mangoes, poppyseed, and almond paste. Many's the night I'd stop in there on my way home to dinner and eat two of 'em. I was an iron man."

"You still are," I comforted him. "Anyone who's lasted as long as you in Hollywood must have the constitution of a yak."

"No more," he said. "I'm all shot—a bundle of nerves. Sometimes, after a day at the studio, I'm so hypertensed I can barely find my own Mercedes in the parking lot." Then he added thoughtfully, crumbling a saltine, "Yep, everything's different, here and out on the Coast, too. How long since you been in Hollywood?"

"Pretty near three years."

"You wouldn't know the place," said Federbush. "All those torpedoes who used to run the industry are gone; everybody's an aesthete. Nowadays, they only make two kinds of pictures there—encyclopedic Russian novels and biographies of famous artists. Take this *War and Peace* hassle, for instance. It's eighty-six years since Tolstoy published it and nobody once thought of turning it into a flicker. All of a sudden, four different impresarios are rushing it into production—Mike Todd, David Selznick, Metro-Goldwyn-Mayer, and an Italian team, Ponti-De Laurentiis, in association with Paramount. Both Todd and the ginzos claim that Marshal Tito promised them the Yugoslavian Army for their battle sequences, and they'll probably go to court about it. The other day, Stravinsky indignantly denies a statement by the Italians that he's doing their score. The word around Chasen's, however, is that Julie Styne has already written it on the q.t. That'll give you a dim inkling of what's going on."

"But why is everyone filming the same story?" I demanded.

"My argument precisely," said Federbush. "I said to one of those donkeys last week, 'Branch out, for Crisakes,' I said. 'Why don't you make some other Russian masterpiece for a change? A good lively musical of *Dead Souls*, let's say, with Piper Laurie and Tony Curtis.' Well, I was just hollering down a rain barrel. He never even heard of the property."

"The famous painters are my dish of tea, though," I said. "First Rembrandt, then Gauguin, then Toulouse-Lautrec. Now I read in the paper that M-G-M's busy on a life of van Gogh. You know, it isn't going to be easy persuading José Ferrer to slice off an ear."

"Personally, I doubt whether Ferrer's available for the role," said Federbush. "As soon as he's through being Mahatma Gandhi, he's scheduled to play Goya. Don't tell me you haven't heard about *that*." I confessed ignorance and sued for details. "It all started a few weeks back with Joseph L. Mankiewicz," he disclosed. "Right after he announced he was producing a life of Goya in Spain for United Artists. Within twenty-four hours, an Italian outfit named Titanus Films began squawking. According to them, they had planned the same thing for two years and were lining up Ferrer as Goya and Gina Lollobrigida as the Duchess of Alba. The payoff, though, is that neither Mankiewicz or these jokers know about the third version."

"Which is what?" I asked, confused.

"The one *I've* been working on under cover," he replied, removing a cigar from a small aluminum dirigible. "Keep it dark, but I'm readying a sensational Goya script using these same two mummers. The only difference is in mine Lollobrigida plays Goya and José Ferrer is the Duchess."

"Rather revolutionary casting, isn't that?" I ventured.

"Not necessarily," said Federbush. "Ferrer has impersonated

women before. Don't you remember him in *Charley's Aunt?* That was how I got the idea. . . . Why, don't you like it?"

"Oh, sure, sure," I said quickly. "I was merely wondering whether you wouldn't lose—ah—certain romantic overtones by transposing the sex of the characters."

"Don't be obtuse," he returned. "Basically it's still the same story—two people overwhelmed by a reckless tidal wave of passion which it snaps its fingers at the petty-bourgeois standards of the time."

"Only the girl happens to be a Spanish court painter and the boy's a duchess," I said reflectively.

"Correct," said Federbush. "After all, how many people in your audience know whether Goya was a man or a woman in the first place?" His face became animated. "The beauty of my setup is that one sizzling situation piles on top of the next. Like when Goya—that is, Lollobrigida—is painting the Duke of Wellington. All of a sudden, the bluff old war dog digs the fact that his limner is a woman—a beautiful, desirable woman—and he makes a pass. As she's struggling and pleading for mercy—"

"Wait a minute," I broke in. "Why does she struggle?"

"For conflict, goddam it," snapped Federbush. "If she didn't, you wouldn't have any picture. Don't interrupt me . . . So while she's pushing over taborets and refectory tables to stem his advances, we cut to Ferrer in a lavish suite of the ducal palace, all dittied out in a black lace mantilla and surrounded by these scantily clad duennas that they're ministering to his wants. Naturally, they never dream the Duchess is a man, which of course opens up a myriad opportunities for good hoke comedy and maybe even a tug at the heartstrings. Anyway, some powerful empathy between the lovers warns Ferrer that his sweetheart Goya is in jeopardy. He hastens to her studio, arriving just as Wellington is rendering apart her smock, and we climax with a battle royal wherein José kayoes the Iron Duke."

"Sounds plausible," I said. "How are you handling the busi-

ness of the two portraits? I mean the study of her in the nude
and the one Goya painted to show her husband."

"That incident, candidly, I had to drop," he admitted candidly. "It didn't fit in with my approach. Between you and me
and the Breen office, I don't think the world is thirsting for a
shot of José Ferrer naked on a bearskin rug. When he was six
months old, yes, but not now."

"Well," I said. "To be honest, I can't quite visualize Lollobrigida as an Old Master, but I suppose all those wars and bull-
fights and court intrigues Goya was mixed up in offer lots of
scope for drama."

"Brother, you can embroider that on a sampler," said Federbush warmly. "One of my most gripping scenes is where she
defies the command of Charles IV to use egg tempera on the
famous portrait of the royal family. 'Sire,' she says, flinging
aside her maulstick and drawing herself up proudly. 'You may
swing me from yon gibbet, break me on the wheel, suffer crows
to peck out mine eyes, but by my maidenhead, I shall never
use egg tempera.' That sequence is pure TNT, if I say so myself. By the way, what *is* egg tempera?"

"Search me," I replied. "But before it gets to celluloid, you'd
better do some fast research at the Art Students League."

"Ach, it don't matter," he said carelessly. "It's the sense of
the thing I'm after—the clash of wills. What really bothers me
is how to end the story. I wanted to have the two of them going
away to Tahiti to begin a new life together, but I'm not so sure
it's believable."

"No, it seems out of key with the rest of it," I agreed. "Have
you hit on a title yet? You mentioned the Iron Duke a second
ago. How about *The Tinfoil Duchess?*"

Federbush shook his head. "Uh-uh," he said. "It has to evoke
Goya's work somehow—you know what I mean? For the time
being, I'm calling it *The Disasters of the Heart.*"

"I'll buy that," I said. "Yes sirree, I'll underwrite that." I arose and extended my hand. "Well, Jacques," I said. "I hate to run, but I promised to pick up my wife at a *vernissage* at five, and she ought to be nearly dry by now."

"It's been a treat," said Federbush simply. "I needn't tell you that if you ever come out to the Coast—"

"And I needn't tell you that if you ever come East again—" I echoed.

We left it like that, neither of us predicting what might happen. With people like Federbush and me, almost everything is tacit. Or will be from now on. You can lay money on that.

I'll Always Call You Schnorrer, My African Explorer

BORNE ON THE NORTHEAST GALE that had whipped Narragansett Bay into icy froth all through a February night in 1916, a freezing rain beat down relentlessly on Westminster Street, main artery and Rue de la Paix of Providence, Rhode Island. Inside the box office of the Keith-Albee Theater, the town's principal vaudeville stand, the house manager gnawed his nails and stared glumly at a rackful of unsold tickets. It was almost three o'clock; there were seventeen patrons out front, five of them cuffed in on Annie Oakleys, and the curtain had been up half an hour on the most disastrous matinée in the history of show business. Just as he was preparing to issue forth to Farcher's drugstore and end it all with two minims of prussic acid, a curious homuncule scurried into the lobby. He wore a reach-me-down mackinaw, a pair of mismated overshoes, and a yellow sou'wester by courtesy of Scott's Emulsion, and his twelve-year-old face—if, indeed, it could be so dignified—was beef-red with excitement.

"The holley had a trot-box!" he panted. "I mean, the trolley had a hatbox—I had to run all the way from Chalkstone Avenue! Are they on yet?"

"Is who on?" growled the manager, surreptitiously burning a pastille to neutralize any infection around his wicket.

"The head-hunters," the other babbled. "I mean, the head-liners—the Four Marx Brothers in their sidesplitting extravaganza, *Home Again*, a funfest for young and old." Before the showman could produce his vouchsafer and vouchsafe a reply, the youth had fumbled a knotted bandanna from his jumper and spilled out a cache of greasy nickels. Then, snatching a ticket, he bounded up the stairs to the peanut gallery.

To recall with any degree of clarity the acts I saw on gaining my balcony perch would, of course, be impossible across the gulf of thirty-six years. Out of the haze of memory, however, I remember Fink's Trained Mules, Willie West & McGinty in their deathless housebuilding routine, Lieutenant Gitz-Rice declaiming "Mandalay" through a pharynx swollen with emotion and coryza, and that liveliest of nightingales, Grace Larue. All these, though, were mere appetizers for the roast. The *mise en scène* of the Marx Brothers piece was the Cunard docks in New York, an illusion conveyed by four battered satchels and a sleazy backdrop purportedly representing the gangway of the *Britannic*. Garbed in his time-honored claw-hammer coat, his eyes shifting lickerishly behind his specs and an unlit perfecto in his teeth, Groucho irrupted onstage accompanied by his presumptive wife, a scraggy termagant in a feather boa. Behind him came Gummo, impersonating his cocksure son, and Harpo and Chico, a pair of shipboard cronies. Groucho's initial speech set the flavor of the proceedings.

"Well, friends," he observed, stifling a belch, "next time I cross the ocean, I'll take a train. I'm certainly glad to set my feet on terra firma. Now I know that when I eat something, I won't see it again." This earthy confidence, understandably, evoked a paroxysm from the audience (a small paroxysm, to be sure, in view of its size), and Groucho began to expand on his trip abroad. Heckled at almost every turn by Gummo, he at length remarked waspishly, "Nowadays you don't know how much you know until your children grow up and tell you how much you don't know." According to Groucho, no pundit has ever been able to explain exactly what the foregoing meant or why it always elicited cheers and applause; apparently the customers sensed some deep undercurrent of folk wisdom he himself was unaware of. At any rate, after considerable horseplay in which Harpo disgorged the entire ship's cutlery from his sleeves and inspected the lingerie of several *zoftick* fellow passengers, Chico approached Groucho with hand extended.

"I'd like-a to say goombye to your wife," he proposed, in what was unquestionably the paltriest dialect ever heard off Mulberry Street.

"Who wouldn't?" riposted his brother. This boffo ushered in the second scene, laid without any tiresome logical transition at Groucho's villa on the Hudson. The plot structure, to be candid, was sheerest gossamer; vague reference was made to a stolen chafing dish, necessitating a vigorous search by Harpo of the corsages of two showgirls drifting unaccountably about the premises, but on the whole there were few nuances. Following a rather soupy rendition of "The World is Waiting for the Sunrise" by Harpo, Chico played "Chopsticks" on the piano with grueling archness, and the pair exited rear stage left in a papier-mâché boat on wheels, knocking down three members of the troupe. Those who remained thereupon joined in a stylish chorale entitled "Over the Alpine Mountains E'er So Far Away," and, as the orchestra segued into von Suppé's "Light Cavalry Overture" to herald the acrobats, I descended to

Farcher's Drugstore for a double banana split with maxixe cherries.

The years slipped away in their usual fleet fashion, leaving an impressive residue of silver in the hair and none whatever in the pocket. I heard no more of Groucho and his tatterdemalion crew, and I assumed they had drifted into some other field where their inadequacies handicapped them less. What was my surprise, therefore, to receive a long-distance call not long ago from Groucho in Hollywood.

"Well, well," I said encouragingly, "and what are you doing now? Working in some sort of restaurant or garage?"

"The deuce I am," he sneered. "I'm on Main Street now. I'm making a flick with William Bendix and Marie Wilson, and what's more," he added boastfully, "I've got my own radio and television show."

"Of course you have," I said soothingly. "What's afoot?"

"Well," he said. "I was just thinking it's time you came out of your shell. You're bored, restless, fed up with civilization and its hollow pretense—right?" I had to admit he had divined my mood. "Then why not fly out for a couple of days with me— at your own expense, of course? If you want to see unspoiled, primitive people, we've got some here who've just begun to walk erect."

"M-m-m," I said reflectively. "It does sound appealing, but I can't get away. There's my secretary, for one thing." I'd acquired an absolute whiz of a typist shortly before, kind of a younger Boots Mallory, and the problem of how to keep the child off my lap wrung my withers, word of honor.

"Couldn't you stand up and dump her off?" he suggested. It was typical of the man's audacious imagination, his refusal to bow to convention, that he should go straight to the core of things. Within forty-eight hours I had severed my obligations and was disembarking at the Los Angeles airport, and within another twenty-four, had reached the film colony. Slightly unsteadied by a cup of puréed avocado and a chickenfurter, I betook myself to R-K-O, where Marx was filming *A Girl in Every Port.* The set to which I was directed, a faithful replica of a battleship, hummed with activity; hordes of extras in navy blue were absorbed in scratch sheets, electricians on all sides feverishly worked to draw inside straights, and high on a camera parallel, two associate producers, arms clasped about each other, were busily examining their pelts for fleas. Groucho, as was his wont, was in the very thick of the melee. He was sprawled blissfully in a director's chair, having his vertebrae massaged by Marie Wilson, a young lady whose natural endowment caused a perceptible singing in the ears. I promptly drew up a chair next to her and confided that I too was suffering from a touch of sacroiliac, but the fair masseuse appeared to be hard of hearing.

"Did you bring any coffee with you?" demanded Groucho abruptly. I asked whether he realized that I had just flown across the country. He countered with a peevish snort. "That's neither here nor there," he snapped. "Anybody with a smidgen of decency would have brought me a cup of coffee from Lindy's. The stuff out here's pure slop."

"Then why do you stay here?"

"Where else can you get Marie Wilson to rub your back?" he asked. "A little lower down, dear—there, that's better."

"I haven't met the young lady yet," I remarked pointedly.

"No, and you're not likely to, you sneak," he retorted. "I know when I'm well off. Well, what's the chatter on Broadway?" In a few incisive phrases, I summed up recent developments there, such as Olga Nethersole's resounding success in *Sappho*, the razing of Hammerstein's Victoria, and the emergence of A. Toxen Worm as leading drama critic, and, to bolster his spirits, revealed that Milton Berle's TV show had a much larger following than his own. He was visibly pleased. "Let's get together before you leave town," he said, wringing my hand warmly. "I'd like you to poison some moles in my lawn." At this juncture, the lunch gong pealed, and leaving an effigy of himself with

Miss Wilson to rub until his return, Groucho bore me off to the commissary. His outsize Corona and eyeglasses were somewhat at variance with his nautical dress, but he lent a maritime tang to the meal by snarling out an occasional "Belay there, ye scut" and dancing a hornpipe with the waitress. Bendix, also clad in sailor suit, spent the lunch chewing meditatively on the foreleg of an Angus steer. He is a hearty trencherman, as befits a man of his girth, and has been known to consume a firkin of butter and a hectare of gherkins in less time than it takes to say "Bo" to a goose.

"You know, Mr. Bendix," I said enviously. "It must be hilarious, making a movie with a topflight comedian."

"Yeah," he agreed. "I'd love to do it some day."

"But I—I don't understand," I persisted. "You must roll on the floor when he gets off those repartees of his."

"Who's that?" he queried, detaching his eyes slowly from the steer. I indicated his co-star. He masticated pensively for a moment. "It's a living," he grunted. During our exchange, Groucho had seized the opportunity to couple his check with mine. On my expostulating, he unleashed such a torrent of sniveling and abuse that I finally paid in disgust. The mercurial temperament thrives on petty triumphs; at once he became ardent, solicitous of my welfare, determined to accord me every hospitality.

"Now listen," he said forcefully. "From here in, it's strictly my treat. What about dinner at my place and a night ball game afterward?" I agreed readily, and he pondered. "Where are your grips?"

"I left them with the cop at the main gate."

"Good," he said. "I've got a big, roomy house out in Beverly. Pick up the bags and take them to Schwabacher's used-car lot on Exposition Boulevard. You can sleep for nothing in one of their old jalopies."

"I have to clean up, take a shower," I protested feebly.

"Who takes a shower to go to a ball game?" he asked with

irritation. "Lot of cheap swank." He scribbled on a card. "O.K., give this to my maid and she'll let you in the bathroom, but take it easy on the hot water—I'm not made of money. Did you bring a towel?"

"Only a fiber one I muckled from the plane."

"We-e-ll," he said grudgingly, "I guess we can loan you one, providing you sign for it. See you later, then; dinner at seven sharp." As I moved toward the door of the commissary, I felt myself the cynosure of countless envying eyes. A great star had bared his heart to me. What idiosyncrasies, what foibles I could divulge were I not bound by the journalist's sacred code. But my lips were sealed, and if Groucho's cuisine was as toxic as I anticipated, it would be worth my life to open them even a fraction.

At seven-thirty that evening, in the playroom of a repossessed hacienda on Hillcrest Drive, a couple of middle-aged gallants racked with sciatica descended painfully from their bar stools and linked arms with two statuesque actresses. The mood of the quartet was distinctly festive; tongues loosened by copious draughts of loganberry cocktails, their flushed cheeks and sparkling eyes marked them incontrovertibly as devotees of Bacchus.

"Shay, Groucho," I hiccoughed. "Thish a grea' party. Le'sh not go ball game; le'sh have s'more logleberry cocktails. Wha' shay, girls?" My host quickly snatched an aquarium from my path and threw open the door of the dining room.

"Bring him in here and we'll get some grub into him," he directed. "Watch out—he's scraping the piano."

"That's not all he's scraping," muttered my partner, disentangling my arm from her waist. "Where'd you find this crumb, anyway?"

"On the old Fall River Line," said Groucho plausibly. "Used to be a whitewing, I think. I gave him a lavish tip and he's been bleeding me ever since." He propped me up in a chair and retired to a side table to carve the roast. Inwardly I smiled a

197

small, secret smile. My ruse was working perfectly; beneath a seemingly tipsy exterior, I was razor-keen, studying them as objectively as specimens under a microscope.

"You're too softhearted, Groucho," chided Queenie, the more buxom of the duo, thoughtfully crumbling her roll. "Silly boy, why do you leave grifters like this milk you? You need a woman to take care of you." Groucho was immediately all ears, so much so that he almost sliced one of them off.

"That's what I was just thinking," he said, swiftly circling the table. "What did you have in mind?"

"Oh, I don't know," she said coyly.

"You *don't?*" he demanded, rounding on her. "Then what do you mean by teasing me to the brink of madness, mocking me with a mouth like a scarlet hound?" He flung aside his knife with a bitter laugh. "Do you know what it means to stand here night after night, sawing away at a cheap pot roast and thirsting for a coquette's kisses?"

"Hey, this meat is awful dry," complained Chiquita, our other dryad. "Isn't there any gravy?"

"Gravy, gravy!" shouted Groucho. "Everybody wants gravy! Did those six poor slobs on the *Kon-Tiki* have any gravy? Did Scipio's legions, deep in the burning African waste, have gravy? Did Fanny Hill?"

"Did Fanny Hill what?" I asked.

"Never mind, you cad," he threw at me. "I'm sick to death of innuendo, brittle small talk, the sly, silken rustle of feminine underthings. I want to sit in a ball park with the wind in my hair and breathe cold, clean popcorn into my lungs. I want to hear the crack of seasoned ash on horsehide, the roar of the hydra-headed crowd, the umpire's deep-throated 'Play ball!'" So graphically had he limned the color and excitement of the game that the three of us hung there with shining eyes, too rapt even to spurn the paper-thin, parsimonious slices of meat he had served us.

"Golly!" breathed Chiquita. "I feel like as though I had really witnessed the game!"

"So do I," said Groucho, yawning, "and I'm pooped. I'll thank you two harpies to clear out and take that lush with you. I've got to be on the set at eight." Courtly as one of George Cable's antebellum planters, he stood in the doorway and waved us farewell. I turned from the curb for a last glimpse of him, and somehow it seemed to me his gesture of parting had a peculiar tremulous quality. I looked again; yes, he was scratching himself. I called to him, but already his thoughts were far away, intent on the copy of the *Partisan Review* with which he invariably concluded his day. Softly I tiptoed out into the smog.

"ALL RIGHT, settle down, everybody—this is a take!" bawled the director. "Hit the wind machine, and remember, Groucho, bend down into his ear and plead with him." A hush fell over the turbulent sound stage, technicians exchanged a last crisp monosyllable, and the transparency screen behind the set lit up to reveal half a dozen race horses plunging toward us. In front of them, in jockey's silks, sat Marx and Bendix on two amazingly lifelike steeds molded of rubber. As the machinery underneath them began churning, the horses came alive; their necks elongated, manes and tails streamed in the breeze, muscles rippled in their flanks and bellies. The riders plied their mounts with whip and endearments, straining forward into the camera to steal the scene from each other.

"Cost twenty-five grand to build those bang-tails," the producer confided to me in the darkness. "We rent the pair of 'em for five hundred a day. But it's worth it. When they go to see the picture, they'll swear it's a real horse race."

"What happens if they don't go to see the picture?" I asked, fascinated. He turned deathly pale, and excusing himself, stumbled off to the studio psychiatrist. A few minutes afterward, rid of his makeup and in jaunty spirits, Groucho met me at the door of his dressing room. The picture was finished, and he was at last free to resume his passionate avocation, the collecting and cross-fertilization of various kinds of money. To celebrate its completion, he had suggested a final lunch at Romanoff's. Over our risotto, I inquired about his future plans.

"Who knows?" His smile was charming, and seeing his teeth, one would have sworn they were real. "I shall, of course, travel; I do think travel tends to broaden, don't you? Marriage? No, I hardly think so. Babies? No, I hardly think so."

"Chutney?" put in the waiter.

"No, I hardly think so," said Groucho. "Wait a minute—that comes with the *plat du jour*. Give me a double portion, and I'll take some home in a bag."

"What advice would you give a young person just starting out in the theater?" I asked.

He ruminated awhile, and his face softened.

"You know what I'd say?" he mused. "I'd take that young girl by the shoulders, I honestly would, and I'd say, 'Honey——'" He looked up alertly as Marilyn Monroe, in a diaphanous pink blouse, passed the table bound for a rear booth. There was a sudden uprush of air beside me, and a scant fifty minutes later he returned, wry bewilderment on his countenance. "Talk about coincidence," he marveled. "It seems that kid was just starting out in the theater, too, and she asked me the very same thing."

"What did you tell her?"

"Oh, just trivialities." He coughed. "Naturally, in so brief an encounter, I didn't get a chance to grapple with her particular problems. We're meeting at the Mocambo tonight to discuss them further."

"Well, Groucho," I said huskily, reaching for my hat, "it may sound fulsome, but I can testify you've got a heart as big as all outdoors. If you ever come to Bucks County, there'll always be an extra bed for you at the George S. Kaufmans'."

"My boy," he said, and his voice shook slightly, "a very wise old man once said that there are two things money cannot buy—nostalgia and friendship. He died in the poorhouse. Don't forget to square that tab on the way out." He gripped my hand hard and was gone, a gallant freebooter who had made his rendezvous with Destiny. As his skulking, predatory figure faded from view, I bowed my head in tribute. "Adieu, Quackenbush," I whispered. "Adieu, Captain Spaulding. No man ever buckled a better swash." Then, through a mist of tears, I soberly signed his name to the check and went forth to a workaday world.

One Comely Babe,
Piping Hot

IT MAY SEEM startling put into words, but it was a matter of
common knowledge to any wide-awake youth in New England
about 1920 that millionaire orgies were frequently held in Paris,
France, at which naked showgirls emerged from pies. The self-
same youth, under prodding—and often quite gratuitously—
could reveal a wealth of other odd and absorbing information—
for instance, that the ownership of famous gems like the Hope
diamond, the Kohinoor, or the Cullinan entailed almost certain
disaster; that astronomers had established the presence of
canals on Mars, clearly the work of sentient beings; that domestic felicity was rare among New York society's "400"; that
brutal Cossacks busied themselves in the dungeons of the Cheka
knouting their beautiful White Russian captives; that the eyes
of a common housefly, magnified to the size of the Woolworth

Building, had myriad facets; and that an Indian maharajah had climaxed a fabulous dinner at Monte Carlo by circulating liqueurs to his guests on a toy train of solid gold, operating on silver tracks.

The origin of all this folklore, of course, was the Sunday supplement of the Boston *American*, which compounded sin and science into such a heady negus that it has taken me nearly four decades to sober up. While I still horripilate pleasurably every so often at the memory of *Secrets of the Sureté*, by H. Ashton-Wolfe, or that perennial favorite, the Hindu fakir palpitating on his bed of nails, the voodoo of Mr. Hearst's kerosene-scented pages has pretty well receded—or so I thought until recently, when his most hallowed legend popped up to confront me. It appeared in a treatise on Victorian morals by Cyril Pearl, published here several months ago, called *The Girl with the Swansdown Seat*. Discussing a widely celebrated courtesan named Cora Pearl, who I gather was no relative, the author had this to say: "Money from vaults that seemed inexhaustible showered on her bed; she was burdened with jewels; her apartments were crammed with a muddle of treasures and rubbish, Boule, ormolu, gilt, tapestries, mirrors, bronzes, such as one encounters in a stall at the Flea Market; she danced a cancan on a carpet of orchids and bathed before her guests in a silver bathtub filled with champagne. . . . She would spend £500 on a dinner for twenty men, and sometimes, the chroniclers say, offer herself as the *plat du jour*, naked, on a silver platter in a large pie." Evidently, Mr. Pearl sensed a need to amplify about so unique an entrée, because he went on animatedly: "Many gourmets claim to have encountered this unusual dish. The Marquis de Vellavieja described it to his cousin the Baroness de Stoeckel, wife of a Russian Minister to Washington. He was dining *chez* Cora, when—'the door flew open and four footmen in her livery brought in a life-size dish with a cover. They placed this in the middle of the long table and on taking off the cover there lay Cora Pearl nude. . . . She had such a wonderful figure . . . that all the guests gasped with admiration. . . .'" Nor was this penchant for tureens, it appears, an idiosyncrasy of Cora's alone. "La Belle Otero," expatiated Mr. Pearl, "claims in her autobiography that she was served thus at a banquet at St. Petersburg, for the diversion of some Russian officers who fell on their knees before the beauty of the spectacle, and the American cotton king MacFadden is reported to have ordered a similar *bonne bouche* at Maxim's, with the refinement of having the naked girl served in a delicate pink sauce."

As the reader sponges the saliva from his neckerchief and, fortified by a pinch of yohimbin, reflects on the foregoing, he may find himself, as I did, a prey to perplexity. Granted the boundless ingenuity and resources of the chefs involved, it must have been no minor engineering feat to assemble a pastry with an *au-naturel* filling. One wonders, pardonably, how much shortening and flour these delicacies required, how the ladies inside protected against asphyxiation, and whether the kitchen staff was temporarily blindfolded while at work or, in buccaneer fashion, put to the sword afterward. Where do you buy those life-size dishes, with covers, that Cora Pearl reposed in, and how do you serve them up with dexterity and *élan* at the critical instant? Lacking a ouija board powerful enough to communicate with the roisterers themselves, we might fall back on —or at least lean against—the following dramatic exegesis in a contemporary setting, highly unsuitable for production in public schools. Douse the lights, someone, and if any Nosy Parkers start asking questions, tell 'em we're conducting a séance.

SCENE, *the combination workshop and scenery loft of Susscraft Studios, builders of stage settings, theatrical props, department-store displays, and similar ephemera. A thunderous cavern in what seems to be anarchic disorder, the shop is actually a hive of disciplined activity. Half a dozen painters on a scaffold at rear labor over a backdrop representing medieval battlements for a play which, unfortunately, has folded the previous night in New Haven. Another pair, armed with spray guns, are frosting the roof of a transparent igloo, commissioned for his Christmas windows by a clothier who, excluding a miracle, will be in receivership long before then. A chair and table roughly thirteen feet high—the Gargantuan type of furniture employed in dream sequences to make actors look like pygmies —is being sanded by a craftsman on a stepladder; several other artisans are occupied in festooning Daliesque lobsters with watches and men's garters, in assembling manikins whose heads consist of spirals of wire or wicker, and in kindred weighty pursuits. As the curtain rises, Wagnerian, the foreman of the shop, is hunched over a set of blueprints downstage, frowning and chewing a cigar. Lapwing, a scenic designer, regards him impatiently.*

LAPWING: What's so complicated about it? It's just an ordinary Byzantine palace staircase, with a giant candelabrum on each side.

WAGNERIAN: I know, but where the hell will I find the mother-of-pearl you want for these steps?

LAPWING: Call up a button factory, or a jewelry-supply house. All we need is fifty or sixty yards.

WAGNERIAN: Hmm. That could run into money.

LAPWING: What difference does it make? Nobody's going to be paid anyway.

WAGNERIAN: Yeah, I guess you're right. O.K., you'll have it in time for your opening in Wilmington. (*As Lapwing turns to go*) By the way—if they decide to cut this scene out of the show, will somebody give us a ring?

LAPWING: Well. I'm pretty busy, but I'll try to remember. (*He exits. As Wagnerian furls the blueprints and lights his cigar stump, Susskind, chief of the organization, enters. He is a wan, harassed individual with a distended nostril and a briefcase to match, earmarked for misfortune from birth.*)

SUSSKIND: My God, isn't that igloo finished yet? I promised it last Tuesday!

WAGNERIAN: I told you, Mr. Susskind—it's the door that held us up. If we make it big enough for a person to enter without stooping—

SUSSKIND: You don't have to. They decided to use a midget Santa Claus.

WAGNERIAN: But how can he get the reindeer in, like you said?

SUSSKIND: They'll be fox terriers, with little antlers taped on. . . . And speaking of dogs, we're in a fine jam over that St. Bernard suit of yours—the one Rusty Gulliver's wearing in *Tickle Me Pink*. The head caught fire again in his dressing room last night.

WAGNERIAN: I warned him not to smoke in it. He knew we couldn't flameproof the ears.

SUSSKIND: Well, he wasn't badly scorched, but you know actors. By the time he walks into Sardi's, he'll look like Claude Rains in *The Invisible Man*. I won't collect a dime from that production. (*Miss Bechtel, his secretary, appears, followed by two gentlemen of executive bearing in costly Homburgs. She mutely indicates her employer and withdraws.*)

FIRST GENTLEMAN: How do you do, sir? My name's Hennepin, and this is my colleague, Mr. Poteat. I believe we talked with you on the phone some weeks ago in regard to a—harumph—a testimonial pie?

SUSSKIND (*blinking*): Come again?

POTEAT: You remember, the life-size pie for the banquet honoring Mr. Floyd Geduldig, our associate in the utilities field.

SUSSKIND (*a light dawns*): Oh, yes, now I dig you. Well, it's almost ready—and let me tell you, it was a devil of a job to build without specifications. Am I right, Wagnerian?

WAGNERIAN: I'll say. The whole thing was guesswork. Nobody told us how much the dame inside's gonna weigh—what her measurements are—

HENNEPIN (*nervously*): No doubt, no doubt. However, in such a delicate matter, you can't very well expect us to put anything on paper. The slightest breath of scandal—

SUSSKIND: What's scandalous? You're throwing a feed where a bimbo comes out of a pie. Whose business is that?

POTEAT: Ha ha—quite—of course. May we have a look at what you've done?

SUSSKIND: Sure. Right over here. (*Dismissing Wagnerian with a wave, he crosses to a tarpaulin-shrouded object at left, whisks off the canvas, and discloses an oval terrine the size of a small dory, covered with papier-mâché crust, reposing on a couple of sawhorses.*) There you are, gents. Pretty nifty, isn't it?

HENNEPIN (*his face clouding over*): Um . . . Frankly, I envisioned something a good deal smaller.

POTEAT: So did I. Like a—well, like a large *vol-au-vent*, about three feet in diameter.

SUSSKIND: Three *feet*? (*Whipping out a pocket rule*) Listen, Jack, I don't know how *zoftick* this party you got in mind is, but even now, she'll have trouble squeezing in—

HENNEPIN (*overriding him*): And another thing. Didn't we agree you were to furnish us with a genuine biscuit crust—of real pastry?

SUSSKIND: Yes, but you overlooked one little point. How's anybody going to pop out of here on cue if they're sealed in by ninety pounds of dough reinforced with chicken wire?

POTEAT: I see his objection, Hennepin—it does sound a bit unwieldy. Will this cover of yours lift off readily?

SUSSKIND (*with a superior smile*): Watch. (*He presses a button and the crust jackknifes upward like a clamshell, revealing a torsion spring within at the further end.*) Easy as rolling off a log, hey?

HENNEPIN: Very ingenious, but suppose it fails to respond at the psychological moment, when everyone's on tenterhooks?

SUSSKIND: What do you mean? You saw it open just now, didn't you?

POTEAT: Still, if something went wrong—if the mechanism jammed and the—er—young person didn't emerge, we'd have a dismal anticlimax.

HENNEPIN: Not to speak of a nice little lawsuit.

SUSSKIND (*bristling*): Look here, my friend, when I give you a personal guarantee that a prop of mine will work—

HENNEPIN: I'm afraid that's hardly sufficient. This banquet's taken a lot of organizing, Mr. Susskind, and we've got to safeguard every detail.

SUSSKIND (*overwrought*): Crisakes, what do you want me to do—get inside and demonstrate it for you?

POTEAT: Oh, come, come, no need to lose our tempers— (*Susskind, lips compressed, strips off his jacket, and quivering with indignation, clambers into the terrine.*) Really, Mr. Susskind, nobody was questioning your integrity. . . .

SUSSKIND (*curling up*): Pull down the cover. Go ahead, never mind the schmoos—pull it down! (*His clients exchange doubtful glances; then Poteat, with a shrug, complies. He is just about to press the release button when Hennepin stops him.*)

HENNEPIN: Wait a second, Malcolm. I wonder if we haven't gone off half-cocked.

POTEAT: I don't follow you.

HENNEPIN: I mean the whole idea of a testimonial dinner, with speeches and entertainment and all that nonsense. Doesn't it seem awfully ostentatious, on second thought?

POTEAT (*ruminating*): Well, it *could* make for very poor public relations, coming at a time when we've just raised our rates.

HENNEPIN: Precisely. Why not salute Floyd Geduldig's achievement in a more simple, dignified manner—with a handsome onyx desk set, say, or a nice traveling clock? (*Susskind's voice, calling some muffled request, is heard from inside the terrine.*) I suggest we go up to Mark Cross without further ado—

POTEAT (*uncertainly*): But hadn't we better let this chap out of there?

HENNEPIN: What for? He's got plenty of air—look at that row of holes around the edge.

POTEAT: Just the same, I imagine he'd like some token payment for the pie—

HENNEPIN (*taking his arm*): Now don't get sentimental, Poteat. (*Sleekly*) After all, it's not as though we put anything on paper, did we? (*They exit. A stifled bellow, accompanied by hammering, proceeds from the terrine, and it rocks on the sawhorses. A moment or two later, Wagnerian enters, absorbed in another blueprint, and collides with Miss Bechtel hurrying in.*)

MISS BECHTEL: Where's the boss?

WAGNERIAN: Knocking around here somewhere. Why?

MISS BECHTEL: A water main just burst at the Gaiety in Philly, all over the scenery. It's a total loss.

WAGNERIAN: How'd you find out?

MISS BECHTEL: The way we generally do. The producers stopped our check.

WAGNERIAN (*philosophically*): Well, that's the theater for you. There's no spot those guys can't wriggle out of.

MISS BECHTEL: That's what I'm always telling Mr. Susskind. You've got to be a regular Houdini to stay in business today. (*As they go their separate ways, leaving Susskind to unravel his dubious destiny—*)

CURTAIN

CLOUDLAND REVISITED:

"M" Is for the Migraine
That She Gave Me

If, in the tradition of *Asmodeus, or The Devil on Two Sticks,* you and the Prince of Darkness had happened to be flapping around over Sheridan Square one chill December evening in 1925, rubbering down at the human spectacle below, you might have seen the present writer bent over a drawing board in his hall bedroom, laboriously inking in a comic sketch. It portrayed a distraught gentleman careering into a doctor's office, clutching a friend by the wrist and whimpering, "I've got Bright's disease and he has mine." How I had gravitated into this seedy locale, to subsist meanly on a pittance from a humorous weekly that rejected everything I drew, is not especially germane, yet, by and large, my lot did not seem to me

210

insupportable. The temperature of the cubicle was subarctic, the pens and brushes kept fouling in the quilt draped over my head, and a week thence I was fated to collapse with scurvy from living exclusively on crullers, but I hummed a little song as I worked. Parnassus, I had convinced myself by incredible sophistry, was just over the next rise, and my tendons were not even fluttering.

At any rate, I had blown a layer of fixative over my handiwork and was holding it off at arm's length to admire it when I heard the sound of a woman's sobs issuing through the wall of the room adjoining. So piercing was her woe, fraught with such immediacy and heartbreak, that I sat aghast. The voice, I knew, was that of Ivy Spicer, a chlorotic, auburn-haired graduate of Mount Holyoke who earned her cakes editing the society page of a Newark morning newspaper and wrote alexandrines on the side. In our few encounters, I had found her pretentious, too often addicted to the Gioconda smile and the quotation from James Elroy Flecker, but she was obviously *in extremis* now and I reacted as Jeffery Farnol would have wanted me to. Sprinting out into the hall, I beat a hasty tattoo on her door and entered. Ivy, enveloped in a Japanese kimono and obi that had probably belonged to Lafcadio Hearn, lay sprawled on a day bed, weeping convulsively. The candlelit room was heavy with the odor of sandalwood and there was no lack of icons.

"G-go way," she snuffled in response to my overtures. "You're a nasty little hypocrite, like all the rest of them." Interpreting her words as those of a woman betrayed, I declared with as much dignity as the quilt over my head permitted that I, for one, was not given to seducing ladies and abandoning them. Instantly, Ivy's sorrow changed to exasperation. "What are you foompheting about, you idiot?" she snarled. "I'm not crying over any man. I just saw *Stella Dallas*." She then made it clear, as if addressing a Queensland aborigine, that the movie of that title, unknown to me, was a masterpiece second only to the *Götterdämmerung*, and its star, Belle Bennett, the greatest tragedienne since Clara Kimball Young. Luckily, before she could recount the plot some sixth sense warned our landlady, an incorrigible snooper, that two lodgers of opposite sex were fraternizing abovestairs behind a closed door, and she began ululating outside. I made my retreat by the fire escape, and subsequently, when I could afford a visa to cross Fourteenth Street, went to see the picture. Its effect, I had to admit, was cataclysmic. Blinded by scalding tears, I groped my way downtown and confessed to Ivy that she was right. I got precisely what I deserved. She deadpanned me, and, observing that my taste was execrable, enjoined me to read James Elroy Flecker.

As ONE WAY of outwitting bailiffs and remaining incommunicado for a spell from the tensions of existence, I recently slipped into a projection room at the Museum of Modern Art, where, by a coincidence, *Stella Dallas* was being screened. Lacking a notebook, I jotted down on the film curator's collar some memoranda which he has kindly allowed me to transcribe before sending it to the Chinaman. If they seem slightly incoherent, I can only plead that they were written in the dark on a slick celluloid surface and that the wearer kept squirming around in the most inexplicable fashion. Perhaps he had caught his pinkie in the spring mechanism of his chair, or possibly he had seen the picture before. It comes to about the same thing.

Ostensibly, *Stella Dallas* treats of mother love and the tremendous self-sacrifice it is legendarily capable of; actually, it is the story—told with a degree of mawkishness such as only three virtuosi of bathos like Samuel Goldwyn, Henry King, and Frances Marion were capable of—of a vulgar, ostentatious woman who bedevils her husband and daughter so relentlessly that she loses them both. Unfortunately, whatever twisted satisfaction one might derive from this payoff cancels out, since the husband is a prig and the daughter a snob. If any movie ever had a more offensive set of characters than *Stella Dallas*, I'd

212

like to know its name. No, I wouldn't, really. I just said that out of nervousness.

Stephen Dallas (Ronald Colman), a pharisaical young squirt with the visage of a plaster saint, has been in love since childhood with Helen Dane (Alice Joyce), one of those unbearable girls whose faces are always transfigured by an inner radiance. (Any enlightened premedical student knows that this condition stems from a disordered bile duct, but no matter.) When Stephen's father is detected in embezzlement, and suicides, the son flees to an obscure mill town and there succumbs to the wiles of a frivolous, rather sluttish creature named Stella Martin (Belle Bennett). Soon after their marriage and the birth of a daughter, Stella develops social ambitions and a taste for gaudy clothes that pain Stephen immeasurably. While he pursues his legal duties at the plant, we see her at the country club sipping tea with a group of matrons whose genteel derision she excites by her extravagant ostrich plumes and killing manner. To make matters worse, she openly hobnobs with Eddie Munn, the club's riding master (Jean Hersholt), a greasy and overaffable tinhorn shunned by the ladies. Eddie's buffooneries—he drolly pretends to swallow a table knife, advertising the feat as "a little parlor trick Eve tried on Adam's apple" —horrify the gathering, but Stella thinks him beguiling and invites him home to dinner. They have uncorked a bottle of beer and are very much *en famille* when Stephen comes in from work. His sniffish displeasure at seeing a stranger posturing about in his wife's hat eventually penetrates to Eddie. "Well," remarks the latter, sheepishly resuming his jacket, "like the roof says to the cyclone, I'm off now." In the domestic squabble that ensues, Stephen involuntarily provokes a tantrum from Stella by announcing his transfer to New York. She refuses to accompany him; they wrangle about the custody of the infant, a curious diversion considering that it is patently a doll rented by Mr. Goldwyn for the occasion, and finally Stella wins the little effigy on the understanding that she will bring it to New York at some undisclosed date. At about this juncture, the curator I was scribbling on lit a match, which struck me as temerity in a man with a celluloid collar, and I had a moment of anxiety for my notes. However, nothing untoward happened, and shortly both of us were again nodding to the hypnotic drone of the projector.

The next couple of reels are a somnambulistic exposition of the child's girlhood; Stella, progressively blowzier and more enamored of Eddie Munn, vegetates in the small town, but her daughter Laurel (Lois Moran) regards her mother's suitor as intolerably boorish and pines for Stephen. Her tenth birthday is ruined by her expulsion from Miss Philiburn's private school, the headmistress having followed Stella and Eddie to New York and seen them enter an unsavory rooming house. Needless to say, they are guiltless of wrongdoing, and the scene in which Laurel and her mother await the guests who never arrive is a sentimental holocaust on a par with the death of Little Nell. I had a strong impulse to blubber, and let me tell you, Dick, I don't blubber easily. Stephen Dallas, meanwhile, has rediscovered Helen, his early flame, now a widow with three sons, and is pressing Stella for a divorce. She has broken with Eddie, by this time a decrepit wino who shambles about chewing a bunch of scallions for some arcane low-comedy reason, and she clings obstinately to her marital status, fearful that Laurel may throw in with her father. Eight or nine years pass in this gloomy state of emotional disequilibrium, and then, at a spa, the girl falls head over heels for a blueblood named Richard Grosvenor, played in his most whippy vein by Douglas Fairbanks, Jr. Their exquisite rapport—dramatized in a febrile montage of tennis, hiking, and various aquatic sports under the caption "Days that flew on swallows' wings"—is short-lived; mortified by Stella's parvenu clothes and deportment, Laurel precipitately terminates their stay. Homeward bound on the train, Stella by chance overhears several women chuckling over her deficiencies, cruelly referring to her as a millstone around Laurel's neck and a major obstacle to Grosvenor's marrying her. Comes now the actor's dream, the big obligatory scene of self-abnegation as Stella seeks out Helen Morrison and, amid more nose-blowing than a school of sperm whales, begs her to wed Stephen and adopt Laurel. "I couldn't rob a mother of her only little girl," Helen protests, all swollen with nobility like Bertha Kalich. Whether from Helen's proximity or because her own bile duct is beginning to kick up, Stella's face becomes transfigured with that old inner radiance. "But you don't understand, Mrs. Morrison, I've thought it all out," she implores. "When you get married, your name will be Mrs. Dallas, too, and when Laurel gets married, the wedding invitations will read right. I'd like people to think she's yours. You're the kind of a mother she could be proud of. I—I ain't. She'll never be nobody, Mrs. Morrison, with me shackled around one foot." Well, sir, you can imagine the weeping and the kissing and the slobbering this brings on. And as though it weren't gruesome enough, they have to top it with a shot of Stella pausing impulsively at a bouquet, asking "May I take a rose to remember you by?" and imprinting a kiss on the bolster of the bed Laurel is to occupy. I vum, it makes a man come all over queasy.

In case anybody thinks these lachrymose doings prefigure a squeeze, though, he doesn't know a false climax when he sees one. After Stephen and Helen have been united in what looks like a warehouse for aging bourbon, Laurel comes to stay with them and inadvertently learns of Stella's sacrifice. She returns to the maternal roof, and, as hallowed movie custom requires, keels over with brain fever. While wielding a palmetto fan at her bedside, a peerless method of inducing pneumonia in an invalid, her mother peeks into Laurel's diary and discovers she still languishes after Richard Grosvenor but fears the union to be hopeless on account of Stella. Why she doesn't strangle the brat then and there is unclear, except that it presents a juicy opportunity for further histrionics. She seeks out Eddie

Munn, who has drunk himself into oblivion, peremptorily declares her intention of marrying him, and abstracts one of his early photographs. She then hastens back to apprise Laurel of her impending nuptials, feigning immense exuberance and cooing sticky endearments to Eddie's picture. The stratagem succeeds; Laurel hurtles back to Stephen and his family, and there is an orgy of reconciliation, climaxed by the reappearance of Richard—an older, more understanding Richard, with a new dignity about him. This time he has a mustache.

The closing section of *Stella Dallas* is, I suppose, more familiar to more people on the weather side of forty than "Tipperary." The mansion ablaze with lights on the night of Laurel's wedding, the throng clustered outside in the rain-swept street, and finally Stella, in sodden rags held together by a giant safety pin, clinging to the fence and yearning upward for a last glimpse of her child—boy, that's catharsis like Mother used to make. The beating Sam Goldwyn inflicted on his heroine and his audience surpassed anything that Gus Flaubert ever did to Emma Bovary. He gave anguish a new dimension, lifted nausea into another sphere, with the juxtaposed shot of the bride nearing the altar on her father's arm and Stella being pried away from the gate by an inexorable policeman. "I'm going," ran the immortal subtitle. "I was only seeing how pretty the young lady was." No restorative in the world can counteract the effect of a line like that, except maybe a cherry smash.

Like a delayed-action mine, however, the full impact of the picture did not hit me until hours later—dinnertime, to be exact. In the role of paterfamilias, which I play with considerable *brio*, I was carving a Smithfield ham and suddenly found that I needed an extra plate for the nubbins. Without slackening rhythm, I directed a fifteen-year-old baggage on my right, currently home from boarding school, to fetch it from the kitchen. At least thirty seconds passed while Sleeping Beauty sat gaping at the ham, her thoughts far away. I ripped out a more forcible command, couched in the idiom of the quarter-deck. "I'm going," she said resentfully. "I was only seeing how pretty the cloves were." The cadence of her words sharply evoked all the misery I had been closeted with that afternoon; I let fall the cutlery and, burying my face in the crook of my elbow, broke down.

The baggage stared at me mystified. "What's wrong with *him*?" she asked her mother. "Is he jingled?"

"No more than usual," said the mem kindly. "Probably been nosing around a film vault again. Eat your squash."

In a short while, I was right as rain again and had everybody in a roar pretending to swallow a table knife. It's a trick I picked up from some movie or other whose name escapes me. If you think of it, do me a favor, will you? Thank you.

You're My Everything,
Plus City Sales Tax

Do I take it everybody's familiar with a magazine called *Town & Country*? (If I know my luck, it'll turn out that there *is* no magazine called *Town & Country*, or else that there are five with nearly identical titles—*Town & Poultry, Hound & Gentry, Grouse & Peltry*, etc.) Anyhow, the one I mean is a fashionable paper costing six bits that chronicles the activities of the quality, and hence doesn't circulate around the Luxor steam baths or most of the other places I do. Several weeks ago, though, while waiting for the lacquer to dry on a new toupee at my wigmaker's, I noticed a copy of the September issue on his credenza and began thumbing through it. Before I could determine what cotillions were upcoming or which supper clubs the Braganzas favored, my attention was impaled on a singular advertisement for Dayton Koolfoam Pillows. In case you're a square like me, who never heard of it, the Dayton Koolfoam isn't just a conventional bolster; in the eyes of its sponsors it's a whole *mystique*, almost a philosophical system. "Yes, Dayton Koolfoam is *more* than a pillow . . . it's a *way* of life," the text announced with marked exaltation, "for its relaxing sleep-ability rejuvenates you for another day. And it's *more* than *foam*, for its patented process gives a unique, velvety 'open-pore' surface that assures ever-changing fresh air." What corralled me specifically, however, was the superimposed color photograph of a patrician young person musing over a note from some impassioned gallant that contained the following bit of meringue: "Betty dear . . . being away from you makes every day seem like a week, every week like a month. But here's a kiss . . . tuck it under your Koolfoam and dream of me."

This inveterate disposition of the advertiser to cuddle, to yoke his product to the consumer's emotional life and stability, is, of course, nothing new. Brand Names Foundation, Inc., a fellowship dedicated to making the public label-conscious, has been piping away on the same theme for quite a while now. Its most touching effort, perhaps, was the advertisement a year or so back that showed a family moving into a new home in a strange city, friendless and utterly without roots. Everybody was thoroughly woebegone, but, said the copy, there was no occasion for despair. Close at hand were nationally advertised wares to restore a sense of kinship and continuity—old cronies, I gathered, like the O-Cedar Mop for Mom, the cheerful red tin of Prince Albert for Dad, Kiwi Shoe Polish for Junior, and Mogen David Wines for Sister. And, it might have added, a full selection of dependable roscoes, like the Smith & Wesson, if things got really unendurable.

Granting the fact that Koolfoam has pioneered in cross-pollinating love and commerce, my sole objection to its romantic correspondence is that it tantalizes instead of enlightening; no sooner does it start a provocative hare than it inexplicably abandons the chase. Just what, I wonder, is the status of the lady's pen pal that he speaks so jauntily of her pillow? Most men in the early stages of courtship, at least, haven't the faintest idea whether their sweethearts sleep in Utica or in burlap, and, even after a *modus amandi* is established, rarely quiz them about their preference in pillows. To be sure, she may have thrown hers at him in a hoydenish moment while larking around her *garçonnière*, but nobody with red blood in his veins studies labels at a time like that . . . I beg pardon? . . . Oh, I thought you said something. If, on the other hand, the charmer is intended to be a young matron, are we to assume that she and her husband routinely exchange love letters freighted with advertising? The whole thing becomes more cryptic the longer you speculate on it, and since everyone knows that intense speculation can easily unhinge the reason, I'd like to make a proposal. I have here, by a coincidence that those prone to stagger may regard as staggering, a series of letters very similar in content to Koolfoam's, and I think their perusal might reward the peruser. They came out of a desk I acquired at a country auction last weekend, whose previous owner, a bachelor friend of ours, emplaned quite precipitately before the sale for an extended stay in Europe. Ordinarily, I would hesitate to publish the letters because of their intimate flavor, but as he left no forwarding address and has undoubtedly changed his name by now, I consider I'm not violating any confidence. The lady concerned can fend for herself. She seems to have done ably thus far.

SEPTEMBER 8

GUY DARLING,

I suppose you'll think I'm a silly little goose to write this, but I felt I simply *had* to apologize for Eliot's behavior the other evening at dinner. Also, I can't resist any opportunity to use my new Parker 51, which, as you know, takes the drudgery out of correspondence. Did you realize, by the way, that its patented Vacuum-Flo suction barrel, embodying a revolutionary concept in pen styling, guards against seepage? Yes, it's goodbye to ink-stained fingers and annoying blots. The stationery, of course, is Eaton's Wedgwood, obtainable in eleven inviting colors. It's sort of a hallmark with fastidious people like myself, those who appreciate the finer things. Guy, you'd adore their fascinating free booklet, "The Romance of Paper." Why not send for it today?

I'm afraid Eliot made a perfectly horrid impression on you when you arrived, but the poor dear caught cold on his way home from the office and, instead of employing Vicks Inhaler, your doctor's recommendation at the first sign of sniffles, drank practically a fifth of Haig & Haig. That's his very own favorite, and I guess it's the choice of the discriminating everywhere, because it's light without being heavy and just smoky enough so it isn't clear. Well, the old green-eyed monster always comes out in Eliot whenever he's had one too many, and he started grilling me in this relentless fashion about where I'd met you, etc. Fortunately, I know those moods of his; had I spilled the fact that we'd sort of picked each other up in the lobby of the Bellevue-Stratford, he'd have brained you the moment you walked in. So I acted real vague—classmate-of-my-brother double-talk —and he quieted down pronto. All that glowering of his, and the playful pass he made at you with the carving knife, was just his way of showing off. Speaking of the knife, did you notice our dinner service? It's Gorham's Damascene pattern, and the apogee of elegance from a hostess's point of view. Master craftsmen have lavished years of experience on this loveliest of all cutlery.

Are you by any chance free this Thursday? Eliot has to fly out to Cincinnati overnight for some tiresome insurance symposium, and I thought you might like to buzz over and take potluck. Of course, it won't be very exciting, just the two of us, but I'll get one of those divine Hormel hams—and they *are* scrumptious, with their mouth-watering goodness sealed into each tin in gigantic pressure ovens—and afterward we can laze around the fire and talk if we have to. I've been dying for a chance to flaunt my new negligee from Bergdorf Goodman's. It's so sheer that Eliot won't let me wear it when we have company. Still, I don't think it's fair for anyone way out in Cincinnati to impose his whim on people, do you? Let's teach him a lesson.

Affectionately,

BRENDA

SEPTEMBER 17

DEAREST GUY,

I'm sure you'll never forgive me for popping into your secluded bachelor retreat yesterday afternoon without warning, and I do hope you won't think me terribly forward. Needless to say, I wouldn't have dreamed of acting that impulsively except it seemed the only way out of my dilemma. I was so wet and spent after getting lost on those twisty back roads that when I saw your mailbox, I almost sobbed with relief. And when you insisted on bundling me out of my damp things and sharing that hot brandy punch, I could have hugged you. Or did I? It's all a bit fuzzy, but definitely on the enchanted side. Is that your impression?

Incidentally, I love the upstairs part of your lair, the imaginative way you've treated the walls and ceilings—Kem-Tone, isn't it? It gives such a satisfying patina, and contractors no less than homeowners swear by its durability. So washable, too; cobwebs and lint scamper at the flick of a dustcloth. Everything you've done, in fact, is calculated to extract "oh"s and "ah"s, with a single exception. Will you disown me if I make one teeny-weeny criticism, lover? In poking around the kitchen, I noticed your refrigerator needs defrosting. Now, Guy, we both know that false icebox economy spells whopping electric bills, as unbiased surveys conclusively reveal. Don't put off that visit to your Westinghouse dealer's to see his dazzling new line of 1957 models. The most generous trade-in allowance in years now makes it possible in some instances to get not only a factory-fresh unit but a cash dividend of several hundred dollars as well. My, can't you just hear everyone's budget purr?

I'll tell you a secret if you swear not to repeat it: I'm becoming the least bit concerned about Eliot. He flies into the most jealous rages over positively nothing. Last night, for instance, he suddenly rounded on me and demanded where I'd found the Madras sports shirt from Brooks that you loaned me. Darned if he didn't catch me off balance and I almost told him, but some instinct saved me. I said the laundry'd sent it back with his by mistake. He kept staring at it all evening, trying to place it, because of course you'd worn it the night he met you. Isn't that hilarious? I knew it'd amuse you.

A clairvoyant little birdie just whispered something in my ear. He said that next Monday, about two-thirty, I'd be in the bar of the Carverstown Hotel, at one of those rear tables in the dark, looking for mischief. If you happen to be driving through Carverstown around then, it might be fun to see whether he's right. Aren't you dying of curiosity? I am.

Expectantly,
BRENDA

OCTOBER 1

SWEETIE,

I've never known anything so uncanny as our running into each other in Bloomingdale's upholstery section yesterday morning. Of course, I knew you often ran up to New York for the day, but of all the unlikely places to encounter one's neighbors! We didn't get very much shopping accomplished, though, did we? And I saw ever so many tempting things as we were leaving—those stunning nine-by-twelve Gulistans whose rich, glowing designs complement your furniture whatever its period, the new Waring blender that whips up foamy puddings and sauces when unexpected guests drop in, a whole cornucopia of sturdy gadgets to gladden the housewife's heart.

Promise me to browse through their kitchenwares the *very* first chance you get.

The *escargots* in your little French restaurant on Fifty-third Street were delectable, and as for their stingers, I don't even recall leaving the place. Where on earth did we progress to afterward? I have a hazy recollection of an automatic elevator and your fussing with a shoelace, and the next I knew, the conductor was shaking me and calling out Flemington Junction. Eliot was fit to be tied when I rolled up in the taxi. Seems he'd left the car for me at the station as we'd agreed at breakfast, but I could barely focus, let alone remember a trivial detail like that. To make matters worse, some busybody—Ailsa Spurgeon, I'll bet, she's always hated me—had called up and reported that she'd spotted us reeling out of the Carverstown Hotel last week. Well, you should have seen the fireworks. All kinds of wild threats about breaking every bone in your body and hiring a private eye and Lord knows what—sheer bluff, naturally, since he hasn't a blessed shred of evidence except the monogrammed belt buckle you left behind the night he was in Cincinnati. I thought of mentioning it to you afterward, but I hate postmortems, don't you? So dampening.

I may be attending an alumnae luncheon in Philadelphia Wednesday—at least, Eliot's convinced I am, and it seems pointless to disillusion him. Shall we say the theology section of Leary's Bookstore at one? I'll look properly demure to fit the surroundings, but I could turn into a bacchante in the right environment. Here's a kiss . . . tuck it under your Chemex and heat your coffee on it.

Consumingly,
BRENDA

OCTOBER 6

MY POOR LAMBIE,

No words can convey how *pulverized* I was at the news. I'm absolutely shattered, but obviously I can't rush over to nurse and otherwise console you, because Eliot hasn't stirred out of the house for two whole days and keeps watching me like a lynx. However, I'm slipping this to the handyman, and with luck you'll get it tomorrow.

You must have been petrified when Eliot barged into Leary's out of the blue and began punching you, but you can't say I didn't warn you; he's a fiend when aroused, and tricky as he can be. I'm convinced after putting two and two together that he must have steamed open my last letter—which I see now I should never have given him to mail—and then sent me a phony wire from Mother luring me up to New York. I wouldn't believe he could be so base; it shows you can't trust *anybody*. Did he really blacken both your eyes, as he keeps cackling to me? When the swelling goes down, try brushing the discolored areas with Max Factor's Pan-Cake. You'll be amazed how this smoother, *balmier* makeup irons out crow's-feet and restores tissue tone. Small cuts and nicks, too, yield to its snow-flake touch. At better drugstores and beauticians everywhere.

As soon as you're presentable, why don't you drop over here early some afternoon for a cozy little drinkie? Or, if you'd rather, I could wander by your chalet. Don't be apprehensive about Eliot. He has these tantrums from time to time, but they usually blow over. Oceans of love, and, whatever you do, don't forget to claim

Your baggage,
BRENDA

Is There a Doctor
in the Cast?

He has a true humanist's care for the wholeness—the mental and physical health—of individuals. . . . It is not surprising, therefore, that in his youth Mr. Kaye wanted to be a doctor. . . . That childhood ambition has, indeed, remained with him, but reduced to its necessary proportion. Interest in healing is a sideline with him, though a sideline for which he cares intensely. . . . He is neither frightened nor repelled by disease; and his interest in it, and in its cure, is no more morbid than a doctor's.

An extraordinary incident—without precedent, surely, in the history of the London Palladium—occurred in Mr. Kaye's dressing-room last Saturday night. It occurred shortly before ten o'clock—about ten minutes before he was due to appear in the second house. At such moments, most entertainers must be undisturbed; many of them are "bundles of nerves."

Mr. Kaye had begun to put on his makeup. Suddenly his door

burst open. A man rushed in, crying "Hey, Danny! Can you do anything for Louis? He's very bad." He dragged in a dancer, in stage costume, whose face was grey and agonised. He was suffering, he said, from a migraine-type headache.

"Sit down," said Mr. Kaye, standing behind a chair. "Rest your head against my body." He then went to work on the man's neck and face and scalp, in the manner of an osteopath. In perhaps three or four minutes the job was done: the man still looked unwell, but he said that the pain was gone. Mr. Kaye only remarked "Let me know a bit earlier next time"; went on making up; and was on stage on time.—*From an article on Danny Kaye in the* New Statesman & Nation.

NEW YORK, SEPTEMBER 12

I feel such a sense of guilt—can it really be two months since I made the last entry in these pages? How strange that every time I temporarily desert show business, the same thing should happen. The moment I take some noxious little job to keep myself going between parts, my ego deflates and I can't bear to face my diary. The reason's perfectly obvious, of course; the theater is my whole life, and while the name of Bruce Menafee on a marquee right now wouldn't draw flies, one day it'll be up there with the greats like Maurice Barrymore, Maurice Evans, and Maurice Schwartz. Still, you can get pretty discouraged in these wretched doldrum periods, when you're reduced to posing for mail-order catalogues, ushering at the Music Hall, or working as night watchman at an embalmer's, frantically making the rounds of the managers' offices meanwhile. This last break of mine was typical. I was all ready to go back to Antioch and teach Freshman Drama, to marry some vapid booby and resign myself to perpetuating the human race. Then, out of the blue, Alec Fragonard, who played the second leper in the road company of *Father Damien's Chickens* last season, called up to say there was a bit in *On You It Looks Good,* which had just started rehearsals Monday. I hot-footed right over, auditioned for Ronnie Castlemaine, the director, and,

227

wondrous to relate, was chosen from among thirty applicants. The pay is scale and the role isn't especially large, but I do think it's rather impressive histrionicwise. I make my first entrance in white flannels, carrying a tennis racket with rhinestone strings, in an ensemble number called "Forte Love" that introduces Louella Grope, our female lead. I next appear in the Newport houseparty scene, impersonating a tipsy English butler; not much dialogue here except trifles like "Hic" or "Shay, Countess, lesh you and me dansh," but I'm confident I can work out some amusing horseplay. My real chance to shine is the Casbah sequence halfway through the second act, where I come on as Osmani el Fatoom, an Arab soothsayer who unwittingly unites the lovers. It's a ticklish characterization in that I'm not supposed to know I'm doing it and neither are they —kind of a mystic slant, with overtones of "The Passing of the Third Floor Back." As yet, I haven't quite got my teeth into it, but I plan to contact the author and have him build up the precise nuances I have in mind.

Thus far, there's nobody in the cast, with one exception, whom I'd describe as particularly *simpatico*. Fletcher Kumyss, our star, is a pompous ass who's forever flexing his biceps at the showgirls, one of those standard romantic leads whose semicircular canals are deafened by the sound of his own voice. Louella Grope, who plays opposite him, is a real torn-down piece from Memphis, all moonlight and magnolias on the surface but pure brimstone underneath. The rest of the company is routine, either wide-eyed worshipers of Stanislavski or hopheads. The only person with any sensitivity, I'd say is, is Rags Meiklejohn. He's a tall, dreamy chap, with a poetic face in which you sense enormous compassion, a connoisseur of beauty and an omnivorous reader. Unlike the others, who drug themselves with comic books, he spends every spare moment poring through Huysmans, Cabell, Firbank, and Anatole France (he's supposed to have read *Jocasta and the Famished Cat* four times). I was surprised to learn, though, that his real preoccupation is medicine. From earliest youth, he confessed to me the other morning, he has yearned to be a healer, to assuage bodily and emotional distress. "Funny, isn't it?" he reflected, with a wry smile. "Here I am in jester's motley, distilling yocks out of exploding cigars and pratfalls, when deep down and basically I'd give everything to be another Schweitzer, to don an operating gown and rehabilitate my fellow man."

I commented on his long, sensitive fingers—better suited to wield a scalpel, I ventured, than the traditional pig bladder of the buffoon. "Who knows?" I speculated. "You might have been a world-famed surgeon had the opportunity arisen."

"It still may, Menafee," he said, his eyes gone pensive. "After all, is there any man jack amongst us, basically speaking, which he can prognose what the future holds in store?"

An unusual personality, Meiklejohn—more than a touch of the visionary in his makeup. I've a curious feeling there was something prophetic about his words.

NEW YORK, SEPTEMBER 15

My instinct was right; Meiklejohn *is* psychic. Scarcely twenty-four hours after our conversation, he got a chance to use his therapeutic gift and rose to it nobly. It happened day before yesterday during the Andalusian scene. Fletcher Kumyss—who, for plot purposes, is disguised at this point in the show as Louella's chaperon, though she and the audience are unaware of it—was perched on a stepladder being serenaded by Jackie Renoir, the second lead. I guess the director's attention was elsewhere, but at any rate our ballerina, Gemze de Lapidari, did a sudden *tour jeté* downstage, accidentally grazed against the ladder, and over went Fletcher into the orchestra pit. There was a simply appalling crash as he struck the music stands; it sounded exactly like my Uncle Ned backing through the wrong end of our garage the time he got drunk on zinfandel.

Well, all hell instantly broke loose. Everybody was milling around, shouting advice and scrambling for smelling salts, when Rags Meiklejohn stepped into the breach.

"Keep cool, folks!" he sang out. "Nothing wrong with Mr. Kumyss—just a little stunned, that's all. The main thing is to restore his circulation right away. Here, someone help me get him back on his feet."

There was an immediate outcry, a number of the company protesting that it was risky to move the man before determining whether he had a spinal injury. An old wives' tale, rejoined Rags crisply; overwhelming medical evidence showed that the sooner you became ambulatory following an accident, the better, and that any delay might result in the direst consequences. He spoke with such authority that opposition melted at once. Fletcher, disheveled and mumbling, was assisted off to his dressing room, and the rehearsal continued. Somewhat later, however, he unaccountably lapsed into a dead faint, and our producer, Mr. Finsterwald, decided to implement Meiklejohn's opinion with a professional one. The doctor he called in—derisively referred to by Rags as a quack from a nearby theatrical hotel—promptly dispatched Fletcher to the Polyclinic Hospital, where his X-rays revealed a dislocated collarbone, three broken ribs, and a fractured spleen.

"Moonshine!" snorted Rags when I approached him for an explanation. "Didn't have a scratch at the time I examined him. Between you and me, the ambulance probably hit a lamppost on the way to the clinic."

Have decided that for the nonce, at least until the show opens out of town, I shall hang on to my night-watchman job at the Golgotha Funeral Home. The duties aren't too onerous, and I've been able to put in some concentrated work on the role of the Arab soothsayer. I expect to use the merest soupçon of a French accent, with an inscrutable smile flickering around my lips—somewhat the expression Tony Glaucoma wore when he played the second goldsmith in *Father Cellini's Chickens*.

With a black Vandyke and pale olive makeup, it ought to be quite effective.

NEW YORK, SEPTEMBER 22

This has been a fairly momentous week, fraught with tension and portents that our dramatic craft may encounter squalls before it arrives safe in port. The first came when Ronnie Castlemaine, irritated by Louella's Southern accent, acidly requested her to take the boll weevils out of her mouth, whereupon she threw a container of coffee in his face. Fortunately, it was cold, and other than momentarily blinding him, caused no irreparable damage. Just the same, it took hours to smooth everyone's ruffled plumage, and, knowing Louella's vengeful nature, I doubt she'll ever wholly forgive Ronnie. A much more ominous complication, though, has been the mounting antagonism between Mr. Finsterwald and Rags Meiklejohn. Rags—animated by what are plainly the most altruistic motives—has been treating the cast for various minor ailments like colds and sprains; in fact, he has converted the prop room into an informal dispensary and busies himself between scenes cauterizing abrasions, massaging pulled tendons, and rendering all manner of first aid. While the majority of his cases have responded beautifully, two or three have developed puzzling symptoms such as traumatic shock, gangrene, etc., which have necessitated Mr. Finsterwald's replacing them on very short notice. His exasperation with Rags reached a pitch yesterday when two showgirls in the Aztec ballet, after receiving medication for heartburn arising from pastrami sandwiches, fell into a near-epileptic state and had to be removed on stretchers. Thus far, Mr. Finsterwald has avoided any public denunciation, but to judge from his labored breathing and phrases one overhears through the flats, like "You and your goddam chemistry kit!" managerial ire is aflame.

Basil Clingstone, last seen locally as the second sculptor in *Father Praxiteles' Chickens*, has taken over Fletcher Kumyss's role. Though less incisive dictionwise, Clingstone is a more cerebral actor than Fletcher, and his cleft palate gives his portrayal of the stalwart Canadian Mountie who dares all for love an interesting added dimension. My conception of the Arab soothsayer, by the way, is also fast taking on light and shade; I intend to sport a monocle and an amber cigarette holder, and to space my words so deliberately that the audience must needs hang on every syllable. "Towering above his mediocre colleagues, Bruce Menafee gave a sharply etched performance—vibrant, witty, dynamic. Not since John Carradine has a personality held us so spellbound. . . ." Daydreams, perhaps, and yet some small inner voice bids me have faith in my destiny. Next week, Philadelphia.

PHILADELPHIA, SEPTEMBER 29

It may be too soon to make predictions, but *On You It Looks Good* does not seem slated for an easy success. Four of the five critics who attended our opening here Monday ranged from lukewarm to negative, deeming the production "a nightmare," "three hours of unmitigated cretinism," and "the most noisome swill since *Bertha, the Sewing-Machine Girl.*" The fifth reported that a handful of taxpayers had inadvisedly sought refuge from a rainstorm at our attraction the previous evening, a classic example of leaping from the frying pan into the fire. Mr. Finsterwald nevertheless refused to be disheartened; he immediately ousted the author, composer, and lyricist, imported several television writers from New York, and the show is now being revamped into a Mormon folk operetta. Inasmuch as some of our parts have not yet been changed—I still appear in my burnous in the Salt Lake Tabernacle, but speak the English butler's lines—the audience must be a whit confused. Luckily, we have been drawing moderately small houses during this transition period, so the confusion has had no chance to spread.

A propos of opening night, we almost had a crisis—averted, in the nick of time, by Rags Meiklejohn's quick-wittedness. One of the Conquistadors, Norman Trebizond, was unable to remove his helmet while making a change; evidently it had lodged over his ears, constricting the blood supply, and the poor man was in mortal agony. Just as the stagehands were struggling to loosen it, Rags came by and instantly diagnosed the trouble as a slipped casque. He commandeered a hammer, gave the helmet a few expert taps, and in a twinkling Norman was free. Ultimately, malicious rumors got around that he developed a concussion as a result, but when I queried Rags, he seemed unperturbed. "Quite possible," he said, looking up abstractedly from his copy of *The Skin Around Us.* "That's what we practitioners call a calculated risk. After all and basically, we don't pretend to be miracle men, you know."

Mr. Finsterwald has turned the most alarming color lately—a deep Burgundy shade with streaks of purple—and the cigars he gnashes between his teeth rustle like cornstalks. I fear he is not at all well.

BOSTON, OCTOBER 11

The past few days have been exceptionally trying ones, so much so that it demands every ounce of fortitude to chronicle them in any logical order. Following Mr. Finsterwald's sudden decision to move to the Hub City, our company was sent up here in three buses, and we rehearsed madly in the laundry of the Hotel Touraine while the scenery was being hung. Thanks to the clouds of steam and the wet wash brushing against their faces, most of the singers came down with laryngitis and croaked like a chorus of frogs at the première last night. From the moment the overture struck up, in fact, it was evident that a hoodoo was pursuing the show. A couple of Conestoga wagons someone had hoisted into the flies to conserve space came unstuck, raining spokes and whiffletrees on the musicians with such force that three of them were knocked senseless. In the meantime, a truly shattering incident was taking place backstage. A trained bear, which I understand was scheduled to appear in a new gypsy sequence in Act II, somehow worked out of its cage, grabbed hold of Basil Clingstone, and began waltzing him about, trampling the sets to matchwood. The crew clobbered the animal unmercifully with fire extinguishers and brooms, but by the time he relaxed his hold, Basil was in hysterics and his understudy had to go on. Everything considered, it was amazing our performance got the reviews it did. Mergenthaler of the *Globe*, who can be devastating if he dislikes a play, gave us only two onions and a leek, and the *Post* hailed us as "indispensable mulch for a bounteous theatrical season."

As regards my personal status, the future does not engender optimism. I now appear but twice, first as a Sioux hostage who declines to disclose the whereabouts of his tribe, and later as a Trappist monk, which, as I took occasion to point out to Mr. Finsterwald today, reduces me entirely to pantomime. His answer was rather incoherent, possibly because he had just surprised Rags in process of giving Basil Clingstone a tetanus shot, but it was something to the effect that trains left Back Bay Station hourly for New York. I think I acquitted myself with laudable dignity. I extracted my monocle and screwed it into my eye, surveyed him with the same withering scorn Yankel Frobisher displayed as the second plenipotentiary in *Father Metternich's Chickens*, and stalked away. When he shows up in my dressing room tonight, groveling and stammering apologies, I shall be austere, reserved, faintly sardonic. "Yes, Mr. Finsterwald, I will continue in your wormy little attraction," I envision myself saying, "but first let us discuss salary and billing. Here is my ultimatum. . . ."

NEW YORK, OCTOBER 14

What a sense of utter calm enshrouds the Golgotha Funeral Home at this hour; except for the measured ticking of the clock and the faint, pervasive scent of formaldehyde, one might well fancy himself on some remote South Sea island. Candidly, I did not anticipate returning here quite so soon, but circumstances beyond my control made it obligatory. Suffice to say they have been referred to an attorney who will teach a certain producer that actors cannot be booted down a circular iron stairway with impunity. Sawdust puppets though we are considered, some of us *do* have feelings.

Ran into Rags Meiklejohn on Sixth Avenue this morning as I was emerging from a cruller shop. Oddly enough, he, too, is at liberty, though he confided that interests outside the greenroom increasingly claim his attention; indeed, he was just en route to the New York Academy of Medicine to read a paper. He tapped the stethoscope protruding from his pocket with a mischievous smile. "On me it looks good," he observed archly. An engaging cuss, Meiklejohn, and a rare specimen of the *genus homo*. The stage lost a great personality when he took up medicine.

Hungarian Goulash, with Battered Noodles

WHY THE MEMORY of a screen actress named Constance Talmadge should cause, after two highballs and three decades, a constriction in the throat and misty vision is something I can't readily explain. I suppose it is one of those idiosyncrasies I must accept as normal nowadays, along with progressive penury and the vertigo that attends lacing my shoes. Though I realize such belated homage crackles like a paper of ancient snuff, I may as well 'fess up that yesteryear I was spoony over Miss Talmadge to the point of idolatry. I wallowed in every picture, major or minor, she deigned to appear in, and, when called upon, could instantly furnish authoritative data on her birthstone, favorite flower, and bust measurement. It seems singular, therefore, that with such a financial and emotional investment in this quicksilver creature, the only movie of hers I could recall until recently was a boudoir farce called *The Duchess of Buffalo*, and that merely because of the circumstances under which I first saw it. One autumn afternoon in 1926, I dropped in to visit a former college classmate of mine, Steamy Welch, who was employed as a copywriter in some vast advertising agency near Grand Central. Steamy, said my informants, was the coming man in the agency, an embryonic tycoon, and it sounded credible; he had been a big wheel under the elms, a miracle of scholarship and co-ordination, and classified, in the jargon then stylish, as a snake, or suave operator with the ladies. I still retain a clear image of him at a Junior Week tea dance, clad in a four-button jacket of unbleached sisal and pants with twenty-two-inch bottoms, expertly weaving his partner through the intricacies of the toddle. The orchestra, full of saxophones and tenor banjos, was playing either "Dardanella" or "Wildflower," and when Steamy whirled to complete an arabesque, you caught the glint of an octavo-size metal flask in his hip pocket. There were no flies on Steamy.

At any rate, I found my schoolfellow in one of a maze of tiny glass cubicles, moodily biting his knuckles and trying to evolve some dithyrambs for a process cheese. He hailed me effusively and confirmed the rumors of his success. He was now earning a salary well in excess of twenty thousand a year—without bonuses, of course—and expected to be made vice-president of the firm shortly. He had just acquired a Spanish hacienda at Rye, in the yacht basin of which he proposed to moor a forty-five-foot yawl. Actually, he confessed wryly, he never knew a moment's leisure; all manner of pestilential bores like Charlie Schwab and Eugene Grace kept badgering him for advice on their securities, and he was debating the idea of leasing a grouse preserve in Scotland as a way of escaping them. Did I have any more cogent suggestion, he asked with appealing candor. Just as I was studying the problem, the door flew upon and a forthright gentleman entered without bothering to remove his hat.

"Hi ya, Welch," he said, consulting a notebook. "You're two months behind on that suit of clothes. Cough up a double sawbuck or we'll hang a judgment on you." As my friend, glowing like a bed of phlox, slowly fished out his wallet, his nemesis scrawled a receipt and gave him a short, incisive lecture on the ethics of installment buying. When he had departed, Steamy looked so shopworn that I suggested a small libation on the altar of Silenus. Three or four shells of needle beer restored his *amour-propre*, and by easy stages we gained a Hungarian restaurant in Yorkville, where I remember downing a great deal of synthetic Tokay and dancing a czardas in a rather abandoned fashion. There was a fuzzy interval outside a phone booth while Steamy vainly besought two nurses on Staten Island to join us in making whoopee, and then I was in a neighborhood movie house, blinking ponderously at Miss Talmadge's antics and wondering how a film called *The Duchess of Buffalo* came to be laid in Russia. Steamy had vanished to fulfill his portion, which, the last time I heard, was managing a lubritorium outside Spearfish, South Dakota.

A FEW DAYS AGO, while peaceably traversing West Fifty-third Street, I was set upon by a hooded trio lurking in the entresol of the Museum of Modern Art, forced at pistol point upstairs into the film library's projection room, and compelled to see *The Duchess of Buffalo* again. The press gang gave no clue to its motives in shanghaiing me, but it was made clear that I could expect reprisals against my loved ones should I fail to report my findings. If, consequently, an apprehensive note steals into the following recapitulation from time to time, the reader will understand I speak under duress. Here and there, from sentences patently meant to be read backward, he will glean some conception of the ordeal I underwent. Honestly, my hand still shakes whenever I light up a strip of film.

Hungarian playwrights always having been pre-eminent in the field of laborious fun, *The Duchess of Buffalo* was derived from a piece written by two Hungarian playwrights and adapted for the screen by a third. The megaphone and the production reins were handled by two local boys named, respectively, Sidney Franklin and Joseph M. Schenck, but their contribution was so much of a piece with the authors' that if I were aedile, I would have conferred honorary Hungarian citizenship on them. As for the cast supporting Miss Talmadge, it was nothing if not cosmopolitan—Tullio Carminati, Edward Martindale, Rose Dionne, Chester Conklin, and Jean de Briac, all of them gustily impersonating Russians of every degree of eminence from Grand Duke to hotelkeeper. Mistaken identity, of course, was the theme, and it was exploited with such tenacity that for seventy minutes the chills never stopped rippling down my spine. To be sure, the gun that was kept pressed against it throughout didn't help any.

The plot of *The Duchess of Buffalo*, woven of summerweight thistledown, concerns the obstacles surmounted by a wellborn young dragoon, Lieutenant Orloff (Carminati), in wedding Marian Duncan, an American ballerina from Buffalo (Miss Talmadge). As we fade in on the latter's triumphant recital before an audience of St. Petersburg swells, the opening title sets the mood: "Marian Duncan danced in America with a veil. Then she tried Russia without a veil, and oh boy-ovitch. She was so good that two visiting Scotchmen forgot their change at the box-office." One gathers from the spectacle onstage, which resembles a spring pageant in the secondary schools, that the Muscovites are ravenous for entertainment, but it presently develops that Marian is the magnet of every eye, and in particular that of a seasoned voluptuary named the Grand Duke Gregory Alexandrovitch (Edward Martindale). His surreptitious ogling and mustache-twirling, under the very nose of the jealous Grand Duchess Olga Petrovna (Rose Dionne), are guaranteed to tickle anyone's risibilities—save those, possibly, of a man with a Colt in his back—and the camera now leaps to another spectator, even more deeply interested, Marian's lieutenant. Orloff, a dashing youngster from the tips of his well-polished boots to his paleolithic forehead, has been chaperoning his ladylove from the wings, tremulous lest she discard her ultimate veil. Fortunately or otherwise, the *corps de ballet* interposes itself as she does, the curtain falls, and, by the time the lovers grapple, Marian's charms have been fireproofed in a baggy leotard clearly improvised from a suit of heavy woolen underwear. In this decent if oppressive garb, she receives from Orloff a ring plighting their troth, and amid protracted twittering the couple finalize plans to marry at once.

As anyone conversant with dragoons is aware, a Russian dragoon desirous of matrimony must first obtain his Grand Duke's consent, so next day, piling Marian into a sleigh, Orloff sets about procuring it. His superior, abstractedly selecting a diamond brooch to be sent to Marian, at first views the petition with favor but, on learning the name of the prospective fiancée, harshly forbids alliance with a dancer. "Then," says Orloff, unbuckling his sword with the *élan* any dragoon worth a hoot in Hollywood would be expected to display, "I must ask to resign my commission."

Well, sir, if there is one art at which a czarist noble excels, it is dealing with insolent puppies. Placing his arms akimbo— the akimbo position is mandatory in all productions budgeted at three hundred dollars or over—Gregory Alexandrovitch icily rejoins, "You are to be detained in your quarters three days. Perhaps you will have changed your mind by then." Marian, meanwhile, has driven home to order dinner. With rare insight into the native character, not to say political clairvoyance, she realizes that once those Russkis get to jawing, a person may as well grab herself a hot meal.

The misunderstandings now begin to sprout like forsythia; the Grand Duke hurries straightway to Marian's scatter, where she tenderly awaits Orloff, in the belief that *he* has sent her the brooch, and there is a passage of kittenish lovemaking to congeal the blood as the two, separated by a folding screen, tickle each other delirious. Eventually, her fingertips surprise his beard—the same classic dénouement in which Charley Chase or Larry Semon discovers he has been stroking a runaway lion—and she is compelled to dampen his ardor without alienating him altogether. The Grand Duke, nevertheless, refuses her entreaties to spare Orloff and exits majestically, not suspecting that Marian, a hoyden to the last, has pinned the brooch to his cape. Incredibly enough, someone neglected to add the obligatory hilarious scene of his wife stumbling on the bauble and foaming like a Seidlitz powder. For an instant, I had a flicker of suspicion about the scenarist's real nationality. Ferenc Molnar never would have muffed an opportunity like that.

Presumably desolated by this impasse, Marian sends word to her lover urging him to forget her and departs for Orel, a step that provokes a wholesale migration to that city. Orloff breaks arrest to follow her, the Grand Duke conceives the notion of renewing his courtship there, and his Duchess, suspecting that he is philandering, decides to pursue and eavesdrop. We thereupon cut to the manager of Orel's leading hotel, Chester Conklin (obviously sheepish about his role in this enterprise), reacting to a telegram reserving space for the Grand Duchess and commanding secrecy. In the tradition of Hungarian farce, he of course instantly disobeys. He confides the secret to his staff, confuses Marian with the patrician visitor, for no earthly reason, and installs her in the imperial suite. Orloff has meanwhile overtaken Marian and suggests they flee to Paris. Before they can do so, though, the local company of dragoons insists on tendering a banquet in honor of the putative Grand Duchess, which, nobody needs to be told, is the signal for the Grand Duke to step back into the plot. Playing on Marian's fear of exposure—she has used her influence to shield Orloff from arrest—he caddishly enclasps her waist in public and begs indulgence of the officers to retire, as he and his lady are fatigued from their journey. Knowing the monkeyshines this portended, I sagged down in my seat in the projection room with a dolorous sigh, but my escorts were plainly diverted. "Hot spit!" chuckled one of them under his hood. "Let's see you crawl out of *that* one, sister." I hinted, as unobstrusively as I could, that she undoubtedly would. "Shaddap," he ordered, prodding my spine with his roscoe. "Pipe down if yuh know what's good fer yuh." I don't, but I piped.

The sequence that follows is the sort of demented inter-bedroom frolic Avery Hopwood used to write with his left hand while feeding himself aspirin with his right to deaden his sensibilities. The alarums and excursions in the imperial suite, the headlong buffooneries as the Grand Duke and Orloff pop in and out of closets manhandling Marian and evading each other, generate the same cast-iron glee as *Getting Gertie's Garter* and *Up in Mabel's Room*. Whenever my contemporaries are disposed to bemoan the decline of the theater, by the way, they might profitably recall that these high jinks and the dramas of Eugene Walter were the only available pabulum in their youth. Anyhow, at the height of the carnage the real Grand Duchess comes blundering in like a bluebottle, the lovers manage to smuggle her husband offscene and establish their bona fides, the Grand Duke benevolently excuses Orloff's desertion, and everything ends copacetically with a Greek Orthodox wedding presided over by an archimandrite from the Central Casting Agency.

I fatuously imagined that the psychic welts left by *The Duchess of Buffalo* had subsided until, somewhat later the same day, I stopped by the New York Public Library to renew a card that had lapsed. It must have been a purely instinctive response, but when the clerk demanded my occupational status for the application, I replied, "A hostage."

After a wary silence, during which she pretended to examine my references but actually fumbled for a buzzer under the counter, she cleared her throat. "We don't recognize that as a vocation," she said. "Just what is the nature of your work?"

"Golly, I don't know," I pondered. "I guess you might call me a snapper-up of unconsidered trifles, but right now I'm in jeopardy on account of a movie. You see, it's like this—" Before I could expatiate, a uniformed man with a rather burly neck took me by the collar and guided me to the Forty-second Street exit. All around, a hell of a day, though I have one thing to be thankful for. At least I didn't run into Steamy Welch.

Who Stole My Golden
Metaphor?

⊂≣

I HAD A SUIT over my arm and was heading west down Eighth
Street, debating whether to take it to one of those 24-hour dry-
cleaning establishments or a Same-Day Cleaner or even a place
that might return it before I left it, when I ran smack into
Vernon Equinox in front of the Waffle Shop. Fair weather or
foul, Vernon can usually be found along there between Mac-
Dougal Street and Sixth Avenue, scanning the bargain Jung
in the corner bookshop or disparaging the fake Negro primitive masks at the stationery store. His gaunt, greenish-white
face, edged in the whiskers once characteristic of fisher-folk
and stage Irishmen and now favored by Existentialist poets,
his dungarees flecked with paint, and his huaraches and massive turquoise rings clearly stamp Vernon as a practitioner of

the arts, though which one is doubtful. The fact is that he favors them all impartially. He writes an occasional diatribe for magazines called *Neurotica* and *Ichor*, paints violent canvases portraying one's sensations under mescaline, dabbles in wire sculpture, and composes music for abstract films as yet unphotographed. He derives his sustenance, if any, from a minuscule shop on Christopher Street, where he designs and fashions copper sconces and jewelry, but since the place is open only from six-thirty in the evening until eight, its revenue is nominal. It has been whispered, late at night in Alex's Borscht Bowl, that Vernon holds a Black Mass now and again in his shop. How he can get a naked woman and a goat into that tiny store, though—let alone himself—is a puzzle.

Anyway, there he was outside the Waffle, staring at the three rows of Dolly Madison ice-cream cones slowly revolving in the window before a background of prisms, and his contempt was magnificent to behold. It was a pretty unnerving display, actually; the ice cream was so obviously pink-tinted cotton and the cones themselves made of the plywood used in orange crates that you instinctively shuddered at the oral damage they could inflict. As he turned away from the window with an almost audible snarl, Vernon caught sight of me.

"Look there," he said furiously, pointing at the multiple rosy reflections shimmering in the glass. "That's what you're up against. Is it any wonder Modigliani died at thirty-three?" I stood transfixed, seeking to fathom the connection between Dolly Madison and the ill-starred Italian painter, but Vernon had already hurdled his rhetorical question. "I give up! I throw in the towel!" he proclaimed. "You spend your whole life trying to imprison a moment of beauty, and they go for borax like that. Gad!"

"When did you get back?" I asked placatingly. There was nothing in his appearance to indicate that he had been away at all, or even exposed to direct sunlight for the past six months; still, it seemed a reasonably safe gambit.

"End of January," he said with a morose backward look at the window.

"Er—how did you like Haiti?" I asked. That too was a wild stab, but I dimly remembered being waylaid outside the Bamboo Forest in an icy wind and told of up-country voodoo rites.

"Haiti?" Vernon repeated, with such withering scorn that two passers-by veered toward the curb. "That tourist drop? Nobody goes there any more. I was in Oaxaca. Not Oaxaca proper, mind you," he corrected, anxious to scotch the impression that he frequented resorts, "a tiny village about sixty miles north, San Juan Doloroso. Completely unspoiled—Elspeth and I lived there for three pesos a day."

"Oh, yes," I said fluently. "Henry Miller mentions it in *Tropic of Capricorn*." From the quick look Vernon gave me, I knew I had planted the seeds of a sleepless night. "Well, old boy," I inquired, giving his shoulder an encouraging clap, "what are you up to these days? When are we going to see a show of those nereids made out of pipe-cleaners?"

"I'm through with that dilettante stuff," said Vernon. "I've been designing some nonobjective puppets. It's a combination of dance and mime. Schoenberg wants to do the music."

"I'd let him," I recommended. "It sounds exciting. Tip me off before the recital, won't you?"

"There isn't going to be any," he said. "The puppets are suspended in zones of light and the music comes over. That is, it's superimposed. We're trying to establish a mood."

"Very definitely," I agreed. "I'm sure it'll work out. Well, good luck, and—"

"I'd have finished it months ago if Truman Capote hadn't sabotaged me," Vernon went on irascibly. "The aggravation I suffered from that episode—well, never mind. Why burden you?"

Arrested by the bitterness in his tone, I turned back. "What do you mean?" I asked. "What did he do?"

"Come in here and I'll show you," said Vernon, propelling

me into a coffeepot a few doors away. After extensive byplay with the counterman involving the preparation of a muffin, obviously calculated to heighten the suspense, he drew a clipping from his wallet. "Did you read this interview with Capote by Harvey Breit? It came out in the *Times Book Review* around a year ago."

"Why, yes," I said vaguely, scanning the text. "It was rather tiptoe, but then, most of the publicity about him is. I didn't notice anything special."

"Nothing except that the little creep helped himself to my whole style," said Vernon with rancor. "Things I said at different parties. It's the most barefaced—"

"Wait a minute," I interrupted. "Those are blunt words, neighbor. You sure of your facts?"

"Ha *ha!*" Vernon emitted a savage cackle. "I just happen to have about two hundred witnesses, that's all! People who were there! Look at this, for instance." He ran his forefinger down a column. "Breit asked Capote to describe himself, and what do you think he said? 'I'm about as tall as a shotgun—and just as noisy. I think I have rather heated eyes.' "

"He's rumored to have ball-and-claw feet too, like a Queen Anne dresser," I returned, "but why should *you* get worked up?"

"Because it's a straight paraphrase of a thumbnail sketch I gave of myself," said Vernon tigerishly. "You know Robin Nankivel, the ceramist—the girl who does the caricatures in porcelain? Well, it was in her studio, next to the Cherry Lane Theater. I remember the whole thing plainly. They were all milling around Capote, making a big fuss. He was wearing a chameleon silk vest and blue tennis sneakers; I could draw you a picture of him. Arpad Fustian, the rug-chandler, and Polly Entrail and I were over in a corner, discussing how we visualized ourselves, and I said I was about as tall as an Osage bow and just as relentless. Right then I happened to look over, and there was Capote looking at me."

"I guess his eyes *are* really heated, though," I said. "The only time I ever saw him, in the balcony of Loew's Valencia, they glowed in the dark like a carnation."

"At first," continued Vernon, too full of his grievance to encompass anything outside it, "I didn't associate this puling little simile of his with my remark. But after I read on further, where he analyzes his voice and features for Breit, I nearly dropped dead. My entire idiom! The same unique, highly individual way I express myself! Here it is—the end of the paragraph. 'Let's see,' he (Capote) said. 'I have a very sassy voice. I like my nose but you can't see it because I wear these thick glasses. If you looked at my face from both sides, you'd see they were completely different. (Mr. Capote demonstrated.) It's sort of a changeling face.'"

I studied the photograph imbedded in the letterpress. "A changeling," I said, thinking out loud, "is a child supposed to have been secretly substituted for another by elves. Does he mean he's not really Truman Capote?"

"Of course he is," said Vernon irritably, "but read the rest—"

"Hold on," I said. "We may have uncovered something pretty peculiar here. This party admits in so many words that he's not legit. How do we know that he hasn't done away with the real Capote—dissolved him in corrosive sublimate or buried him under a floor someplace—and is impersonating him? He's certainly talking funny."

"God damn it, let me finish, will you?" Vernon implored. "It's this last part where he copied my stuff bodily. Listen: 'Do you want to know the real reason why I push my hair down on my forehead? Because I have two cowlicks. If I didn't push my hair forward it would make me look as though I had two feathery horns.'"

"Great Scott!" I exclaimed, a light suddenly dawning. "Don't you see who's talking? It's not Capote at all—it's *Pan*. The feathery horns, the ball-and-claw feet—it all ties together!"

"He can be the Grand Mufti of Jerusalem for all I care,"

snapped Vernon. "All I know is that I was having brunch at Lee Chumley's one Sunday with Karen Nudnic, the choreographer, and she was wearing a bang. I said she looked like one of those impish little satyrs of Aubrey Beardsley's, and that just for kicks she ought to do up her hair in points to accentuate it. Well, I don't have to tell you who was in the next booth with his ear flapping. Of course, I never thought anything of it at the time."

"It's open and shut," I said. "The jury wouldn't even leave the box."

"Ah, why sue ϵ guy like that?" he replied disgustedly. "So I'd expose him publicly and get six cents in damages. Would that recompense me for my humiliation?"

I tried not to appear obtuse, but the odds were against me. "I don't quite understand how he hurt you," I said. "Did any of your friends spot this—er—similarity between Capote's dialogue and your own?"

"No-o-o, not until I wised them up," admitted Vernon.

"Well, did they avoid you subsequently, or did you lose any customers as a result of it?"

"*What?*" he shouted. "You think that twirp could make the slightest difference in my life? You must have a lousy opinion of my—"

"Hey, you in the back!" sang out the counterman. "Pipe down! This ain't Webster Hall!"

"No, and it's not Voisin's either!" Vernon snarled. "The coffee here's pure slop. Who are you paying off down at the Board of Health?"

As the two of them, spitting like tomcats, converged from opposite ends of the bar and joyfully began exchanging abuse, I recovered my suit and squirmed out into Eighth Street. The Dolly Madison cones were still revolving turgidly in the Waffle Shop, and a light spring rain fell on the just and the unjust alike. All at once, the fatuity of dry-cleaning a garment that would only become soiled again overcame me. How much more sensible to put the money into some sound cultural investment, such as a copy of *Other Voices, Other Rooms,* for instance, thereby enriching both its talented author and one's own psyche. I instantly directed my steps toward the corner bookshop, but as luck would have it, halfway there I ran into a young bard I know named T. S. Heliogabalus. The story that kid told me!

CLOUDLAND REVISITED:

It Takes Two to Tango, But Only One to Squirm

⊂⊒

By CURRENT STANDARDS, the needs of a young man-about-town in Providence, Rhode Island, in 1921 were few—an occasional pack of straw-tipped Melachrinos, an evening of canoeing on the Ten Mile River, with its concomitant aphrodisiac, a pail of chocolate creams, and a mandatory thirty-five cents daily for admission to the movies. My fluctuating resources (most of the family's money evaporated in visionary schemes like a Yiddish musical-comedy production of *The Heart of Midlothian*) often forced me to abjure tobacco and amour, but I would sooner have parted with a lung than missed such epochal attractions as *Tol'able David* or Rudolph Valentino in *The Four Horsemen of the Apocalypse*, and I worked at some very odd jobs indeed to feed my addiction to the cinema. One of them, I recall, was electroplating radiators in a small, dismal factory that turned out automobile parts. It was an inferno of dirt and noise; half a dozen presses, operated by as many scorbutic girls whose only diet seemed to be pork pies, were kept busy turning out the honeycomb radiators used in several cars at that time, and it was my task to baptize these artifacts in a huge vat filled with boiling acid. The fumes that rose from the immersion were so noisome that within a month I lost eleven pounds and developed nightmares during which I shrieked like a brain-fever bird. Compelled under parental pressure to resign, I wheedled a job as clerk at the baked-goods counter of Shepard's, a department store that dealt in fancy groceries. Overnight, my anemia magically vanished. Cramming myself with cinnamon buns, broken cookies, jelly doughnuts, ladyfingers, brownies, macaroons—anything I could filch while the floorwalker's back was turned—I blew up to fearful proportions. When not folding boxes or discomposing customers, I transported fresh stock from the bakery on the top floor of the building, a function that eventually led to my downfall. One afternoon, spying a beguiling tureen, I snatched a heaping ladleful of what I thought was whipped cream but which proved to be marshmallow. Just as I was gagging horribly, I heard behind me the agonized whisper "Cheese it, here comes Mr. Madigan!" and the floorwalker appeared, his antennae aquiver. He treated me to a baleful scrutiny, inquired whether I was subject to fits, and made a notation on his cuff. The following payday, my envelope contained a slip with a brief, unemotional dispatch. It stated that due to a country-wide shortage of aprons, the company was requisitioning mine and returning me to civilian life.

After a fortnight of leisure, my bloat had disappeared but so had my savings, and, unable to wangle credit or passes from the picture houses, I reluctantly took a job selling vacuum cleaners from door to door. The equipment that graced my particular model must have weighed easily three hundred pounds, and I spent a hideous day struggling on and off street-cars with it and beseeching suburban matrons to hold still for a demonstration. I was met everywhere by a vast apathy, if not open hostility; several prospects, in fact, saw fit to pursue me with brooms. Finally, a young Swedish housewife, too recent an immigrant to peg a tyro, allowed me to enter her bungalow. How I managed to blow all the fuses and scorch her curtains, I have no idea, but it happened in an *Augenblick*. The next thing I knew, I was fleeing through an azalea bed under a hail of Scandinavian cusswords, desperately hugging my appliances and coils of hose. The coup de grâce came upon my return to the warehouse. It transpired I had lost a nozzle and various couplings, elbows, and flanges, the cost of which I had to make good by pawning the household samovar.

IT WAS more or less inevitable these early travails should return from limbo when, as happened recently, I settled myself into a projection room at the Museum of Modern Art with a print of *The Four Horsemen of the Apocalypse*. Actually, I would have much preferred to reinspect another vehicle of Valentino's called *Blood and Sand*, which co-starred Nita Naldi, down whom it used to be my boyhood ambition to coast on a Flexible Flyer, but the ravages of time had overtaken it. (Miss Naldi, *mirabile dictu*, is as symmetrical as ever.) *The Four Horsemen*, however, provided the great lover with a full gamut for his histrionic talents, and a notable supporting cast, containing, among others, Alice Terry, Wallace Beery, Alan Hale, Stuart Holmes, Joseph Swickard, and Nigel de Brulier. It was difficult to believe that only thirty-two years before—only yesterday, really, I told myself comfortingly—it had kept me on the edge of my chair. Ah, well, the chairs were narrower in those days. You positively get lost in the ones at the Museum.

The Four Horsemen, as any nonagenarian will remember, was based on Vicente Blasco Ibáñez's best-seller. It was released on the heels of the First World War, and its pacifist theme was unquestionably responsible for a measure of its success, but Valentino's reptilian charm, his alliances with Winifred Hudnut and Natacha Rambova, the *brouhaha* about his excesses and idiosyncrasies were the real box-office lure. An interminable, narcotic genealogy precedes his appearance in the film, establishing a complex hierarchy of ranchers in the Argentine dominated by his maternal grandfather, an autocratic Spanish hidalgo. Julio Desnoyers (Valentino) is French on his father's side and the patriarch's favorite; he has German cousins being groomed as legatees of the family fortune, and the sequence pullulates with murky domestic intrigue. Petted and indulged by the old man, Julio grows up into a sleek-haired finale hopper who tangos sinuously, puffs smoke into the bodices of singsong girls, and generally qualifies as a libertine. In the fullness of time, or roughly six hundred feet of minutiae that remain a secret between the cameraman and the cutter, Julio's mother inherits half the estate and removes her son, daughter, and husband to Paris, where they take up residence in a Gallic facsimile of Kaliski & Gabay's auction rooms. Julio dabbles at painting—at least, we behold him before an easel in the manner of those penny-arcade tableaux called "What the Butler Saw Through the Keyhole," sighting off lickerishly at some models dressed in cheesecloth—and, in more serious vein, applies himself to seducing Marguerite Laurier (Alice Terry), the wife of a French senator. The role must have been a nerve-racking one for Valentino. Not only did he have to keep an eye peeled for the senator but the production was being directed by Miss Terry's husband-to-be, Rex Ingram. No wonder the poor slob fell apart when he did.

To provide Valentino with a setting for his adagios, the affair gets under way at a fashionable temple of the dance called the Tango Palace, packed with gigolos and ladies in aigretted turbans swaying orgiastically; then Marguerite, apprehensive of gossip, makes surreptitious visits to her lover's atelier. He, intent on steam-rollering her into the Turkish corner, is oblivious of all else, and there is a portentous moment, embroidering the favorite movie thesis that mankind always exhibits unbridled sensuality just prior to Armageddon, when his male secretary tries to show him a newspaper headline reading, "ARCHDUKE FERDINAND ASSASSINATED AT SARAJEVO," only to have Julio petulantly brush it aside. The symbolism now starts to pile up thick and fast. The secretary, croaking ominously, exits to consult a mysterious bearded philosopher in a Russian tunic (Nigel de Brulier), who, it has been planted, dwells upstairs. No reliable clue to this character's identity is anywhere given, but he seems to be a mélange of Prince Myshkin, Savonarola, and Dean Inge, possesses the gift of tongues, and is definitely supernatural. His reaction to the murder is much more immediate, possibly because he doesn't have a girl in his room. "This is the beginning of the end," he declares somberly. "The brand that will set the world ablaze." Downstairs, meanwhile, Marguerite's scruples are melting like hot marzipan under Julio's caresses, and it is manifest that the duo is percale-bound. The camera thereupon cuts back to the oracle extracting an apple from a bowl of fruit. "Do you not wonder that the apple, with its coloring, was chosen to represent the forbidden fruit?" he asks the secretary, with a cryptic smile. "But, when peeled, how like woman without her cloak of virtue!" I don't know how this brand of rhetoric affected other people of my generation, but it used to make me whinny. I secretly compared it to the insupportable sweetness of a thousand violins.

Before very long, Marguerite's husband ferrets out her peccadillo, wrathfully announces his intention of divorcing her, and challenges Julio to a duel. The scandal never eventuates, happily; in response to a general mobilization order, the senator joins his regiment, the Fifth Calvados Fusiliers, and his wife, seeking to make atonement for her guilt, enrolls as a nurse. "The flames of war had singed the butterfly's wings," explains a Lardnerian subtitle, "and in its place there was—a

255

woman, awakening to the call of France." Excused from military service because of his nationality, Julio dawdles around Paris making an apathetic pitch for Marguerite, which she priggishly rejects on the ground that venery is unseemly while the caissons roll—a view diametrically opposed to that of another nurse in the same conflict described in *A Farewell to Arms*. Throughout the preceding, the soothsayer in the attic has been relentlessly conjuring up double-exposure shots of the apocalyptic horsemen and their sinister baggage, and a funereal pall descends on the action—not that it has been a Mardi Gras thus far, by any means. Julio's father (Joseph Swickard) has been taken prisoner at his country house by a detachment of uhlans commanded by Wallace Beery, who proceeds to stage one of those classic Hearst-Sunday-supplement revels with bemonocled Prussians singing *"Ach, du lieber Augustin,"* girls running around in their teddies, etc. At the height of the debauch, a frosty-eyed general (Stuart Holmes) enters and is revealed as Desnoyers' own nephew; i.e., a cousin of Julio's from the Argentine. Touched by the old man's plight, the officer displays unusual clemency and has him confined to a small, airy dungeon all his own; then, unbuckling his sword, he broaches an especially choice jeroboam of his uncle's champagne for the staff. Julio and Marguerite, in the meantime, continue their marathon renunciation in, of all places, the grotto at Lourdes, where she is nursing her husband, now blind and, of course, totally unaware of her identity. With a tenacity verging on monomania, Julio still hopes to con his sweetheart back to the ostermoor, but she is adamant. At length, he sickens of the whole enterprise—a process one has anticipated him in by a good half hour—castigates himself as a coward unworthy of her love, and rushes off to enlist. And just in the nick, it may be added, for what scenery hasn't been blasted by the foe has been chewed beyond recognition by the actors. Next to Mary Miles Minter laundering a kitten, nobody in the history of the silent screen could induce mal-de-mer as expertly as Valentino when he bit his knuckles to portray heartbreak.

The ensuing sequence is a bit choppy, occupying itself with Julio's heroism under fire and his parents' vicissitudes, though the only indication we get of the former is a shot of him, in a poilu helmet, fondling a monkey at a first-aid station. (However, the animal may conceivably have been afflicted with rabies.) Papa Desnoyers eludes his captors and visits the young man at the front with news that Marguerite pines for him but is devoting herself unsparingly to the senator, which can hardly be classified as an ingenious plot twist. There obviously remains but one situation to be milked to dramatize the irony of war—a battlefield encounter between Julio and his German cousin—and, blithely skipping over the mechanics of how a general falls into a shell hole in No Man's Land, the scenario maneuvers the relatives into a death grapple. I rather suspect that at this point a hurried story conference was called on the set to debate the propriety of allowing Valentino to be strangled. No doubt it was argued that the spectacle might cause mixed emotions in the audience, and a compromise was evolved wherein, before the outcome is resolved, we whisk to Marguerite's bedroom as she prepares to abandon her husband for Julio. Suddenly her lover's image materializes, suffused with an unearthly radiance, and she realizes the issue is academic. The rest of the picture is a lugubrious wash-up of the incidentals, climaxed by a graveside meeting between the elder Desnoyers and Julio's former upstairs neighbor, the apparition in the fright wig. Their conclusion, as I understood it, was that things were going to be a great deal worse before they became any better, but confidentially I found it hard to keep from whistling as I raced the projectionist to a *bourbonnerie*, around the corner from the Museum. After all, come sunshine or sorrow, it was extremely unlikely I would ever have to see *The Four Horsemen of the Apocalypse* a third time.

With the fatuity of middle age, I imagined I had exorcised the ghost of Valentino for keeps, but in some inexplicable fashion his aura must have clung to my person or otherwise put a hex on me. An evening or so later, my wife exhumed from the attic a Spanish shawl and several filigree combs she had been hoarding until she could get the right offer from a thrift shop. As she was executing an impromptu fandango to the strains of "Siboney," employing a pair of coasters as castanets, I was jealously impelled to demonstrate my superior co-ordination. "Watch this, everybody!" I sang out, flourishing a roll of shelf paper. "My impression of a matador winding himself in his sash, as created by the immortal Rudy Valentino in *Blood and Sand!*" I wrapped one end of the paper around my midriff, ordered a teen-age vassal to pay out some twenty feet and steady the roll, and, with a wild "*Ole!*" spun gyroscopically in her direction. Halfway, I ran full tilt into a peculiar blizzard of white specks and, to weather it, grabbed at a student lamp for support.

I got the lamp, all right, and plenty of time to regret my impetuosity. Lazing around the house with my tweezers, subsequently, probing for slivers of glass, it occurred to me all at once that maybe Valentino used a double in moments of hazard. Maybe I should have, beginning way back around 1921.

Calling All Addlepates

There's nothing so pleasing and nothing so teasing—if I may borrow the first line of a frisky couplet the quotation of whose second would bring the postal watchdogs down on me faster than they descended on Charles Ponzi—as an annual conclave of experts. No matter what their specialty, from hair styling to sheep genetics, the authorities in every field nowadays seem to regard it as obligatory to convene in a sacred grove once a year, divide into as many panels as possible to insure a maximum of obfuscation, enshroud each other in verbal cobwebs, and, finally, issue to the press a conclusion any newspaper reader could have reached without leaving his bathtub. The latest group of savants to check in thus, I learned from the New York *Times* the other morning while wielding my loofah, was the Institute of Traffic Engineers, which met recently in Buffalo. After a powerful lot of chin music, its membership announced that daydreams are a major crash factor on superhighways. Your ordinary motorist never could have figured that out. It takes an expert to go right to the heart of the matter.

Ironically enough, if you read on in the *Times* account—and the counter-impulse in my case was so overwhelming that I whipped the water to a froth—the party responsible for the daydreaming isn't the driver but these very experts themselves. It was grudgingly conceded by the traffic wizards that in abolishing so-called normal hazards like sharp curves, intersections, traffic signals, and pedestrian and railroad crossings they had substituted the peril of deadly monotony. The meeting was urged to develop some practical method of jostling the autoist from his reveries when danger of collision impends, and a number of brain waves were forthcoming—"jiggle bars," or concrete castings, safety slogans at intervals, serrated highway patterns producing unusual nonrhythmic sounds, and so on. The one that arrested my loofah in midair, though, was "a special band radio broadcasting with package programs devised by trained psychologists to stir the daydreamer out of his lethargy." An adroit solution, you would think, but evidently the experts held otherwise. Speaking for the New Jersey Turnpike, its chief traffic engineer reported that "while special radio programs had merit, the Authority rejected their use because it believed that a two-hour program necessary to hold drivers' attention over the full 118 miles of the route would cost too much."

As a masterpiece of logic, the statement deserves to be chiseled in Wheatena on every overpass the length of the Turnpike. The Authority, if I construe its meaning accurately, has no particular qualms about the millions spent in evolving those dizzying ribbons of cement, but feels that hiring a writer and a couple of actors to keep the public from flying off them would border on the spendthrift. No doubt it envisions luminaries like Tolstoy and Louis Bromfield confecting the programs, and players of the stature of Judith Anderson and Sir Laurence

Olivier. I submit, however, that to curb woolgathering on the highway doesn't present any insuperable task and that the job need not be done on a grandiose scale. Handicaps there are, undeniably; the stargazer should be snapped back to reality without overburdening his heart muscles or making him lose permanent control of the vehicle. The program that ideally meets these conditions, to my mind, consists of a series of vignettes involving people whose stability or caprice affects the man at the wheel.

Let's suppose, for the sake of supposing, that an average young couple, Mr. and Mrs. Pedro Gershoy, are New York-bound on an express highway, en route to dinner and the theater. They have left their five-year-old-son, Naushon, with a baby-sitter in whom they repose implicit confidence. Suddenly, as they sit wrapped in blissful anticipation of the evening ahead, the voices of two teen-age girls emanate from the radio band.

FIRST T.-A.: Golly, this is the best bourbon I ever tasted. Don't they lock up their hooch when they go away?

SECOND T.-A.: Sure, but I know where he hides the key. Anyway, I had a duplicate made. I've got keys for everything in this place. Here's one that opens his desk, and that's for the clothes closet—

FIRST T.-A.: Say, I ought to get some for the Muspratts' house —then I could wear her things, too. Who made them for you?

SECOND T.-A.: My boy friend at the garage. You know, the dark, Spanish-looking chap. He learned how in jail.

FIRST T.-A.: He's *cute*. I love the way be rumbas; it reminds me of Desi Arnaz. . . . Hey, not so much! I'll be looping by the time I get home.

SECOND T.-A.: Relax—Ramón'll drive you back. He's coming over in a while, and we'll have a ball.

FIRST T.-A.: Well, all right, but no more of those funny cigarettes for me. The last time you and I—What's *that*?

SECOND T.-A.: I didn't hear anything.

FIRST T.-A.: It was a bump, like somebody falling out of bed.

SECOND T.-A.: Oh, that darn kid again. He generally drops out about this time of night, and always on his head.

FIRST T.-A.: Why don't you feed him the little white pills I give Archie Muspratt?

SECOND T.-A.: I keep forgetting the name. What is it—barcarole or something?

FIRST T.-A.: No, phenobarbital. Strictly terrif. I slip old Arch a few after his folks pull out of the driveway and he's as quiet as a mouse. Just ask that Loomis boy at the drugstore. He'll give you anything you want.

SECOND T.-A.: Listen, I've got an inspiration. Couldn't we phone him to bring some over? He could drive out with Ramón.

FIRST T.-A.: Honey, at times you frighten me. Not only are you good-looking but you're a genius. Where's that phone book?

AN INTERCHANGE like this, I believe, would effectively galvanize most torpid automobilists, especially the parents of five-year-old boys, and alert them to any threat of collision lurking in the area.

Should the driver—still the hypothetical Gershoy, for convenience—resist the stimulus, the pressure intensifies in the next duologue. The speakers here are a couple of individuals who, in a line or two, characterize themselves as an employer and his office manager. After a brief, funereal passage establishing the decline of profits in the preceding quarter, the conversation gets down to brass tacks.

OFFICE MANAGER: Look, J. B., we both know what the answer is. The organization's full of driftwood. Cut and cut deep is what I say.

EMPLOYER: But we've weeded out practically everybody we can.

O.M.: Nonsense. I could name half a dozen deadheads around here who don't pull their weight. That young What's-His-Name, for instance. The one who's usually daydreaming at his desk.

EMPLOYER: Yep, I've had my eye on him for some time. Living way beyond his means, isn't he?

O.M.: A regular Champagne Charlie. Always touring around the roads, going to the theater, the best of everything. Why, he burns up more in gas than you and I earn in a month.

EMPLOYER: Well, that doesn't prove anything. Maybe his wife's got money.

O.M.: Not a dime. I checked up on the q.t. in his neighborhood. Fourflushers from way back—in hock to everybody. They even owe the obstetrician who delivered their baby five years ago.

EMPLOYER: Um-m-m. Kind of hate to fire a man with a small child.

O.M.: Lay off the "Hearts and Flowers," J. B. In this business, it's dog eat dog.

EMPLOYER: Still, maybe if I talked to him, gave him another chance—

O.M.: Waste of time. There's only one thing worse than an old fogy, chief, and that's a young old fogy. Boot him out.

EMPLOYER: We-ell, you know best. Give him his notice in the morning.

O.M.: Why not tonight?

EMPLOYER: Good grief, Torquemada, have some consideration. It's after hours. You can't call up a man at home and discharge him.

O.M.: He's not at home—he's roaring along a turnpike somewhere. However, if it bothers you, I'll compromise. Let's send out a police call for him.

EMPLOYER: Since you insist, but don't press any charges. I wouldn't want him to get the third degree.

By the time the broadcast reaches this point, whatever castles in Spain Gershoy has been building are certain to have crumbled, and unless he's very phlegmatic indeed, he steers down the nearest exit, gulping to offset the pressure on his eyeballs. The possibility always exists, though, that he may be impervious to ordinary threats, in which case a real depth charge must be exploded. Behind the guarded voices of the man and girl engaged in the next exchange we hear the characteristic sounds of a neighborhood bar—a tinkle of glassware, juke-box music, etc.

MAN: What do you mean, it's sneaky? He sent you the letters, didn't he? He promised to marry you, give you a Cadillac, a mink coat—

GIRL: Oh, yes, but that was back in '47. Now he's got a wife, and a nice home, and a different job. He forgot the whole thing long ago.

MAN: That's the beauty of it, dope. We're just going to refresh his memory a little. As a matter of fact, he'd probably *like* to buy those letters back, to keep them as souvenirs. I'm only acting as your agent.

GIRL: Are— are you sure it isn't illegal?

MAN: There you go again. I told you I used to be a lawyer, didn't I? All right, so I'm not a member of the bar association at present, but he won't raise any technicalities. All you have to do is invite him over to your casa for a drink, for old lang syne. I'll handle the rest.

GIRL: He might not want to see me. Did you think of that?

MAN: Tempt him—make it sound worth while. Put on something clinging, sympathize with his troubles, and then, when he's nicely softened up, I'll drop in for a chat.

GIRL: Now, Vito, no rough stuff. You promised me.

MAN: Sugar, I never used an equalizer in my life. Honey and persuasion is my tonic, and they drink it right down. Well, what do you say?

GIRL: O.K., I'll try him tomorrow at his office. Boy, he'll certainly be surprised to hear my voice.

MAN: Yes, surprise is an important element in this line of work.

GIRL: Speaking of that, how did you ever happen to get into it?

MAN: It's a rather long story. Shall we have another round?

BEFORE THE New Jersey Turnpike authority jumps down my throat with all sorts of objections, I grant that they are numerous and valid. The three samples above, beamed at a specific type of motorist, cannot be expected to deter others in the same situation—preoccupied elderly clergymen, for example, or a sedanful of ornithologists, or a Goanese deck steward hurrying to rejoin his ship. If they want universality, they'll simply have to float another bond issue and hire James Michener. I feel constrained to point out, however, that there is one class of driver, of whom I happen to be the prototype, that the program could never reach, and for a curious reason. There is no legislation in this hemisphere, inexplicably, that forces one to switch on a radio. There is also no legislation compelling one to take a bath with the New York *Times*. I guess I deserve anything that happens to me.

CLOUDLAND REVISITED:

Shades of Young Girls
among the Flummery

ONLY AN ASS, and a knavish one at that, would have the temerity to compare himself with Boswell, the brothers Goncourt, Rainer Maria Rilke, or any of the world's other great diarists, but after thirty-three years of standing around on one foot waiting for a crumb of recognition, I trust I may be pardoned for blowing my own horn. Way back in 1920, while *in statu pupillari* at a Rhode Island lyceum, I kept a journal, briefly, wherein I recorded certain ideals and aspirations, judgments on books and movies that had impressed me, and appraisals of teachers and relatives who had not. It is hardly my purpose to dwell here on how trenchant and shrewd were these comments, how utterly devastating and yet how accurate; enough to say that if some perceptive critic like James Gibbons Huneker had been prowling around my bureau and discovered the diary under the porous-knit union suits where it lay hidden, he would have unhesitatingly pronounced it a minor classic. Unfortunately, Huneker seldom got up to New England in those days and never learned of the existence of the diary prior to his death. (Whether he learned of it afterward I have, of course, no way of knowing.) In any case, looking it over a while ago, I ran across an estimate of a movie I had seen called *The Flapper*, produced by Lewis J. Selznick and starring Olive Thomas. "Coruscating entertainment," I said of it. "Adult fare, replete with Frenchy situations and rib-tickling persiflage. With this production, Hollywood dons long pants. A few more of these, and there is no telling what might happen." Events proved me right. Selznick went bust—the ordinary filmgoer was too crass to appreciate caviar—but his sons vindicated him and made celluloid history. Had I wished to capitalize on my foresight, I, too, might have prospered. Alas, I was a brilliant dreamer, a Mycroft Holmes content to view everything as a chess problem.

QUITE RECENTLY, in the course of a medical checkup, I was alarmed to find that my masochism count had dropped below the safety level and that I was becoming impervious to cinema flapdoodle. Sure-shot emetics like Kirk Douglas had lost their potency, and even the sight of José Ferrer in *Moulin Rouge*, foreshortened and busily polluting the memory of Toulouse-Lautrec, had aroused no more than the collywobbles one experiences broadside of an oily swell. Faced with such inescapable danger signals, I quickly repaired to the film library of the Museum of Modern Art and outlined my symptoms.

The curator's answer was unequivocal. "This is no time for half measures," he said, his fingertips beating a tattoo on the desk top. From underneath it, where his factotum was quartered, came an answering tattoo. The curator stubbed out his cigarette. "Clear all projection rooms!" he bawled down. "Break out that print of *The Flapper*, produced by Lewis J. Selznick and starring Olive Thomas!" Off in the background, diminuendo, I heard the strident voices of half a dozen Sarah Lawrence graduates relaying the command to the storage vaults. A quarter of an hour later, I was semi-recumbent in a darkened auditorium, my stomach fluttering auspiciously and perspiration mantling my forehead. It was a slow, uphill fight, but by the end of the sixth reel I was as panicky as a tenor with a fishbone in his throat.

Chronologically, the flapper of Olive Thomas antedated by several years that of Clara Bow; the freewheeling galosh and the Stutz Bearcat, the coonskin coat and the débutante slouch were still to emerge as symbols of the Jazz Age, and the theme of Selznick's opus, if it had any, was the rebellion ostensibly fermenting in the somewhat younger generation. Casting Miss Thomas as its teen-aged protagonist was, incidentally, sheer dramatic license, for her middy blouse was strained like a balloon jib. The same was true of her schoolmates, a clutch of zestful little breastfuls who must have been recruited from a corset showroom. The fact that they wore Peter Thomsons and hair ribbons and bombarded each other with snowballs didn't upset anyone at the time the picture was current; indeed, it heightened the aura of naughtiness, of Gallic spice, that clung to everything surrounding the nickelodeon. Corinne Calvet in a Bikini, nowadays, doesn't have one-third the sizzle of Elaine Hammerstein in a pinafore. Oh, well, two-thirds.

The dramatis personae of *The Flapper* plummet into the opening reel with such velocity that the proceedings make little sense at first, but a design presently emerges. Ginger (Olive Thomas), the madcap daughter of Senator King (Warren Cook), has been perturbing everyone in the hamlet of Orange Springs, Florida, with her boisterous antics. Familial patience ends when she takes French leave of some youngsters assigned to her care and goes speedboating with a vacationing freshman from a Northern military academy, Billy Forbes (Theodore Westman, Jr.). The Senator thereupon packs her off to a misses' seminary—adjoining Billy's school, for plot purposes—whose students are slyly characterized as "limbs of Satan from old family trees." The only evidence of wanton conduct I could detect, however, was a piggish overindulgence in fudge and an occasional typhoon of giggles; on the face of it, Ginger's cronies are as torpid as a moatful of carp, and to alleviate the monotony she breaches the rules and fraternizes with Billy next door. Concurrently, she develops a pash for a mysterious young man named Richard Channing (William P. Carlton, Jr.), who roams the grounds daily on his saddle horse and whom the girls romantically conjecture to be an English lord, a professional gambler, or an actor. (I saw no external evidence to support the last of these, by the way.) "Don't you think he looks like a Greek god?" Ginger observes rapturously to Billy as the stranger canters by. Billy's retort is a squelcher. "He looks like a fried egg to me," he ripostes. Badinage of this stripe has gone out of fashion of late, or possibly I don't know the right teenagers. It must be two or three years since I've heard anybody declare, "I'm the guy who put salt in the ocean," or "You tell 'em, whalebone, you've been around the ladies."

By maneuvering Billy into a sleigh ride and a consequent upset in the snow, a scene that would prostrate anyone with its antics if he were not already horizontal, Ginger scrapes acquaintance with her idol, falsifies her age, and gets him to invite her to a hop at the local country club. The other bimbos are, of course, oxidized with envy as she struts about waving ostrich fans and bragging of her conquests, and her reputation as a *femme du monde* soars. Unluckily, the headmistress learns of the proposed exploit. She turns up at the dance just as our heroine is holding court around the punch bowl; Channing, miffed at his public embarrassment, refers to Ginger in her hearing as a pinfeathered saphead, which compounds the debacle; and on

269

being haled back to school, she theatrically presses a cluster of lilies to her bosom and prepares to hang herself from a chandelier. Meanwhile, the plot—to employ a courtly synonym—has been proliferating in another and more melodramatic direction. A student named Hortense (Katherine Johnston), described as "a moth among the butterflies," has been in league with one Tom Morran, alias the Eel (Arthur Johnston), to rob the school safe. The valuables contained there—as far as I could see, a string of beads and some women's dresses—hardly warrant being kept under lock and key, but anyway Ginger spies the couple descending a ladder with two suitcases and forgets her suicidal impulse. Despite Hortense's disappearance, the premise is advanced that nobody links her with the caper; the headmistress, clearly someone who lives in a world of fantasy if she keeps clothing in a safe, hushes up the affair on understandable grounds, and her charges start packing for their midterm vacation. Just as the picture showed every sign of being moribund, and I was massaging my knee to obviate the nut-cracking sound so embarrassing in a projection room, the story shuddered convulsively and lumbered off again. I would have followed suit if I could have got my knee back into its socket.

Hortense and the Eel, a dissolve reveals, are bivouacked in a New York hotel, in whose lobby they accidentally see Channing, and they now originate the notion of making Ginger the goat for the robbery. Since Channing does not know them, and since, moreover, the theft has been hushed up, there isn't the slightest trace of logic in any of this; I'm merely repeating what danced across the screen. The heavies dispatch a telegram luring Ginger to their suite, where Hortense confides that she and the Eel were eloping when her schoolmate last saw them. Reassured, Ginger is persuaded to tarry the night, and shortly meets Channing in the dining room. He is also bound for Orange Springs, by a rare coincidence, and paternally tries to induce her to take the same train, but nothing happens, just as it has been happening with dizzying regularity all along. In the middle of the night Ginger is awakened at gun point by the confederates, given the suitcases containing the boodle, and ordered to hide them in Orange Springs until they reclaim them. You or I might regard this as rather eccentric behavior; Ginger, however, treats it with aplomb and, after they bolt, settles down, fascinated, to examine the suitcases. Hidden in the clothing is a packet of sultry love letters from the Eel to Hortense, which, announces a succession of titles, give Ginger a delicious idea: "A complete outfit for a woman of experience . . . She might borrow it and vamp Channing . . . She would go home with a manufactured past."

Well, sir, if you think the foregoing is a wee bit daft, the rest of it is more Surrealist than *Le Chien Andalou* or one of those comic-strip nightmares Little Nemo used to get from eating Welsh rabbits. Down in Orange Springs, a staid party of townswomen is convened at the King home, buzzing over the teacups, when Ginger draws up in a calash, sporting a Duchess of Devonshire hat trimmed with osprey feathers, a hobble skirt, and opera-length gloves, and flaunting a court chamberlain's baton. How this finery had found its way into the school safe, unless the headmistress was in the habit of impersonating Lady Teazle after lights-out, is the only suspenseful element I saw anywhere in *The Flapper*. "Howdy, Gushy, old top," Ginger drawls to a neighbor. "How's everything in the little old town?" To their intense alarm—and when those early screen actors registered alarm, the camera tripod shook—the ladies hear the girl confess that she has been leading a double life in New York, gallivanting around till 4 A.M., etc. etc. To intensify the atmosphere of dementia, Billy Forbes rockets in, reacts in horror to the metamorphosis, and races off to berate Channing for having led his sweetheart astray. As the whole thing deteriorates into bedlam, with Senator King distractedly vowing to kill Ginger's seducer, the brat restores the clothes to the valises and endeavors to ship them by railway express to the New York police. The freight agent, suspicious, fetches a detective, who promptly arrests her. (It wouldn't have surprised me in the least, by then, if she had arrested *him*.) A mighty hue and cry ensues in the King household when she is brought back, everyone bellowing and fainting like sixty, but eventually the plainclothesman recognizes the handwriting in the love letters as that of the Eel—am I going too fast for you?—and the mystery is solved. To round matters off neatly, the Eel and Hortense show up to retrieve their swag and are whisked off to pokey, and the last shot, prefaced by a newspaper headline reading, "ORANGE SPRINGS SOCIAL WELFARE WORKERS HORRIFIED OVER SOFT DRINK DISSIPATION," shows Ginger and Billy devouring sodas and cooing to each other.

IT WAS in a state of acute vertigo, as though I had been rotated in a cocktail shaker, that I left the Museum to buy a stirrup cup at Schrafft's for my daughter, herself a student at a New England academy and entraining that afternoon for the fall semester. Over the parfaits, I listened to a breathless recapitulation of her day. She had picked up a bargain autograph of Marlon Brando at a Sixth Avenue pornographer's, priced a star sapphire at Tiffany's and given the salesperson my phone number, and, cannily sensing that prices were at their peak, charged several thousand dollars' worth of gowns suitable for embassy functions. "And what did *you* do today?" she asked solicitously, sponging a tiny bead of fudge from my cravat. On the theory that Ginger's misadventures might furnish a moral lesson, I began recounting the plot of *The Flapper*. Halfway through, she broke in nervously. "Look, I won't hear of you coming to the train," she said. "You're going home to bed this second." With the aid of a mysterious bystander who could have been an English lord, a professional gambler, or an actor but who turned out to be the manager, I was loaded into a calash and sent home. She must have got back to school safely, unless she took off for Orange Springs. You never know which way these modern kids'll jump. Why, when I was her age, I already kept a journal that frankly— But there I go, blowing my own horn.